# Thinking Through SCIENCE

**Arthur Cheney**
**Howard Flavell**
**Chris Harrison**
**George Hurst**
**Carolyn Yates**

*Series editor: Chris Harrison*

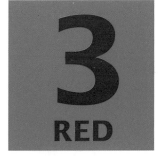

**3**
**RED**

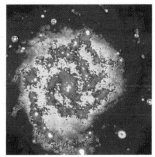

**JOHN MURRAY**

The cover image shows the spiral galaxy M74. It was taken by the ASTRO-1 telescope on board the Space Shuttle. M74 is about 24 million light years from Earth.

Although every effort has been made to ensure that website addresses are correct at the time of going to press, John Murray (Publishers) Ltd cannot be held responsible for the content of any website mentioned in this book.

Papers used in this book are natural, renewable and recyclable products. They are made from wood grown in sustainable forests. The logging and manufacturing processes conform to the environmental regulations of the country of origin.

**Orders:** Please contact Bookpoint Ltd, 130 Milton Park, Abingdon, Oxon OX14 4SB. Tel (44) 01235 827720. Fax (44) 01235 400454. Lines are open 9.00a.m. – 6.00p.m., Monday to Saturday, with a 24-hour message answering service. You can also visit our websites www.hodderheadline.co.uk and www.hoddersamplepages.co.uk

© Arthur Cheney, Howard Flavell, Chris Harrison, George Hurst, Carolyn Yates 2004

First published in 2004
by John Murray Publishers Ltd, a member of the Hodder Headline Group
338 Euston Road
London NW1 3BH

Impression number   10 9 8 7 6 5 4 3 2 1
Year                          2007 2006 2005 2004

Layouts by Stephen Rowling/springworks
Artwork by Oxford Designers and Illustrators Ltd

Typeset in 11/13 Lucida by Pantek Arts Ltd

Printed and bound in Italy

A CIP catalogue record for this book is available from the British Library

**ISBN 0 7195 7857 4**
Teacher's Book Red 3 0 7195 7858 2
CD-ROM 3 0 7195 7859 0

# Contents

# Acknowledgements

**Source acknowledgements**
The following are sources from which artwork and text have been taken:
**p.1** 'I keep six honest serving men...' from *The Elephant's Child*, by Rudyard Kipling. Voyager Books; **p.82** Which? Ltd; **p.116** *Big Bang* by Heather Couper and Nigel Henbest, Dorling Kindersley 1997; **p.156** NETCEN on behalf of DEFRA; **p.200** BBC News Online.

**Photo credits**
Thanks are due to the following for permission to reproduce copyright photographs:

**Cover** NASA, Goddard Space Flight Center/Science Photo Library **p.2** M.I. Walker/Science Photo Library; **p.8** Andrew Lambert Photography/Science Photo Library; **p.10** Andrew Lambert Photography/Science Photo Library; **p.11** *all* John Townson/Creation; **p.18** Laguna Design/ Science Photo Library; **p.27** John Townson/Creation; **p.41** Action Plus/Chris Cole; **p.42** Lunagrafix/Science Photo Library; **p.45** CC Studio/Science Photo Library; **p.51** *l* Rex Features/Sipa Press, *c, r* John Townson/ Creation; **p.56** Jim Varney/Science Photo Library; **p.59** *l* Jeremy Horner/Corbis, *c, r* Mark de Fraeye/ Science Photo Library; **p.60** John Townson/Creation; **p.72** *t* John Townson/Creation, *c* Rex Features/David Hartley; **p.74** Alan Sirulnik/Science Photo Library; **p.76** John Townson/Creation; **p.77** John Townson/ Creation; **p.78** *t* John Townson/Creation, *b* Martyn F. Chillmaid/Science Photo Library; **p.79** *l* Victor de Schwanberg/Science Photo Library, *r* John Townson/ Creation; **p.80** Andrew Lambert Photography/Science Photo Library; **p.82** Sheila Terry/Science Photo Library; **p.84** John Townson/Creation; **p.85** Chris Davies; **p.98** John Townson/Creation; **p.100** Reuters/Corbis; **p.101** *l* Alex Bartel/Science Photo Library, *r* Joseph Sohm; ChromoSohm Inc./Corbis; **p.103** *all* John Townson/ Creation *except br* Cristina Pedrazzini/Science Photo Library; **p.108** *t* George Bernard/Science Photo Library, *b* Library of Congress/Science Photo Library; **p.109** *b* Library of Congress/Science Photo Library; **p.111** NASA/ Science Photo Library; **p.113** NASA/Science Photo Library; **p.115** NASA/Science Photo Library; **p.117** *t* Sanford Roth/ Science Photo Library, *bl* Julian Baum/ Science Photo Library, *bc* Mark Garlick/ Science Photo Library, *br* Mehau Kulyk/Science Photo Library; **p.118** NASA/Corbis; **p.120** NASA/Goddard Space Flight Center/Science Photo Library; **p.123** NASA/Science Photo Library; **p.127** *c* Martin Dohrn/Science Photo Library, *b* John Townson/ Creation; **p.129** *all* John Townson/Creation *except cr* Rex Features; **p.130** *all* John Townson/Creation *except second row l* Grant Smith/Corbis, *second row r* Carl & Ann Purcell/Corbis; **p.132** *cl* Andrew Lambert Photography/Science Photo Library, *cr* John Townson/ Creation, *b* Hodder Archive; **p.135** John Townson/ Creation; **p.139** NASA; **p.140** *all* John Townson /Creation;

**p.142** Colin Garratt; Milepost 92 ½/Corbis; **p.144** David Butow/Corbis SABA; **p.145** Roger Wood/Corbis; **p.146** *t* Mary Evans Picture Library, *bl* Archivo Iconografico, S.A./ Corbis, *br* Robert Harding Picture Library; **p.147** V&A Images; **p.151** *all* John Townson/Creation; **p.152** *l* Dallas and John Heaton/Corbis, *r* Michael St. Maur Sheil/Corbis; **p.153** Hans Georg Roth/Corbis; **p.157** *t* Photodisk, *c* Bob Krist/Corbis, *b* Arte & Immagini srl/Corbis; **p.159** The Art Archive/Bibliotheque de Arts Decoratifs Paris/Dagli Orti; **p.162** Sheila Terry/Science Photo Library; **p.167** Joseph Sohm; ChromoSohm Inc./Corbis; **p.170** *all* Bruce Coleman Collection; **p.173** *tl* Jacqui Hurst/Corbis, *tc* Paul A. Souders/Corbis, *tr and bl* John Townson/ Creation, *br* Maximilian Stock Ltd/Science Photo Library; **p.175** *l* David Cole/Rex Features, *r* Stock Connection, Inc/Alamy; **p.176** *tl* Isopress Senepart/Rex Features, *tr* Astrid & Hanns-Frieder Michler/Science Photo Library, *b* Jeremy Walker/Science Photo Library; **p.177** *l* Bettmann/ Corbis, *r* Archivo Iconografico, S.A./Corbis; **p.185** Dr Jeremy Burgess/Science Photo Library; **p.189** Corbis; **p.190** Mary Evans Picture Library; **p.191** *all* Lester V. Bergman/Corbis; **p.193** *l* Dr Jeremy Burgess/Science Photo Library, *r* Claude Nuridsany & Marie Perennou/ Science Photo Library; **p.199** Saturn Stills/Science Photo Library; **p.203** Science Photo Library; **p.205** Alfred Pasieka/Science Photo Library; **p.206** Bettmann/Corbis; **p.212** *tl* Reuters/Corbis, *tr* Nils Jorgensen/Rex Features, *c* Tom Brakefield/Corbis, *bl* Dewitt Jones/Corbis, *br* Reuters/Corbis; **p.213** *tl and c* Yann Arthus-Bertrand/ Corbis, *tr* Photolibrary/OSF/Mark Hamblin, *b all* John Townson/Creation; **p.214** *all* John Townson/Creation; **p.215** *all* John Townson/Creation; **p.216** CNRI/Science Photo Library; **p.224** Sheila Terry/Science Photo Library; **p.225** *t* Elizabeth Lippmann/Rex Features, *b* Theo Allofs/ Corbis; **p.231** *tr* Barry Batchelor/PA Photos, *bl* Martin Bond/Science Photo Library; **p.233** Science Photo Library; **p.234** Getty Images/Stone; **p.236** *t* Bettmann/ Corbis, *b* John Townson/Creation; **p.238** *all* John Townson/ Creation; **p.239** Topham Picturepoint; **p.241** Sam Ogden/ Science Photo Library; **p.244** Charles O'Rear/Corbis; **p.251** Andrew Drysdale/Rex Features; **p.252** Dewitt Jones/Corbis; **p.254** *from left to right* Guy Motil/Corbis, Picimpact/Corbis, Klaus Guldbrandsen/Science Photo Library, Otto Rogge/Corbis; **p.257** Mary Evans Picture Library; **p.263** *l* Bojan Brecelj/Corbis, *r* Firefly Productions/ Corbis; **p.265** Stefano Bianchett/Corbis; **p.274** Sheila Terry/Science Photo Library; **p.276** Francoise Sauze/Science Photo Library.

*l* = left, *r* – right, *t* = top, *b* = bottom, *c* = centre

The publishers have made every effort to contact copyright holders. If any have been overlooked, they will be pleased to make the necessary arrangements at the earliest opportunity.

# Introduction

## → Science audit sheet

An audit sheet is a checklist. Draw up a science audit sheet that shows the many skills that you already have.

| SAFETY | | SKILLS | |
|---|---|---|---|
| Know lab rules | ✔ | Read a 0–100°C thermometer | ✔ |
| Light a Bunsen burner | ✔ | Use a measuring cylinder | ✔ |
| Know when to wear safety specs | ✔ | | |
| | | | |
| | | | |
| SET-UP | | TESTS | |
| A mat, tripod and Bunsen burner | ✔ | Know how to test for oxygen | ✔ |
| A series circuit with 2 bulbs | ✔ | Know how to test for water | ✔ |
| | | | |

## → Asking questions

**Key words**
∗ observations
∗ evidence
∗ inference

Science helps us find out more about the world around us and how it works. An important skill in science is the ability to ask questions. The types of question that are important in science are not just the 'What?' questions, but also the 'How?' and 'Why?' questions. It is finding answers to the 'How?' and 'Why?' questions that drives forward ideas in science.

> I keep six honest serving men
> (They taught me all I knew);
> Their names are What and Why and When
> And How and Where and Who
>
> Rudyard Kipling

Let's look at an example. Supposing you found a small animal in a sample of pondwater.

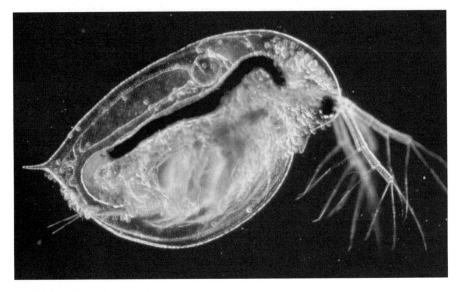

Your questions might run something like this:

What is it?
How is it similar to and different from other
    water animals that I know?
How does it move?
What does it feed on?
How does it manage to find and get that type of food?
What feeds on it?
How does it avoid or escape predators?
How might it move when I shine light on it?
Would it do that in its natural environment?

The answers to some of these questions can be worked out from careful **observations** which can become **evidence** to support ideas. This is strong evidence. Sometimes the evidence is rather weak and we make an educated guess as to what is happening. This is called **inference**.

# → How science works

**Key word**
∗ disproof

In science we make observations. From these and our understanding so far, we make inferences. In looking for more data we might strengthen our evidence for a particular idea. Sometimes more data make us realise that our initial idea was wrong. This is **disproof**, and it is a very important part of how scientists work.

Some questions we can answer from our observations and experiments. The answers to other questions require research in books or on the internet, or finding an expert who can tell you what you need to know. While we have various ways of finding the answers, it's the framing of the questions that is the important first step.

## *Reasoning* *Sycamore*

Look at the drawings and think about what questions you might ask. Here's one question to start with:

Where do the sycamore fruits land when they drop from the tree?

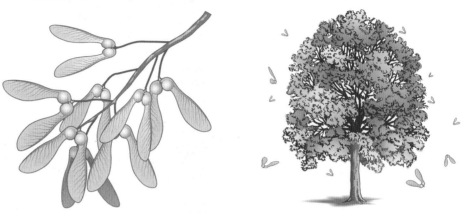

1 Compare your questions with others in your group.

2 Decide on a group list of good questions. Good questions will help you find out more about what is going on with this tree and its fruit.

3 As a group, decide which questions you can answer.

4 Will research help you?

5 Would trying things out help you to find out more?

## *Reasoning* *What happened next?*

1 What is happening in these pictures?

2 Construct a table and put in your observations and inferences. Remember – observations are what you can see, and inferences are what you think is happening.

**3** Look at other pupils' tables and see if they have made the same observations and inferences as you.

**4** Why do you think you have made the inferences that you have?

**5** Could the explanations for what you observe happening be different? Would it help to expand the picture that you are looking at? Would it help to look at the scene later?

**6** Look below to see later scenes of both pictures.

# → Answering questions

Sometimes it is easy to see the answer to a question but difficult to find the words to answer it. Listing all the key words and ideas for that topic helps you select the best ones to use in your answer.

Let's look at an example:

Why is glucose an example of a compound?

Key words in this topic area might be:
atoms, molecules, element, compound, reaction, chemical change, physical change, formula.

A pupil's answer might be:

Glucose has the formula $C_6H_{12}O_6$ which means that it contains carbon, hydrogen and oxygen atoms that are bonded together to form the glucose molecule.

Sometimes questions want us to look at an answer from two different viewpoints. Looking for what is the same between two things is sometimes harder than recognising differences. Let's look at an example:

What is the same and what is different about tap water and seawater?

Listing 'What is the same?' and then listing 'What is different?' provides us with the information that we need to answer the whole question.

| What is the same? | What is different? |
| --- | --- |
| both are liquids | seawater tastes salty |
| both have other chemicals dissolved in them | seawater contains a lot more salt |
| both are solutions | boats float more easily on seawater |
| both have oxygen and carbon dioxide dissolved in them | tap water has been treated to make it safe to drink |

An answer might be:

Both tap water and seawater are solutions, which are liquids that have other chemicals dissolved in them, for example, oxygen and carbon dioxide. Seawater tastes salty because it contains more salt than tap water. This also means that it helps boats float more easily than fresh water. Tap water is fresh water that has been made safe to drink in a purification plant.

*Reasoning* ## Good answers

Work out good answers to the questions below. Each time, list the similarities and differences and use the lists to help you word your answer.

**1** What is the same and what is different about birds and mammals?

**2** Why are saucepans made of metal but their handles made of wood or plastic?

**3** Why do both stirring and heating affect the rate at which sugar dissolves in water?

**4** What is similar and what is different about burning coal and solar heating?

## Answering in steps

To explain an answer clearly we sometimes need to find the steps to answer it. Often we need to select evidence and choose particular examples to explain our answer.

Let's look at an example.

If we were asked:

Is it always true that green organisms photosynthesise?

We would need to ask ourselves:

What happens in photosynthesis?
Which types of organisms photosynthesise?
Why has green been selected rather than blue, red or purple?
What part has the 'greenness' to play in this answer?
Which green organisms do I know that do photosynthesise?
Which green organisms do I know that don't photosynthesise?

If we then worked out ways of answering these questions, we would have the various parts that we need to answer the big question – Is it always true that green organisms photosynthesise?

The answer might be:

Photosynthesis is the way that plants trap the energy from sunlight to make glucose from carbon dioxide and water. Plants photosynthesise because they contain the green pigment chlorophyll. Some animals are green, such as frogs and parrots, but this is not because they contain chlorophyll. Animals do not photosynthesise, and if they are green, it is for some reason other than photosynthesis. So it is NOT always true that green organisms photosynthesise.

---

*Reasoning*   *Is it always true?*

Try to work out clear answers to the questions below. Each time make a list of smaller questions to help you find parts of the answer for the big question.

**1** Is it always true that metals are magnets?

**2** Is it always true that water is a liquid?

**3** Is it always true that mammals give birth to live young?

Write some more questions that challenge whether some statements in science are always true, sometimes true, or true only in some instances. Try out the questions on one another and carefully check that the answers you get match the big question that was set.

# → *Analysing data*

The data in the table below give us information about public health in the nineteenth century. To make sense of the data we need to look at the table very carefully.

**Average ages of death in 1842**

| Type of people | Wiltshire | Liverpool |
|---|---|---|
| gentry, professional people and their families | 49 | 45 |
| farmers, tradesmen and their families | 40 | 39 |
| labourers and their families | 37 | 32 |

1 What does the title of the table tell us about the data?
2 Look at the first column – Type of people. What is the same and what is different about the three groups of people?
3 The first row of the table tells us that the data are about people living in two different places. What is similar and what is different about Wiltshire and Liverpool?
4 Which parts of the table tell us that rich people lived longer than poor people?
5 a) Does the information tell us that people who lived in towns lived longer than those in the countryside in 1842, or that those who lived in the countryside lived longer than those in towns?
   b) Which parts of the table tell us this?
6 Would displaying the data in a graph, bar chart or pie chart help us analyse them? Why?
7 Use your answers to Questions 1–6 to write a summary that would explain what the table of data is showing us.

**EXTENSION** 8 Look at the questions and statements below. Some can be answered or supported by the table of data. In each case explain how the data do or do not provide evidence.

What age was the oldest farmer found in the 1842 survey?

How might a tradesman in the nineteenth century try and improve the lifestyle and health of his family?

Rich people in 1842 were more likely to reach their sixtieth birthday if they lived in the countryside rather than in a town.

Labourers' families lived a hard life in the nineteenth century and often died before they reached adulthood.

More hospitals are found in the towns than in the countryside.

# 1

# *Salts of the Earth*

**In this chapter you will learn:**

→ about the properties of metals and non-metals
→ that different acids react in similar ways with metals
→ that different acids react in similar ways with metal oxides
→ that different acids react in similar ways with metal carbonates
→ that different acids react in similar ways with metal hydroxides
→ how to make metal salts
→ to describe some uses of metal salts
→ how to recognise that a chemical reaction has taken place
→ how to represent elements by symbols and compounds by formulae
→ how to use word and symbol equations to describe the above reactions

**You will also develop your skills in:**

→ describing patterns in qualitative data about reactions
→ using patterns in reactions to make predictions about other reactions
→ devising and evaluating a method for preparing a sample of a salt
→ using models to explain what happens in a reaction
→ using the scientific method

---

➡ ➡ ➡ WHAT DO YOU KNOW?

Magnesium reacting with dilute hydrochloric acid.

Limestone (calcium carbonate) reacting with dilute hydrochloric acid.

**Key words**
* word equations
* symbol equations
* formulae

**1** Both of these chemical reactions produce a gas. Which gas is produced in the reaction between:
  **a)** hydrochloric acid and magnesium
  **b)** hydrochloric acid and limestone (calcium carbonate)?

These are some of the tests that scientists use to identify different gases:

| Test | Method |
|------|--------|
| 1 | bubble the gas through Universal Indicator solution |
| 2 | bubble the gas through limewater |
| 3 | place a burning splint at the top of a test tube of a mixture of the gas and air |
| 4 | place a burning splint into a test tube full of the gas |
| 5 | place a glowing splint into a test tube full of the gas |

In the *Thinking Through Science 1* (Book 1) topic on acids and alkalis, you found that when an alkali (sodium hydroxide) is neutralised by an acid (hydrochloric acid), the neutral solution contains common salt (sodium chloride).

In *Thinking Through Science 2* (Book 2), you used **word equations** to represent chemical reactions. In this chapter, we will look at **symbol equations**. The symbol equation for the above reaction is:

$$HCl + NaOH \rightarrow NaCl + H_2O$$

**2 a)** What are the names of the elements with the symbols:
  **i)** H
  **ii)** Cl
  **iii)** Na
  **iv)** O?
  **b)** Which of these elements are metals?

**3** What are the names of the compounds with the **formulae**:
  **a)** NaCl
  **b)** HCl
  **c)** $H_2O$?

**4** Copy and complete the following table to show the number of atoms in a molecule of each substance. The first one has been done for you.

| Substance | Number of atoms of each type |
|-----------|------------------------------|
| HCl | 1 H    1 Cl |
| NaOH | |
| NaCl | |
| $H_2O$ | |

**5** Use the particle pictures below to answer the following questions.

   **a)** Which picture represents:
     **i)** sodium chloride
     **ii)** water
     **iii)** sodium?

   **b)** Sodium chloride can also be made by a chemical reaction between sodium and chlorine. Which picture represents chlorine?

**A**
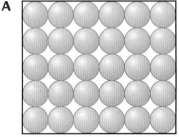

**B**
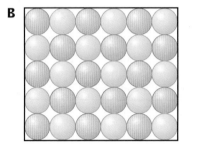

**C**
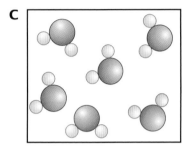

**D**
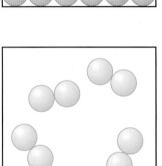

**E**
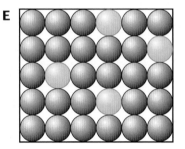

**F**
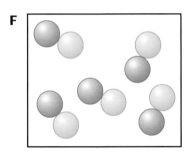

Here are some chemical reactions that you will have come across before:

   petrol + oxygen → carbon dioxide + water
   glucose + oxygen → carbon dioxide + water

In both cases, heat energy is released.

**6** Which equation represents combustion and which shows respiration?

**7** What evidence tells you that a chemical reaction has taken place?

**8** In which of these test tubes do you think a chemical reaction has occurred, and why?

**9** Write down two more chemical reactions that you remember.

# → *What are salts?*

**Key words**
* minerals
* substances
* carbonate
* oxide
* hydroxide

In Books 1 and 2 you will have already come across several salts, such as common salt (sodium chloride), Glauber's salt (sodium sulphate) and plaster of Paris (calcium sulphate). Some of these salts, such as calcium sulphate, are found as **minerals** in the Earth's crust and there is a plentiful supply. Others, such as sodium nitrate, can be found as minerals but they are in very short supply. Some salts, such as copper chloride, are not found naturally.

Scientists have found ways of making these salts by chemical reactions between other **substances**. This is what you will be looking at throughout this chapter.

Common salt is just one example of a metal salt. Many of these salts have important uses:

| Salt | Use |
| --- | --- |
| copper chloride | cures fish fungus |
| sodium chloride | preserving food |
| copper sulphate | cures plant fungus |
| calcium sulphate | plaster casts |
| sodium nitrate | plant fertiliser |

The simplest way to make a salt is to react an acid with either a metal, a metal **carbonate**, a metal **oxide** or a metal **hydroxide**. The pair of reacting substances must be chosen very carefully because some may react explosively, and others may react too slowly or not react at all.

The salt sodium nitrate (Chile saltpetre) is only found in the desert regions of Chile in South America where it hardly ever rains. The salt is very soluble in water, and scientists think that this is why it is only found in this region – it gets washed away by rain in wetter areas.

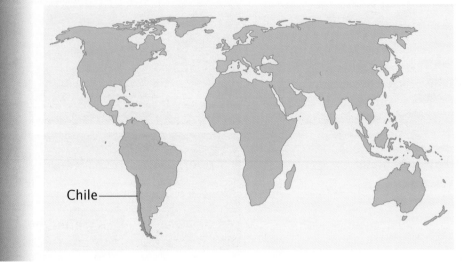

Chile

# Reacting acids with metals

**Key words**
* metals
* non-metals
* periodic table

In Book 2 we saw that all materials are made up of a relatively small number of elements. The elements can be divided into **metals** and **non-metals**.

1 Which of these are properties of metals but not properties of non-metals? Compare your answers with others in your group. Make a group list of the differences between metals and non-metals. Can you think of any differences that aren't listed?

  • conduct electricity
  • always shiny
  • always solids
  • sometimes solids
  • magnetic
  • sometimes soluble
  • never soluble

2 Look at the diagram at the top of the following page. Is it always true that metals are listed in this part of the **periodic table**?

*Research*  Make a card game to help you learn the names and symbols of elements in the periodic table.

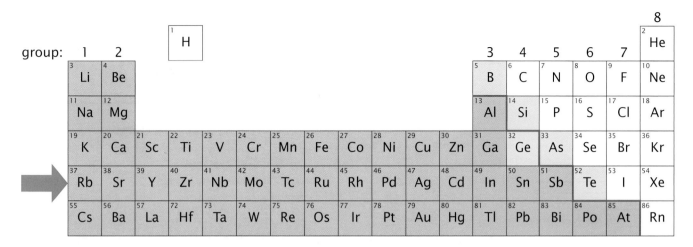

key: ▢ metal

▢ metalloid (have some of the properties of metals)

In Book 1 we saw that the metal magnesium reacts with dilute hydrochloric acid to produce bubbles of the gas hydrogen.

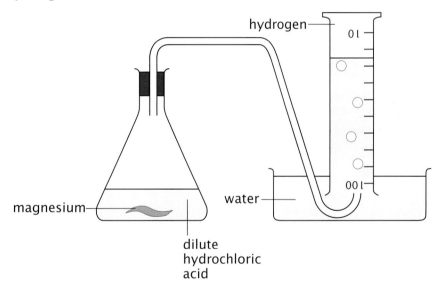

When the reaction is complete, the measuring cylinder contains hydrogen gas and there is no remaining magnesium. From this evidence, scientists can ask questions such as:

1 Do other acids react with metals to produce hydrogen?
2 Where has the magnesium gone?
3 Do other metals react with hydrochloric acid to produce hydrogen?

To solve these questions, scientists can use the scientific method.

**Key words**
* scientific method
* evidence
* hypothesis
* prediction

# The scientific method

Some people think that science is just a list of facts and laws. In fact, science is based on theories and explanations that the scientific community investigates. The **scientific method** is now used by most scientists throughout the world. The process starts with **evidence**, a question or a **hypothesis**.

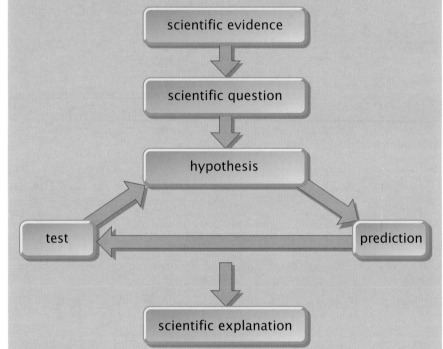

The scientific method.

* *Scientific evidence* is evidence from observations – what you can see, hear, touch, taste or smell. The observations can be repeated by other scientists.
* *Scientific questions* are based on scientific evidence.
* A *hypothesis* is a possible explanation of the evidence.
* *Prediction* – the hypothesis is tested by using it to make a **prediction**.
* *Test* – the prediction is then tested to see if it was correct. If the prediction is not correct, a new hypothesis must be put forward and the cycle of hypothesis → prediction → test is repeated. If the prediction is correct, the scientist may make more predictions and do more tests. Eventually the scientist will publish the results. Other scientists can then test the hypothesis if they wish. From all these different approaches, new scientific explanations arise.
* *Scientific explanation* – if a hypothesis has been tested by different scientists and is always found to be true, it is accepted as a scientific explanation. However, fresh evidence may turn up many years later to prove the explanation wrong, or scientists may reinterpret the ideas. In this case, a new hypothesis must be put forward and the whole process gone through again.

*Enquiry* ## Do other acids react with metals to produce hydrogen?

We can show how the scientific method can be used by thinking about the reaction of magnesium with dilute hydrochloric acid.

**Scientific evidence**

POP!

**Scientific question**

> I wonder if other acids react with magnesium to produce hydrogen...

**Hypothesis**

> Maybe it is just **hydro**chloric acid that reacts because it is the only acid with **hydro** in its name, which means that it contains **hydro**gen.

**Prediction**

> When sulphuric acid is added to magnesium, hydrogen will **not** be formed because the acid does not have **hydro** in its name.

**Test**

> I will add a piece of magnesium ribbon to some dilute sulphuric acid. No gas should be given off, but if it is I will test it to see if it is hydrogen.

**Result**

**1** What do you think will happen? Write down your prediction.

You may have a chance to try out this experiment and put forward a further hypothesis if necessary.

**EXTENSION**   **2** When sulphuric acid is added to magnesium ribbon, a gas is produced. If you test the gas with a lighted splint, it pops. Look back at the cartoon strip and make a new prediction.

# Chemical formulae

➡

In Book 2 we saw that scientists use symbols and formulae as a shorthand to represent different substances. The formula shows us the number of each type of atom in a molecule of the substance. For example:

| Substance | Formula |
|---|---|
| magnesium | Mg |
| hydrogen | $H_2$ |
| water | $H_2O$ |
| hydrochloric acid | HCl |
| magnesium chloride | $MgCl_2$ |
| sulphuric acid | $H_2SO_4$ |
| nitric acid | $HNO_3$ |

Mg represents one atom of magnesium, and $H_2$ represents one molecule of hydrogen.

Particle diagram showing an atom of magnesium and a molecule of hydrogen.

**3** From the above table:
  **a)** which substances are elements?
  **b)** when two or more elements are combined, what is the substance called?
  **c)** which element is common to all three acids?

Magnesium chloride is an example of a metal salt. It has both the elements magnesium and chlorine in it and the number of particles of each element is always the same. The **ratio** of the atoms in the formula of a metal salt depends on the **combining power** of the metal and whatever it is combined with. This combining power can be represented by particle pictures, as shown in the table below. The number of 'arms' that a particle has shows the combining power, and each 'hand' must be occupied when the particle combines with other particles.

| Metal salt | Formula | Combining power pictures | |
| --- | --- | --- | --- |
| | | Separate particles | Combined particles |
| sodium chloride | NaCl | | |
| magnesium chloride | $MgCl_2$ | | |
| aluminium chloride | $AlCl_3$ | | |
| potassium nitrate | $KNO_3$ | | |
| copper nitrate | $Cu(NO_3)_2$ | | |
| aluminium nitrate | $Al(NO_3)_3$ | | |
| sodium sulphate | $Na_2SO_4$ | | |
| calcium sulphate | $CaSO_4$ | | |

In the formula of copper nitrate, the brackets around the $NO_3$ show that there are two nitrates to every one copper. If brackets were not used, the formula would be $CuNO_{32}$ – this means that there are 32 oxygen atoms in the formula.

Like all of the models that we use in science, these combining power pictures are useful but not perfect. Salts, such as sodium chloride, do not actually exist as molecules – the metal and non-metal particles are packed closely together. This packed arrangement is called a giant structure.

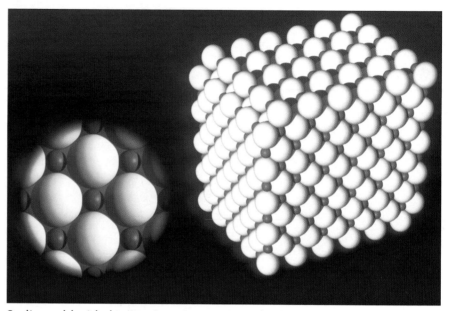

Sodium chloride has a giant structure and so can grow into large crystals.

4 Copy and complete the table below:

| Substance | Type and number of atoms |
| --- | --- |
| Mg | 1 Mg |
| $H_2O$ | 2 H 1 O |
| HCl | |
| $MgCl_2$ | |
| $H_2SO_4$ | |
| $Cu(NO_3)_2$ | |
| $Na_2SO_4$ | |

# *Balancing equations*

To understand how equations balance in chemistry, we need to think about ratios. If you have 60 sweets and divide them equally between three children, each child will get 20 sweets.

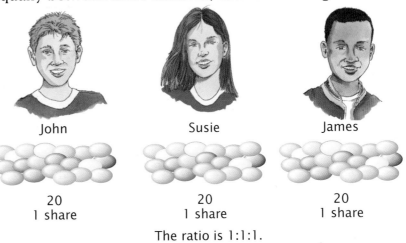

John | Susie | James

20
1 share

20
1 share

20
1 share

The ratio is 1:1:1.

If you decide to give Susie twice as many sweets as the boys, then the share is different.

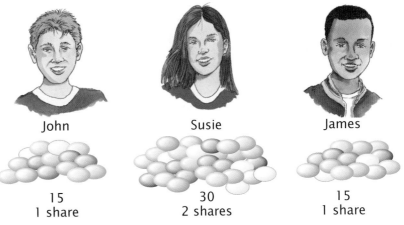

John | Susie | James

15
1 share

30
2 shares

15
1 share

The ratio is 1:2:1.

If you decide to give the boys twice as many sweets as Susie, then the share is different again.

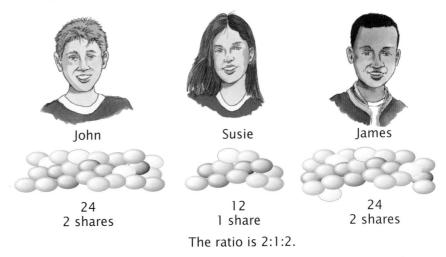

John | Susie | James

24
2 shares

12
1 share

24
2 shares

The ratio is 2:1:2.

We have seen that magnesium reacts with hydrochloric acid to produce hydrogen. Formulae can be used to write symbol equations which are very useful to scientists. The most important rule in writing a symbol equation is that the same number of atoms of the same elements should be on both sides of the equation – it should be **balanced**. To do this you need to work through the following steps:

$$Mg \quad + \quad HCl \quad \longrightarrow \quad H_2$$

1 Mg   1 H   1 Cl           2 H               *not balanced*

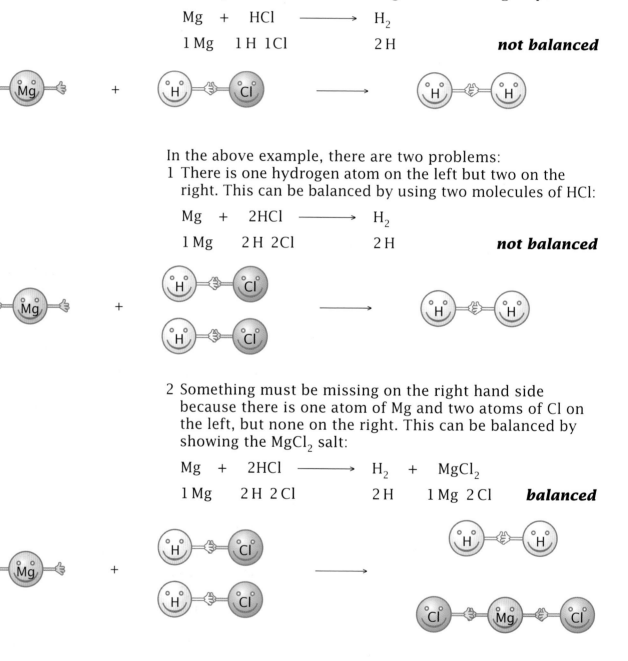

In the above example, there are two problems:

1 There is one hydrogen atom on the left but two on the right. This can be balanced by using two molecules of HCl:

$$Mg \quad + \quad 2HCl \quad \longrightarrow \quad H_2$$

1 Mg     2 H   2 Cl          2 H              *not balanced*

2 Something must be missing on the right hand side because there is one atom of Mg and two atoms of Cl on the left, but none on the right. This can be balanced by showing the $MgCl_2$ salt:

$$Mg \quad + \quad 2HCl \quad \longrightarrow \quad H_2 \quad + \quad MgCl_2$$

1 Mg     2 H   2 Cl          2 H    1 Mg   2 Cl      *balanced*

## Ratio of atoms

| Element | Number of atoms |
|---------|-----------------|
| Mg | 1 |
| H | 2 |
| Cl | 2 |

| Element | Number of atoms |
|---------|-----------------|
| Mg | 1 |
| H | 2 |
| Cl | 2 |

Note that for hydrogen and chlorine there are two atoms of each on the left of the balance. This is because there are two particles of HCl which is shown by the 2 in front of HCl in the equation.

## Ratio of substances

From the particle picture we can see that two particles of hydrochloric acid react with just one particle of magnesium to form one particle of magnesium chloride and one molecule of hydrogen.

*Reasoning* ## *Explaining the formula*

Imagine that a friend has asked you the following question: 'Why is the formula for magnesium chloride $MgCl_2$ and not MgCl?'. Use drawings and notes to explain the correct formula. Read through two or three explanations from others in your group. As a group, decide which parts of the explanations are helpful and which need improvement.

## Summary

A symbol equation:

- should be balanced – the same number of atoms of the same elements should be on both sides of the equation
- is balanced by changing the number of atoms or molecules of the substances on either side of the equation
- cannot be balanced by changing the formulae of the substances.

5 Magnesium also reacts with sulphuric acid to produce hydrogen. Copy and complete the combining powers picture to show the number of atoms in the reaction.
The word equation is:

magnesium + sulphuric acid → magnesium sulphate + hydrogen

A possible symbol equation is:

$Mg + H_2SO_4 \rightarrow MgSO_4 + H_2$

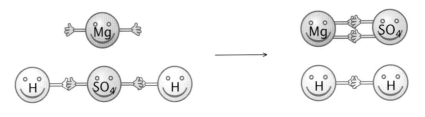

| Element | Number of atoms |
|---------|-----------------|
| Mg      |                 |
| H       |                 |
| S       |                 |
| O       |                 |

| Element | Number of atoms |
|---------|-----------------|
| Mg      |                 |
| H       |                 |
| S       |                 |
| O       |                 |

*Word play*

The word 'balanced' can have different meanings in science compared to everyday use. In which of these statements is 'balanced' used scientifically? Can you add one more scientific use?

1 Peter gave a balanced viewpoint on using animals for testing drugs.
2 Paul is very careful to follow a balanced diet.
3 Molly has successfully balanced the symbol equation.
4 Ahmed was able to balance the see-saw by moving nearer to the centre.

*Reasoning* *Making predictions*

The symbol equation for the reaction of magnesium with hydrochloric acid is:

$Mg + 2HCl \rightarrow H_2 + MgCl_2$

1 Use the symbol equation to form a hypothesis which answers the question 'Where has the magnesium gone?'.

**2** Write a prediction and describe a test which could confirm your hypothesis. Compare your ideas with others in your group.

**3** From what you have seen so far, would you expect metals such as zinc, iron and copper to react with hydrochloric acid in a similar way to magnesium? Explain your answer.

*Information processing*    ## Recognising patterns for metals

The results from a class experiment are shown in the table below.

| Metal | Acid | Observations | Hydrogen formed? |
|---|---|---|---|
| calcium | hydrochloric | fizzing, solid dissolves | ✓ |
| calcium | sulphuric | fizzing, but stops after a while | ✓ |
| aluminium | hydrochloric | fizzing after a while | ✓ |
| aluminium | sulphuric | fizzing after a while | ✓ |
| lead | hydrochloric | no bubbles | ✗ |
| lead | sulphuric | no bubbles | ✗ |

Use the above results and any that you have obtained yourself to answer the following questions:

**1** Do all metals react with dilute acids?

**2** Name one substance that is formed in all of the reactions.

**3** Can you suggest a possible reason why a very reactive metal like calcium stops reacting with sulphuric acid after a short while, even though there is still some acid left?

**4** Can you suggest a possible reason why a fairly reactive metal like aluminium only starts reacting with these acids after a while?

The word equations for two of the reactions in the above table are:

calcium + hydrochloric acid → calcium chloride + hydrogen

aluminium + sulphuric acid → aluminium sulphate + hydrogen

**5 a)** Write word equations for the other two reactions in the table.
   **b)** Copy and complete the <u>general</u> word equation for the reaction of a metal with an acid:

   metal + acid → _____ + _____

**6** When calcium reacts with hydrochloric acid (HCl), the salt formed is calcium chloride ($CaCl_2$). Write a balanced symbol equation for this reaction.

**EXTENSION**   **7** With the help of the combining power pictures shown below, write a balanced symbol equation for the reaction of calcium with sulphuric acid.

# ➡ *Reacting metal oxides and acids*

We have seen that some metals react with some acids to make metal salts. However, this reaction cannot be used to make salts such as copper sulphate, which cures plant fungus, and sodium nitrate, which is used as a fertiliser.

**6 a)** Think of a reason why the 'metal + acid' reaction cannot be used to make the salt copper sulphate.

**b)** Think of a reason why the 'metal + acid' reaction cannot be used to make the salt sodium nitrate.

*Enquiry* ## Using the scientific method

To solve the problem 'How can we make salts such as copper sulphate and sodium nitrate?', we can use the scientific method:

**Hypothesis** To make a metal salt, use a metal oxide and an acid. For example, to make copper sulphate use copper oxide and sulphuric acid.

**Prediction** A metal oxide will react with a dilute acid to form a metal salt. Hydrogen gas will also be produced.

**Test** Working in a group, plan how you will test the prediction. To help you, check that you can answer these questions:

**1** Which metal compounds will you use?

**2** Which dilute acids will you use?

**3** What safety precautions will you take?

**4** What equipment will you use?

**5** What might you expect to see if a reaction occurs?

**6** All metal salts are solids and most are soluble in water. Dilute acid is mainly water, so the metal salt produced will be in solution. How would you get the solid salt from this solution?

**7** The prediction that 'a metal oxide will react with a dilute acid to form a metal salt, and hydrogen gas will be produced' is not fully correct. Can you think of another testable prediction?

*Enquiry* ## Obtaining evidence

We know that metal oxides can be used to make metal salts. The following experimental write-up has been taken from a pupil's exercise book.

### Making a metal salt

30 cm³ of dilute hydrochloric acid was measured out and then poured into a 100 cm³ beaker. The acid was gently warmed until it was about 60°C. One spatula-end of black copper oxide was added while stirring. The black powder dissolved in the acid to form a blue/green solution. Further spatula-ends of copper oxide were added until some copper oxide remained undissolved. The mixture was filtered using a funnel and filter paper. A deep blue solution was obtained. This was partially evaporated by heating and left to cool. Blue crystals of a metal salt were obtained.

**1** Beakers are available in many sizes, for example, 50 cm³, 100 cm³ and 250 cm³. Why was a 100 cm³ beaker best for this experiment?

**2** Why is it dangerous to boil an acid?

**3** What is the evidence that a chemical reaction has occurred?

**4** Why did further copper oxide eventually no longer dissolve?

**5** What substance caused the blue colour?

**6** Why was the solution not fully evaporated?

**7** Use the particle model to explain why the metal salt passed through the filter paper but the unreacted copper oxide did not.

**8** In one experiment, the hot solution was left in a warm room and it cooled down slowly. It formed much larger crystals than another sample that cooled quickly on a cold windowsill. Use the particle model to explain how slow cooling produces large crystals.

**9** Get another group to check your answers, and discuss any that they think are wrong.

*Reasoning* ## Metal oxide equations

In the previous activity, copper oxide was reacted with dilute hydrochloric acid:

copper oxide + hydrochloric acid → copper chloride + water

$CuO + HCl \rightarrow CuCl_2 + H_2O$ **not balanced**

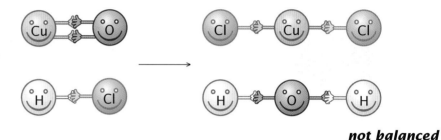

**not balanced**

**1** Write the balanced equation for the above reaction.

**2** Write word equations for the following reactions:
   **a)** zinc oxide + sulphuric acid →
   **b)** calcium oxide + nitric acid →
   **c)** magnesium oxide + hydrochloric acid →

**3** Copy and balance the following incomplete equations:
   **a)** $MgO + H_2SO_4 \rightarrow MgSO_4 +$
   **b)** $Na_2O + HCl \rightarrow NaCl +$
   **c)** $CuO + HNO_3 \rightarrow Cu(NO_3)_2 +$

**4** In all of the above reactions a metal salt is formed. Write a <u>general</u> word equation for the reaction:

   metal oxide + acid → _____ + _____

**EXTENSION** **5** Write a balanced equation for each of these reactions with the help of the combining power pictures below:
   **a)** potassium oxide + sulphuric acid →
   **b)** calcium oxide + nitric acid →

# → *Reacting metal carbonates and acids*

iron carbonate

magnesium carbonate

The results from an experiment using the three common acids (sulphuric, nitric and hydrochloric) are shown in the table below.

| Metal carbonate | Acid | Observations | $CO_2$ formed? |
|---|---|---|---|
| iron carbonate | hydrochloric | fizzing, green solid formed which dissolves | ✓ |
| iron carbonate | nitric | fizzing, green solid formed which dissolves | ✓ |
| magnesium carbonate | hydrochloric | fizzing, white solid formed which dissolves | ✓ |
| magnesium carbonate | sulphuric | fizzing, white solid formed which dissolves | ✓ |
| potassium carbonate | nitric | fizzing, white solid formed which dissolves | ✓ |
| potassium carbonate | sulphuric | fizzing, white solid formed which dissolves | ✓ |

**1** The table is incomplete. For each of the metal carbonates one of the possible reactions with an acid is missing. Write down the name of the metal carbonate and acid and the other observations you would expect.

**2** Is it true that all metal carbonates react with dilute acids to produce hydrogen?

**3** What are the differences between the reactions of metals, metal oxides and metal carbonates with acids?

The symbol equations for three of the reactions in the above table are:

$$FeCO_3 + 2HNO_3 \rightarrow Fe(NO_3)_2 + CO_2 + H_2O$$

$$MgCO_3 + 2HCl \rightarrow MgCl_2 + CO_2 + H_2O$$

$$K_2CO_3 + H_2SO_4 \rightarrow K_2SO_4 + CO_2 + H_2O$$

**4** Rewrite the three symbol equations as word equations.

**5** Copy and complete the following three word equations:

iron carbonate + hydrochloric acid →

magnesium carbonate + sulphuric acid →

potassium carbonate + nitric acid →

**6** Write a <u>general</u> word equation for the reaction of a metal carbonate with an acid:

metal carbonate + acid →

**7** Check that this symbol equation for the reaction of iron carbonate with hydrochloric acid is balanced.

$$FeCO_3 + 2HCl \rightarrow FeCl_2 + CO_2 + H_2O$$

| Element | Number of atoms |
|---------|-----------------|
| Fe      |                 |
| C       |                 |
| O       |                 |
| H       |                 |
| Cl      |                 |

| Element | Number of atoms |
|---------|-----------------|
| Fe      |                 |
| C       |                 |
| O       |                 |
| H       |                 |
| Cl      |                 |

**8** Which question or questions in this activity did you find easy and which ones did you find hard? Do others in your group agree with you?

**EXTENSION**
**9** Balance the following equations by changing the ratio of the substances involved. (Remember that the formula for each compound cannot change, so you may need to have two or three helpings of one substance to balance the other side.)

**a)** $MgCO_3 + HNO_3 \rightarrow Mg(NO_3)_2 + H_2O + CO_2$      ***not balanced***

**b)** $K_2CO_3 + HCl \rightarrow KCl + H_2O + CO_2$      ***not balanced***

**10** Write a balanced symbol equation for each of these reactions. Use the combining power pictures to help you.

**a)** zinc carbonate + sulphuric acid

**b)** sodium carbonate + hydrochloric acid

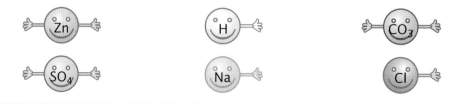

*Time to think*

Here are incomplete word equations that describe how to make metal salts:

metal + acid →

+ acid → metal salt + carbon dioxide + water

metal oxide + acid →

1 Choose one actual example for each of these general reactions and write the word equation and the balanced symbol equation.
2 Make a card game and a set of rules to demonstrate the three sorts of reactions. Your cards must include:

- the formulae of the reactants
- the formulae of the products
- any numbers needed to balance the equation
- an arrow
- plus signs.

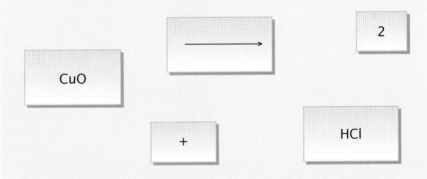

Ask another group to play your game. Did they like it? How would they improve it? How do they know if they have got the right answer?

*DID YOU KNOW?*

You can have too much of a good thing. Excess sodium nitrate on the land washes into waterways causing algal blooms.

*Research*

Why are algal blooms dangerous for water-living animals?

# → *Reacting metal hydroxides with acids*

Metal hydroxides react with acids in the same way as metal oxides:

metal hydroxide + acid → metal salt + water

# Purity

**Key words**
* pure
* impurities
* neutralise
* titration
* burette

When we make a metal salt for a particular use, it must be **pure**. Any **impurities** from the reaction must be removed during the process. For example, copper sulphate is a fungicide – it reduces fungal infections in plants. Copper sulphate is made from copper oxide and sulphuric acid. If the copper sulphate that is produced has some copper oxide mixed with it, it does not do the job as well. For most metal salts, the pure salt is made by adding an excess of metal oxide or carbonate to the acid in order to complete the reaction and **neutralise** all of the acid. This leaves some of the metal oxide or metal carbonate unreacted, but because the metal oxide or carbonate is insoluble in water the unreacted excess can be filtered off. A pure solution of the salt remains, which is evaporated to give the pure solid salt.

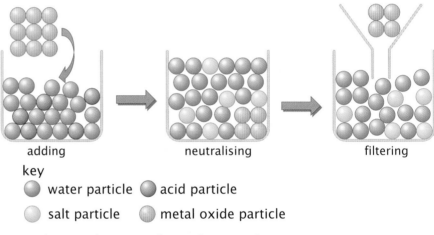

adding      neutralising      filtering

key
- water particle
- acid particle
- salt particle
- metal oxide particle

A simple particle picture for making a salt.

The fertiliser sodium nitrate can be made by the reaction of nitric acid with sodium oxide, sodium hydroxide or sodium carbonate. The pure salt cannot be made by adding an excess of these because they are soluble in water. The resulting solution would contain the metal salt and an impurity of sodium oxide, sodium hydroxide or sodium carbonate. This impurity could harm the plants if the contaminated sodium nitrate is used as a fertiliser. If not enough oxide or carbonate is used, there would be some acid left over in the sodium nitrate. This would also damage the plants.

The answer is to use a special method for preparing salts called the **titration** method. It uses a precise amount of solution of the metal carbonate or metal hydroxide to neutralise the acid.

$$\text{sodium hydroxide} + \text{nitric acid} \rightarrow \text{sodium nitrate} + \text{water}$$

$$NaOH + HNO_3 \rightarrow NaNO_3 + H_2O$$

**7** Explain how a **burette** works.

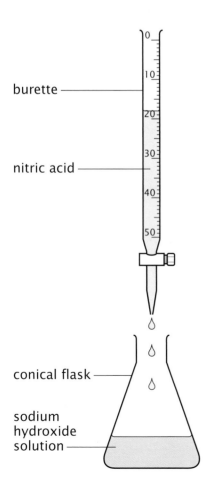

burette

nitric acid

conical flask

sodium hydroxide solution

8 How does the burette differ from a measuring cylinder in accuracy?

9 How could you check that all the sodium hydroxide had reacted with the nitric acid?

---

*Reasoning* ## Metal hydroxide equations

The titration method is also used to make potassium chloride and sodium sulphate salts.

1 Write a worksheet explaining how you would produce one of these salts. Make sure that you include the general word equation for the reaction, and that you give the names of the metal hydroxide and acid needed to make your chosen salt. Include a balanced equation and any safety tips that you think are necessary.

**EXTENSION** 2 With the help of the combining power pictures below, write a balanced symbol equation for the reaction of sodium hydroxide with sulphuric acid.

---

*Research* For each of the following salts, name the two substances that are used to make it, and find out an everyday use of the salt. Use the internet, CD-ROMs, library books or other sources to help you.

- potassium nitrate
- iron sulphate
- magnesium sulphate
- sodium stearate

Use ICT to produce a leaflet or a poster to share your answers.

*Time to think* These are some of the expected outcomes for this chapter. You should be able to:

- recognise when a chemical reaction is occurring, for example, 'the test tube got hotter'
- write word equations for some reactions
- describe the pattern in some word equations and produce a general equation
- work out the number of atoms of each element present in a formula.

Working in groups, write five multiple-choice questions that could assess some of the above outcomes. For each question there should be four answers to choose from. Swap your questions with another group and see if you can answer their questions. Swap answers and see how many each group got correct. Make a note on what you need to revise to get any wrong answers correct in the future.

# 2 Fit and healthy

**In this chapter you will learn:**

→ how the human respiratory, digestive and circulatory systems interact to maintain activity
→ the functions of the human skeleton
→ how diet, drugs, exercise and smoking affect health
→ the difference between fitness and health
→ the role of vitamins and minerals in staying healthy
→ about the effects of stress

**You will also develop your skills in:**

→ collecting sufficient, reliable data to form conclusions
→ plotting, drawing and interpreting graphs
→ evaluating conflicting evidence
→ working collaboratively to carry out a scientific investigation

→ → → WHAT DO YOU KNOW?

**Key word**
∗ fitness

**Fitness** means different things to different people.

What does it mean to you? What does it mean to other people in your group?

How do you stay fit?

Can you be fit but not healthy?

Can you be healthy but not fit?

Working with your group, on a large sheet of paper draw two boxes like this:

In the first box list the five most important things that you must do to stay healthy. In the second box write the five things you think are the biggest dangers to health.

Compare your lists with other groups in your class. Which ideas are similar and which are different?

As a class, decide on the top three factors necessary for good health, and the top three dangers to health. Do you think other classes would agree with you?

*Research*

The internet can help you find the answers to lots of questions about personal health. Use a search engine like Google or Yahoo! and type in some key words, for example, 'kids health'.

Compare some of the websites you find. Which ones do you like best? Why?

# → Fitness

Fitness can be measured by how quickly the heart recovers to its resting **rate** of beating after vigorous exercise. An average healthy heart beats 65 to 75 times a minute. During a race the heart rate will increase to about 180 beats per minute. A fit person's heart rate will return to normal within 3 minutes of the end of the race; it may take up to 10 minutes for an unfit person's heart rate to return to normal.

*Enquiry*  ## Fitness test

In a group, design and carry out an investigation to compare your team members' fitness. Use the fact that fitness is indicated by how quickly the heart rate returns to its normal resting rate after exercise.

1 Think about how you can make your investigation 'fair'.

2 What will be the **independent** (input) **variables**? What **dependent** (outcome) **variables** will you measure?

3 How will you present your data?

4 Results are **reliable** if each time the investigation is repeated you get the same or very similar measurements. The closer the measurements are to each other, the more reliable the data are. How will you make sure your results are reliable?

Ask your teacher to check your design before you carry out your investigation.

# → The human body as a system

A **system** is made up of sets of things or parts which operate together to function as a whole.

1 What parts make up these systems:
   a) a railway system
   b) an education system
   c) the heating system in your house?

Our **digestive**, **respiratory** and **circulatory systems** all **interrelate** (work with each other) to keep us healthy. Our fitness depends on how well our muscles and skeleton function together as a system.

2 Check your knowledge.
   Which organs make up these systems in the human body:
   a) the support and movement system
   b) the respiratory system
   c) the digestive system
   d) the circulatory system?

Below are outline drawings of each of these four systems. Do you know which system is which? Check with a partner which parts you can name in each system.

**3** Which organs help you take in oxygen and give out carbon dioxide?
**4** Which organ pumps blood around the body? Why is blood important to our health?
**5** Where is food digested?

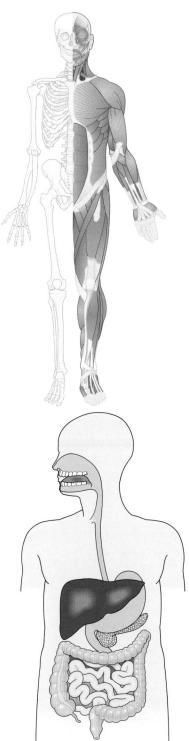

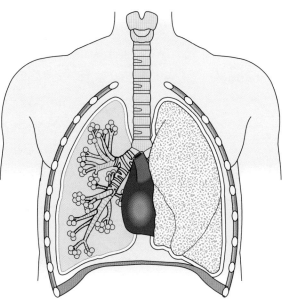

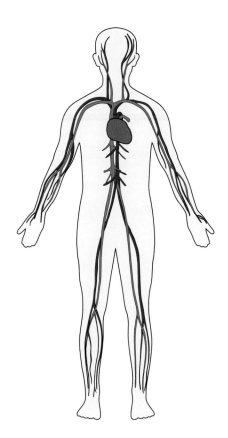

# The support and movement system

**Key words**
* skeleton
* bone
* cartilage
* connective tissue
* ligaments
* tendons
* muscle
* impulse
* contract

## The skeleton

6 Look at the **skeleton** below – name as many parts of it as you can. Check your list with your partner. Who remembered the most bone names? Make a note of those that you did not remember.

7 The skeleton has several functions. What do you think they are? (HINT– Imagine what your body would be like without a skeleton. Think about a jellyfish; it has no skeleton.)

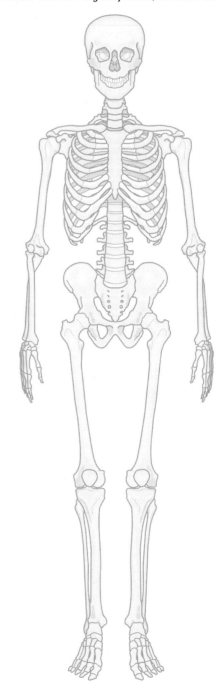

The skeleton is part of the system that moves and supports our bodies. This system is made up of **bone**, **cartilage**, **connective tissue** (**ligaments** and **tendons**) and **muscle**. Ligaments hold the bones together, and tendons attach the muscles to the bone. A nerve **impulse** to the muscles causes them to **contract**. As they contract they get shorter and pull on the bones. This causes movement. Muscles can pull but they cannot push, so they work together in pairs. As one set contracts, it pulls on the bone. The other set of muscles is relaxed. The second set then contracts and the first set relaxes, moving the bone in the opposite direction.

**8** Copy this drawing of a leg and add labels to explain how it moves. The arrow on the drawing shows which way that part of the limb is moving. Indicate which muscles are getting shorter and which are being stretched.

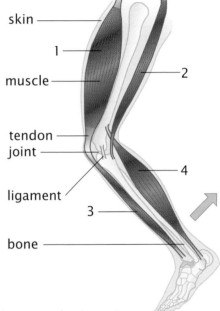

Leg muscles in action.

## Slow- and fast-twitch muscle

Have you ever noticed that in roast chicken there is some dark meat and some lighter, 'white' meat? The meat that you eat is protein, and muscle is made of protein. In 1873 a scientist named Ranvier reported differences in muscle colour in different mammals. The dark meat of turkey or chicken is 'red' or slow-twitch muscle. The white meat is 'white' or fast-twitch muscle. Most animals have a combination of these two fibre types. The slow-twitch muscles have more **mitochondria** packed within the muscle cells – this gives them a darker, reddish colour. Humans also have dark and white meat. Some of our muscles, such as those controlling eye movements, are made up of only fast-twitch fibres. Others, like the ones in the lower leg, are almost all slow-twitch fibres. Most human muscles contain a mixture of both fast-twitch and slow-twitch fibre types. The exact composition of each muscle is **genetically** determined. On average we have about 50% fast-twitch and 50% slow-twitch fibres in most movement muscles, but this varies greatly between people.

Fast-twitch muscle fibres are used when heavy work is demanded of the muscles, and strength and power are needed. They contract quickly, providing short bursts of energy, and are used for high intensity, low **endurance** activities. Fast-twitch muscle fibres become exhausted quickly. Pain and cramps rapidly develop from the build-up of lactic acid, a by-product of **anaerobic** respiration in the muscle cells.

Slow-twitch muscle fibres produce a steady, low intensity, repetitive contraction. They do not tire easily and are used when endurance is needed, for example, for long distance running.

---

*Creative thinking*

## Muscle types

In your group, make an information sheet for a Year 7 class that explains:

- how muscles move bones
- what fast-twitch and slow-twitch muscles are
- what we mean by endurance athletic events and power athletic events.

---

*Reasoning*

## Muscles and sport

1 Some sports are high intensity, low endurance, such as the 100 m track race, and some sports are low intensity, high endurance, such as the marathon. Discuss the difference between these types of sport. Can you think of two more examples of each type?

2 Which type of muscle fibre do you think is most needed by endurance athletes, and which by power athletes?

3 Why do sprinters sometimes collapse in pain when they are running?

4 Why are the muscles that control eye movement made of fast-twitch fibres?

5 Which muscles in our body are mainly made up of slow-twitch fibres? Why?

6 Which type of muscle contains the most mitochondria? Why?

---

*Research*

When people play sports and train seriously they may put a lot of strain on parts of their bodies.

Have you or anyone in your group ever had a sports-related injury? If so, what happened and how did it get better?

*Information processing*    *Sports injuries*

Look at the following bar chart.

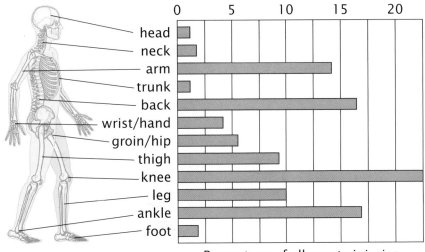

Percentage of all sports injuries

**1** What data do the bar chart show?

**2** Which parts of the body do the data suggest are most likely to be damaged during sports? From your own experience of sport, do you agree or disagree with this?

**3** What types of sport do you think cause these frequent injuries? Why?

**4** Which area of the body is most likely to get damaged if you play:

- squash
- football
- netball?

**5** Swimming-related injuries are not as frequent as injuries from sports played on land. Can you think why that might be?
(HINT– Think about the functions of the skeleton and concepts like gravity and density.)

**DID YOU KNOW?**

There are specially-made swimming pools that can be used for hydrotherapy for injured racehorses.

*Research*

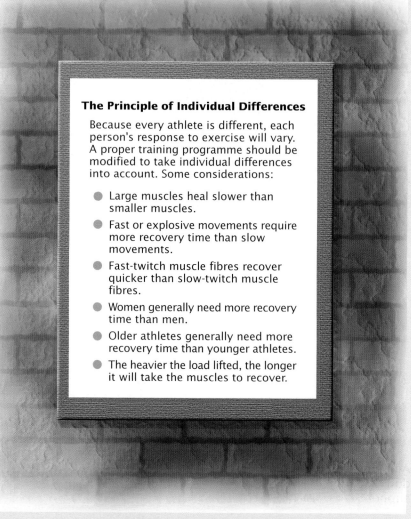

### The Principle of Individual Differences

Because every athlete is different, each person's response to exercise will vary. A proper training programme should be modified to take individual differences into account. Some considerations:

- Large muscles heal slower than smaller muscles.
- Fast or explosive movements require more recovery time than slow movements.
- Fast-twitch muscle fibres recover quicker than slow-twitch muscle fibres.
- Women generally need more recovery time than men.
- Older athletes generally need more recovery time than younger athletes.
- The heavier the load lifted, the longer it will take the muscles to recover.

These are just some of the many differences between athletes. All of these differences have to be considered when deciding what an athlete's training routine should be. You can look up the 'Principle of Individual Differences' on the internet to find out more about the professional world of sports training.

*Information processing* ## Training

Interview your PE teachers to find out how they decide what training each school team needs. Record what you find out – you could use a tape recorder or make notes. Check back with your PE teachers that you have recorded their responses to your questions correctly. Use the information from the interview to write a short article suitable for other pupils on safe training. Your PE teachers will probably be interested to see the article and willing to give you feedback.

# → *Knee joint*

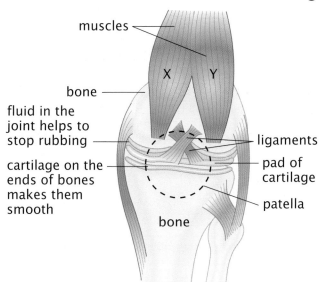

muscles

X   Y

bone

fluid in the joint helps to stop rubbing

cartilage on the ends of bones makes them smooth

ligaments

pad of cartilage

patella

bone

One of the strongest and most complex joints in our body is the knee joint. Normally, both the muscles labelled X and Y in this diagram pull with equal force on the knee bones. In 'runner's knee' one of these muscles is weaker and the knee bone slips to one side causing pain and inflammation, and the knee bone rubs the connective tissues together.

9 Why does the knee joint need to be so strong?

10 What do you think is the function of the two pads of cartilage between the long leg bones?

11 Suggest two other injuries to the knee.

12 When a joint is injured it becomes stiff and hard to move. What is the advantage of this happening?

---

*Creative thinking*  *Ideal footwear*

The diagrams below show some of the injuries that can be caused by wearing incorrect footwear when exercising.

Ankle pain if shoes don't give ankle support.

Instep soreness caused by shoes that rub across the top of the foot.

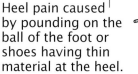

Achilles tendon injury is very painful and is caused by stiff shoes or lack of support at back and top of heel.

Heel pain caused by pounding on the ball of the foot or shoes having thin material at the heel.

Shin splints caused by running on the toes instead of using the whole foot or soft-soled shoes.

1 Sketch and label a design for an 'ideal' running shoe.

2 Which other parts of the body might be injured by wearing incorrect footwear?

3 What type of shoe do you wear during PE?

4 You probably have a pair of trainers – what features made you choose them? Do other people use the same criteria to buy their trainers?

# → *Arm bones*

Shona is having an X-ray of her arm.

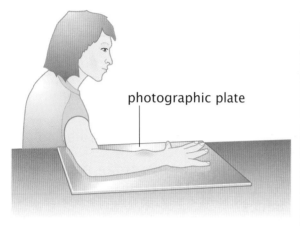

photographic plate

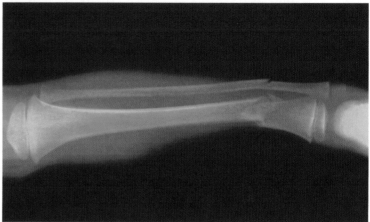

**Key words**
* radius
* ulna
* humerus
* hinge
* slipping
* rotating

This photograph shows the X-ray that was taken.

The two long bones in the X-ray are the **radius** and **ulna**. The ulna is the lower arm bone that joins to the **humerus**. The humerus is the upper arm bone. The joint between the two is a **hinge** joint. The wrist joint is a **slipping** joint, which has limited **rotating** movement.

13 What do you think the doctor told Shona when she saw this X-ray?
14 Copy this diagram of an arm into your notebook and label the bones and joints.

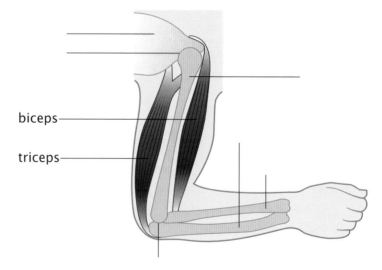

biceps

triceps

15 Describe the movement of a hinge joint.
16 Why are joints needed in the arm?
17 How does the hinge joint at the elbow differ from the wrist joint?
18 How does the hinge joint at the elbow differ from the shoulder joint?

19 Which muscle do you think contracts to move the lower arm up – the biceps or the triceps?

20 What connects muscles to bones – ligaments or tendons?

21 What connects the humerus to the ulna – ligaments or tendons?

*Word play* — Think of an anagram, mnemonic or rhyme to help you remember what tendons and ligaments do.

# The respiratory system

**Key words**
* ribs
* diaphragm

22 Match definitions 1–3 to the processes A–C:

A Gas exchange
B Respiration
C Breathing

1 The process of oxygen moving into the blood from the air in the alveoli at the same time as carbon dioxide leaves the blood and enters the alveoli.

2 The flow of air in and out of the lungs, helped by the movements of the **ribs** and **diaphragm**.

3 A chemical process inside cells that releases energy from glucose.

Check with a partner to see if your answers agree.

## Aerobic respiration

The chemical reaction inside cells which involves oxygen and releases energy from glucose is aerobic respiration. The products of this reaction are carbon dioxide and water. Approximately 15.6 kilojoules of energy are produced from just 1 gram of glucose. When we respire like this we have to breathe in oxygen and breathe out carbon dioxide. We also have to excrete the water produced in our urine.

## Anaerobic respiration

Respiration happens anaerobically when there is less oxygen available. Only 0.65 kilojoules of energy are produced from 1 gram of glucose. When our cells respire anaerobically they also produce lactic acid. Too much lactic acid is thought to cause muscle cramps. Cells can only respire anaerobically for a very short time. Every cell in your body needs oxygen to live – without it, a cell will die after just 4 minutes.

23 Write two word equations to show the differences between aerobic and anaerobic respiration.

24 All living things respire, but do all living things breathe? Name three or four different organisms to answer this question and describe how each gets its oxygen.
(HINT– Remember how we classify living things.)

Your breathing rate is the number of breaths you take in a measured amount of time.

**25** Which of the activities pictured below would increase your breathing rate?

**26** Which activities might cause less oxygen to be available to cells?

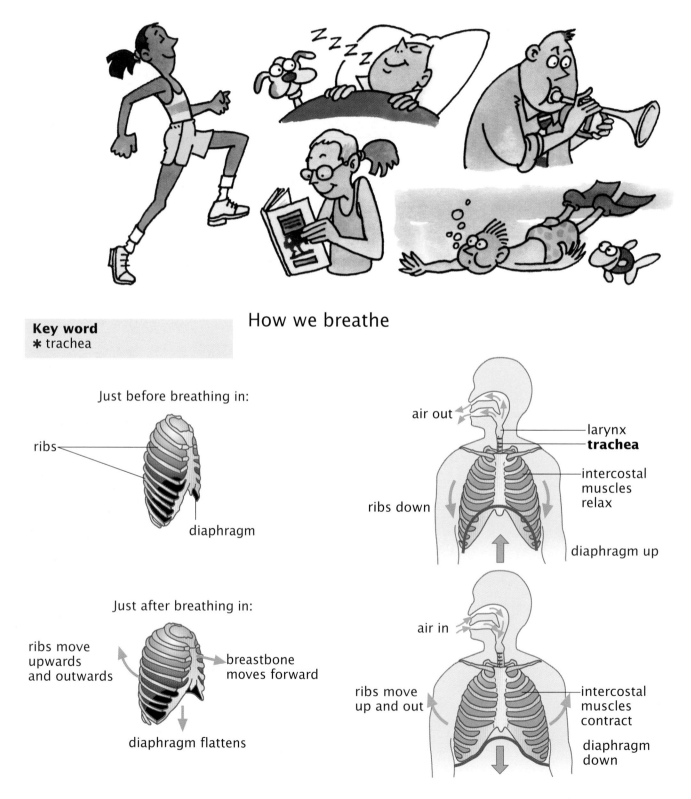

**Key word**
∗ trachea

## How we breathe

Just before breathing in:

ribs

diaphragm

Just after breathing in:

ribs move upwards and outwards

breastbone moves forward

diaphragm flattens

air out

larynx

**trachea**

intercostal muscles relax

ribs down

diaphragm up

air in

ribs move up and out

intercostal muscles contract

diaphragm down

**Key words**
* exhalation
* inhalation
* capacity

27 Write a short description of how air gets in and out of our lungs. Make sure you explain which muscles are involved during **exhalation** and **inhalation**. Which requires more effort?

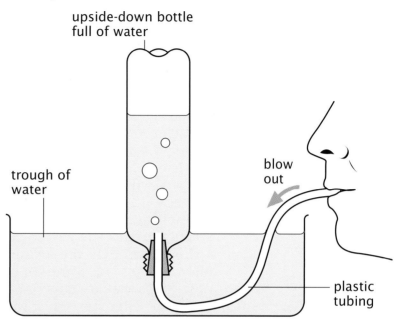

Measuring lung **capacity** the easy way.

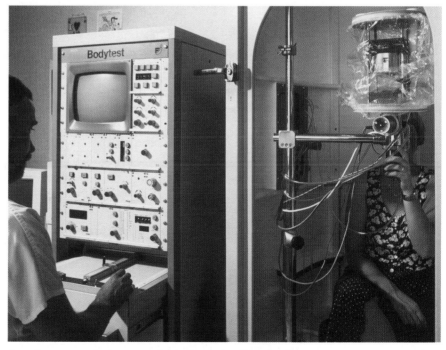

A spirometer being used to measure lung volume.

*Reasoning* ## Lung capacity

Look at the above pictures that show how lung capacity can be measured in a school lab and in a hospital. Talk with a partner to make sure you both know what lung capacity is and how to measure it.

# → *Keeping the respiratory system healthy*

28 In your group, list all the diseases that you know affect the organs of the respiratory system.

## The lungs

Lungs are like huge, delicate pink sponges. The air you breathe into your lungs contains all sorts of things, including bacteria and viruses. It may also contain carbon particles if you live in an area where there is a lot of industry. On average, you breathe in 20 000 million particles of pollution a day. Inhaled air also contains oxygen, which is needed for aerobic respiration.

Special cells line the air tubes (**bronchus** and **bronchioles**) leading to your lungs. These cells make clear, sticky **mucus**. The mucus is **secreted** from the cells to form a slimy layer over the inside walls of the air tubes. Dust and microbes get stuck in it. In between the mucus cells are other cells that are covered in tiny microscopic hairs called **cilia**. The cilia move in a wave, a bit like seaweed in water. They sweep the mucus up towards the mouth and nose, and away from the lungs. It reaches the back of the throat and you swallow it. The digestive system then destroys the dirt and microbes that have been trapped in the mucus. If any dirt or microbes do reach the **alveoli** in the lungs, they are quickly destroyed by white blood cells.

If you have a respiratory infection lots of mucus is produced and it may be thick and greenish or yellow. It clogs up your nose and you may develop a cough to bring it up into your mouth as it is too thick to swallow. This is called phlegm or snot.

There are over 300 million alveoli in the lungs. These are like tiny bags of air with very thin surfaces. If they were all flattened and spread out they would cover an area the size of a tennis court. The oxygen from the air passes through the thin surface of the alveoli into the blood vessels (**capillaries**) that surround them. The alveoli can be very easily damaged, so your body has several methods for protecting your lungs from harmful things.

The diaphragm moving up and down too rapidly can cause hiccups. The longest episode of hiccups was experienced by an American pig farmer. He started hiccuping in 1922 and didn't stop until 1987.

Here is a diagram of alveoli in the lungs. Copy the diagram and complete the labels to show that you understand gas exchange.

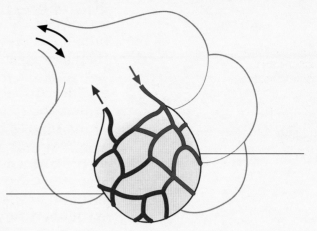

1 Name an airborne microbe that causes a disease that affects the human respiratory system.
2 Which conditions do you think are most favourable for microbes to grow and reproduce rapidly – cold or warm, damp or dry?
3 Which of these conditions describe the inside of your lungs?
4 What chemical process produces carbon particles that might get breathed in? (HINT– Another word for carbon particles is soot.)
5 What makes the lungs look pink?
6 Why are lungs described as being like sponges?
7 How can swallowing mucus get rid of microbes and dirt?
8 When you have a cold, you produce lots of extra mucus. Why?
9 Why do you need to blow your nose when you have a cold?
10 Why might gas exchange be thought of as the link between breathing and respiration?

# Smoking

**Key words**
* pneumonia
* bronchitis
* lung cancer
* nicotine
* addicted

Smoking is the UK's biggest cause of preventable illness and early death. 120 000 people die from smoking every year just in the UK. Hundreds more die from passive or 'second-hand' smoking. Passive smoking is breathing in air filled with smoke from other people smoking in the same environment. Treating smoking-related diseases costs the National Health Service £1.7 billion a year. In America, manufacturers of cigarettes have been successfully sued by people in their sixties dying of cancer who claim that the cigarette companies should have warned them of the dangers of smoking.

The diseases caused by smoking affect the respiratory system, for example, **pneumonia**, **bronchitis** and **lung cancer**. Smoking gives some people relief from stress because cigarettes contain a drug called **nicotine** which stimulates the brain and relaxes the muscles. Nicotine is a habit-forming drug so people who smoke get **addicted** to it.

Inhaling cigarette smoke increases carbon monoxide in the bloodstream. This gas attaches itself to red blood cells in place of oxygen molecules, so the blood cells cannot pick up oxygen. People who smoke are often said to be 'short of breath', as they cannot use the oxygen from each breath they take efficiently.

Among the 4000 chemicals in cigarette smoke are soot and tar particles. These stick to the lining of the respiratory system, building up mucus and causing 'smokers' cough'. This damages the efficiency of gas exchange in the lungs. The heat from inhaled smoke burns the tiny hairs lining the nostrils which would normally help trap dust and dirt, stopping it from getting into the respiratory system. Also, nicotine paralyses the cilia that help move mucus up the respiratory tubes.

Smoking increases the heart rate and blood pressure. This stress can damage the heart muscle. People who smoke double their risk of a heart attack compared with non-smokers. Cigarette smoking is the main cause of sudden cardiac death. Smokers are more likely to die suddenly within 60 minutes of a heart attack than non-smokers. Even people who smoke only cigars or pipes, not cigarettes, appear to have a higher risk of death from coronary heart disease and possibly stroke than non-smokers, even though cigar and pipe smokers do not usually inhale.

*Information processing*   ## Diseases from smoking

Read the above section on smoking again. Discuss with a partner which of these diseases you think smoking is likely to cause, and why:

- bronchitis
- pneumonia
- heart disease
- stress
- lung cancer
- stomach cancer.

*Research*

- What is passive smoking?
- What laws do we have in this country to protect people from passive smoking?
- Do you think these laws discriminate against smokers?
- When did it become law to put health warnings on cigarette packets?
- Are there any government health campaigns being run to help people stop smoking? Collect examples of campaign materials and make a display. Your collection could include posters, video clips or leaflets.
- Find out how cigarettes are made.
- What do cigarettes contain?
- Why do different cigarette brands have different tar ratings?

## Smoking and pregnancy

A woman who smokes when she is pregnant is more likely to have a spontaneous abortion (miscarriage) or stillbirth. Babies born to smokers are usually underweight, so they are not as strong as babies born to non-smokers. They may also be more likely to catch infections as their immune system may be damaged.

**29** Make a list of the damage you think smoking causes. Compare your notes with your group and make one group list summarising the damage to health caused by smoking. Put your list up on the wall and compare it with other groups' work.

*Information processing*  ## Respiratory infections

In the 1980s a study was made of the incidence of infections of the respiratory system in American soldiers going through basic training. 1230 soldiers took part in the study. Look at this table of data. What do you conclude from it about the effects of smoking on health?

| Groups of American soldiers undergoing physical training | Percentage of soldiers in each group who reported respiratory infections |
|---|---|
| soldiers who smoked during their physical training course | 25.5 |
| soldiers who gave up smoking halfway through their physical training course | 36 |
| soldiers who began smoking during their training course | 21.5 |
| soldiers who did not smoke at all | 17 |

The respiratory infections the soldiers reported included coughs and colds.

**1** Work out roughly how much more likely it is for a soldier who smokes to get an infection compared with a soldier who does not smoke.

**2** Why do you think soldiers who smoke are at greater risk of infection?

**3** Suggest a reason for the high figures for infection in the soldiers who gave up smoking halfway through their training course.

**4** If you were the director of a tobacco company, what criticism would you make about this research?

*Reasoning*  ## Correlations

In the 1960s cigarette manufacturers argued that statistics did not prove that smoking causes cancer. They are logically correct – just because there is a correlation between smoking and lung cancer, it does not mean that one causes the other. It would be like saying that eating cereal for breakfast causes car accidents, because out of a sample of drivers who had car accidents 78% had eaten cereal for breakfast. It has been suggested that the correlation between smoking and lung cancer exists not because cancer is caused by smoking, but because the people who become addicted to cigarettes are the kind of people who have a genetic tendency to get cancer.

**1** What sort of investigation would you carry out to show that this is NOT the case?

**2** Which of the graphs below indicate a strong correlation between the disease and smoking?

**3** Which indicate some correlation, but it is not strong?

**4** Which of the graphs indicate no correlation?

**5** How do you think these data were collected?

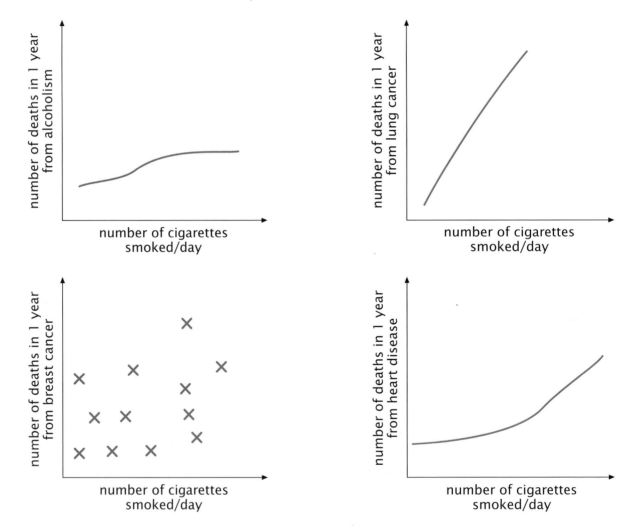

**6** Here are two statements, both of which are true.

'In one year, more people are killed by diseases linked to smoking than die in all the road accidents in that year.'

'Every time you smoke a cigarette you shorten your life by an hour.'

**a)** Which is the best statement for putting people off smoking? Why?

**b)** Which statement would it be easiest to provide scientific evidence for? Why?

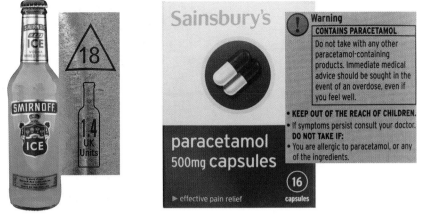

**7** What other products carry health warnings?

## Stopping smoking

Make a health campaign poster that includes a graph showing people how much money they could save if they gave up smoking, and some of the things they could buy with the money they saved. Add any other information you think would help people to decide to give up smoking. Make sure the whole poster is eye-catching and informative.

Look at the posters of other people in your group and together decide which messages are likely to be most effective.

## Smoking

**1** Explain why each of these remarks is unscientific.

**2** Discuss this question in your groups:

If smoking is so bad for you, why do people do it?

## It's not too late to quit

Smokers who quit can reduce the risk of disease. Research shows that 2 years after quitting, the risk of former smokers developing heart disease is reduced by 25%. After 10 years, the risk of developing heart disease is similar among former smokers and those who have never smoked. Quitting is difficult, but it is a positive step towards a healthier heart.

# Drugs

The dictionary definition of a drug is:

'A medicinal substance, used alone or as an ingredient; narcotic, hallucinogen, or stimulant'.

(*The Concise Oxford Dictionary*)

Drugs are chemicals that change the way the body works. Medicines are drugs that help the body when you are sick, but like all drugs they are dangerous if misused. Examples of medicines are painkillers and **tranquillisers**. Cigarettes and alcohol are legal drugs for adults. They are known as **recreational** drugs. In the UK, you have to be 16 to smoke and 18 to drink alcohol. Caffeine is a drug you can have at any age. Other drugs, for example, heroin and Ecstasy, are illegal for everyone in this country.

**30 a)** Decide which of these substances are drugs:

| | |
|---|---|
| ginger | alcopops |
| beer | banana |
| aspirin | ibuprofen |
| caffeine | nicotine |
| wine | tar |
| sage | Vaseline |
| Ecstasy | cannabis |
| penicillin | |

**b)** Do the others in your group agree with you?

**31** Which of the drugs in the list are legal and which illegal to use?

**32** Some of the drugs in the list are restricted to particular groups of people. Which ones? Do you know what the restrictions are?

**33** Some medicinal drugs can be bought in supermarkets and pharmacies 'over-the-counter'; others can only be prescribed by a doctor. Which of the drugs in the above list are recreational, which can be bought over-the-counter, and which have to be prescribed by a doctor?

On the next two pages is a table with information about some drugs that cause damage and are illegal. The amount of damage they cause in young bodies is much greater than in adults because your tissues are still growing. Many of these drugs have very bad effects on brain development, and many lead to addiction. Some can cause death even when taken for the first time. The world of drug taking is a scary and dangerous place.

*Time to think*

**1** Check that you know what these words mean:

- co-ordination
- coma
- tranquilliser
- depressant

**2** In your group, discuss these issues:

- Which drugs do you think are the most dangerous for young people? Why?
- Why do you think that drug addiction is increasing in people under 20?
- What do you think could be done by communities to help young people avoid being tempted by drugs?
- What do you think when you hear some people say that smoking marijuana is not as dangerous as smoking cigarettes?
- What do you think 'addiction' is?
- Why do people get 'hooked' on drugs?

**Key words**
- **\*** depressant
- **\*** hallucinations
- **\*** narcotics
- **\*** coma

| Official name | Other common names | Appearance | How it is ingested (taken into the body) | Effects |
|---|---|---|---|---|
| marijuana – the most widely used drug | cannabis, hashish, Mary Jane, herb, weed, grass, pot, chronic, joint, reefer, skunk | green, brown or grey dried crumbled leaves, like dried parsley | • smoked as hand-rolled cigarettes (a joint or nail) or in a pipe, or in a water pipe called a bong<br>• can be mixed into foods, baked in cakes or brewed as a tea<br>• sometimes mixed with crack cocaine, making it very dangerous | • a **depressant** – slows down the central nervous system<br>• users lose concentration, find it difficult to learn, feel 'chilled out'<br>• raises blood pressure<br>• gives the user red eyes and a dry mouth, can make them sleepy or hungry<br>• can cause paranoia and **hallucinations**<br>• when smoked, it is as damaging to lungs as tobacco |
| heroin – grouped with the pain-relieving drugs known as **narcotics**, which include codeine and morphine, both legally prescribed by doctors | horse, smack, caballo (Spanish), big H, black tar, junk | • white or brown powder with a bad taste<br>• black tar heroin looks sticky or like a hard lump | • can be mixed with crack cocaine – the mixture is called 8-ball<br>• usually injected or smoked<br>• if pure, it can be inhaled through the nose (snorted) | • burst of good feeling (rush) leading to a high level of relaxation, followed by drowsiness and sickness<br>• users can stop breathing and die<br>• repeated injecting leads to scarring called 'tracks'<br>• addicts often share needles, increasing their risk of getting killer diseases such as hepatitis B and HIV/AIDS<br>• can be addictive after only one or two doses<br>• withdrawal symptoms include panic attacks, lack of sleep, chills and sweats, convulsions and seizures<br>• it is easy to fall into a **coma** and possibly die with an overdose |

| Official name | Other common names | Appearance | How it is ingested (taken into the body) | Effects |
|---|---|---|---|---|
| Ecstasy – 3,4-methylenedioxy-*N*-methyl-amphetamine (MDMA) | XTC, X, Adam, E, roll | • made illegally as a 'designer' drug as tablets or powder<br>• tablets may have a popular logo on them (for example, a cartoon character) which makes them look like sweets | • can be swallowed as a pill or tablet, or snorted as a powder | • gives a 'high' by stimulating adrenaline production<br>• can keep user active for days<br>• can kill after one use<br>• causes racing heart, dry mouth, stomach cramps, blurred vision, chills and sweats, sickness<br>• the body can overheat during dancing leading to death<br>• causes a decrease in the salts and minerals in the blood so the brain swells – could cause permanent brain damage<br>• destroys memory and thinking functions<br>• literally 'mind-bending' |
| inhalants – for example, glues, paint thinners, dry-cleaning fluid, some felt tip marker pen inks, hairspray, deodorants, spray paint, whipped cream dispensers (whippets) | whippets, poppers, snappers, rush, bolt, bullet | | • sniffed, snorted from containers or a plastic bag (bagging) or 'huffed' – holding an inhalant-soaked rag in the mouth | • give a 'rush' or 'high'<br>• feelings of being drunk followed by sleepiness, staggering, dizziness and confusion<br>• long-term use leads to headaches and nose bleeds, loss of sense of smell<br>• oxygen to the brain is decreased, so brain function is damaged<br>• can kill on first use |

# ➡ *Addiction*

Addiction can be physical, psychological or both. Drug abuse can lead to addiction.

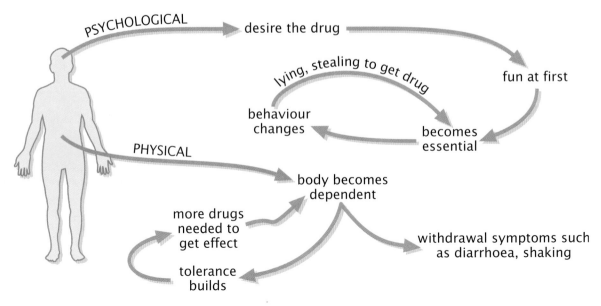

*Reasoning*   *Addiction*

Read this information from a health clinic leaflet.

# How to tell if a friend is addicted:

Have their sleeping habits changed?

They may sleep more or less than usual.

Have their eating habits changed?

Are they always hungry or have they lost their appetite?

Do they complain they are tired?

Do they feel sick?

Are they irritable and unpredictable?

Have they started arguing with their family all the time?

Have they lost interest in sports and hobbies they used to like?

If they are athletic, has their performance got poorer?

Have they become secretive?

Have they become depressed?

Have their school grades or marks got worse?

Are they taking less care with personal appearance?

Spots around the mouth/bad breath/red eyes?

**Overall, are they becoming a stranger to you?**

**1** Do you think this leaflet is helpful?

**2** How could you improve it to make it more helpful to young people?

**DID YOU KNOW?**

Babies whose mothers are heroin addicts can become addicted to the drug before they are born. They have to undergo treatment to wean them off the heroin as soon as they are born. If they are not treated, this addiction can kill them soon after birth. However, nicotine is said to be even more addictive than heroin or crack cocaine.

# Alcohol

Alcohol damages the liver because the liver is the organ which 'cleans' alcohol from the blood. Alcohol gets **concentrated** in the liver, preventing effective cell respiration and so killing the cells. When you drink alcohol its molecules are quickly and easily absorbed into the bloodstream from the stomach and small intestine, and go to the liver. All body cells can break down alcohol molecules in a way similar to the breakdown of lactic acid made during anaerobic respiration, but the liver is the main site for breaking down alcohol. Alcohol molecules are split into water and carbon dioxide.

People who drink too much alcohol get 'fatty liver' as the first indication their liver is being damaged. If they do not cut back their drinking, the liver becomes inflamed and swollen. Then they develop **jaundice**, a blood disease caused by damaged red blood cells. The blood may thicken, increasing the chances of blood clots. This is liver **hepatitis**. Some people with hepatitis will go on to develop **cirrhosis** (pronounced 'si-ro-sis'), where the liver becomes scarred and new cells do not grow. This damage is permanent.

Alcohol is a depressant – it slows **metabolism** and affects the ability to think and speak. It kills brain cells. Large amounts affect balance and can lead to reckless behaviour. It also reduces the ability of the body's immune system to fight off infections, and it stops healthy muscle growth in young children. Being drunk leads to 'hangovers', where the person who has been drinking a lot of alcohol has headaches and sickness after the other effects of the alcohol have worn off. People addicted to alcohol are called alcoholics. They can be violent. A problem related to alcohol is that 'drink driving' (when someone drives after drinking alcohol) causes many car accidents each year.

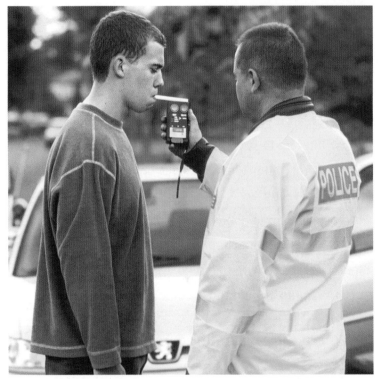

Police use a breathalyser to test if a driver has been drinking alcohol.

*DID YOU KNOW?*

About half the pedestrians aged between 16 and 60 killed in road accidents would be over the legal limit for driving.

*Time to think*

1 Why does alcohol affect every organ in your body?
2 What does the word metabolism mean?
3 Why is the liver the organ most likely to get damaged by excess alcohol consumption?
4 How does the body get rid of the water and carbon dioxide that is produced when alcohol is broken down?
5 Why are alcoholics more likely to get injured than people who do not drink to excess?

## Alcohol and the law

| Age | What is legal | What is illegal |
| --- | --- | --- |
| up to 16 | no alcohol | it is illegal to buy alcohol anywhere, and it is illegal for other people to buy alcohol for you |
| 16–17 | you can buy or be bought beer and cider on licensed premises to drink with a meal in a restaurant area | you cannot drink beer or cider bought for you in the bar area or public spaces |
| 18 and over | you can buy alcohol and consume it in bars and restaurants; people selling you alcohol are entitled to ask for ID showing how old you are | you cannot buy alcohol for anyone under 18 or encourage anyone under 18 to buy alcohol |

*DID YOU KNOW?* Children who start drinking alcohol before they are 15 years old are four times more likely than other non-drinking friends to become alcoholics.

*Information processing*

## Alcopops

Alcopops are being blamed for increasing teenage drinking. The World Health Director General, Dr Brundtland, said:

'By mixing alcohol with fruit juices and energy drinks to make 'alcopops' and by using advertising that focuses on youth lifestyle, sex, sports and fun, the large alcohol manufacturers are trying to establish a habit of drinking alcohol at a very young age. Youth are the key target of marketing for the alcohol industry.'

To see if the evidence supported Dr Brundtland's statement, a sample of 150 Scottish schools was selected. They represented different types of school, for example, comprehensive and secondary modern, single sex and mixed. Of the 150 schools selected, 122 took part in a survey about their smoking, drinking and drug use. Within these 122

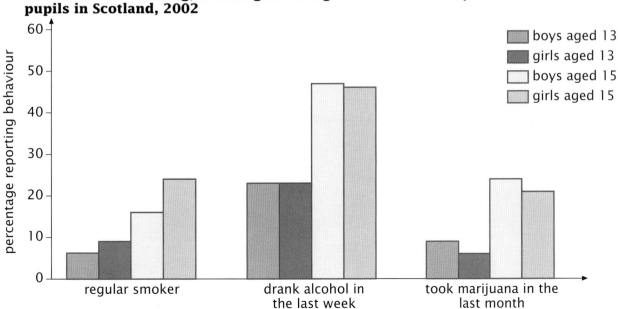

**Prevalence of smoking, drinking and drug use in 13- and 15-year-old pupils in Scotland, 2002**

percentage reporting behaviour

boys aged 13
girls aged 13
boys aged 15
girls aged 15

regular smoker    drank alcohol in the last week    took marijuana in the last month schools, about 70% of the pupils completed a questionnaire. The pupils were brought together in a classroom under the supervision of an interviewer, but with no teacher present.

1 Look at the data displayed in the graph on the previous page. In your group decide what can be inferred about drugs and youth in Scotland.

2 List the independent variables to do with the type of school that were surveyed in this sample.

3 Why was it important to represent different types of school? Are girls more at risk than boys?

4 Are all the drugs being used at the same level?

5 Which do you think present the greatest risks, and why?

6 Why was no teacher present during the survey?

7 Do you think there is evidence to support Dr Brundtland's statements?

8 What would you do next to add more useful information to these data?

**DID YOU KNOW?**

According to the World Health Organisation, one in four deaths among 15- to 29-year-olds is due to alcohol abuse.

---

*Evaluation* **What evidence?**

# Alcopops rot teeth

The controversial fizzy alcopops drinks are so acidic that they can rot people's teeth. The danger came to light when John Brown, a 17-year-old from Huddersfield, went to the dentist complaining that his teeth hurt, particularly the morning after a night out with his friends. He admitted that when he went out he and his friends drank beer and several bottles of alcopops, often vomiting because they got so drunk. His dentist capped his teeth and told him that the damage was caused by the acid in the alcopops mixing with the stomach acid in his vomit. John cut down on his drinking and his teeth have stopped rotting.

1 Do you think it is plausible to assume that the acid in alcopops might cause tooth rot?

2 What else could be the cause of tooth rot?

3 What scientific evidence would you advise the journalist to look for to strengthen the claim that alcopops are causing tooth rot?

4 How could that scientific evidence be collected?

---

*Word play*

Dictionary definitions:

'Seeming reasonable or probable'

'Taken as being true, for the purpose of argument or action'

Which statement defines the word 'plausible' and which defines 'assumption'?

# → *Caffeine*

Caffeine is a drug found in coffee, tea and chocolate, as well as some soft drinks, for example, cola. It comes from tropical plants: coffee comes from a plant called *Coffea arabica*, tea from *Camellia sinensis*, and cocoa from *Theobroma cacao*.

Picking coffee beans.

A tea plantation.

Cocoa pods.

## The symptoms of caffeine poisoning

In very small doses, caffeine mildly stimulates the nervous system. Large quantities of caffeine can cause dizziness, stomach pain, nausea, diarrhoea, elevated pulse rate and low blood pressure, as well as drowsiness. Severe caffeine poisoning causes headaches, insomnia, tremors and constipation. Since caffeine tolerance varies markedly from individual to individual, it is hard to predict just how much caffeine a person can drink before any symptoms are experienced. Luckily, caffeine poisoning is not fatal; moderate consumption is, for many people, one of life's perks. However, some people are very sensitive to caffeine and need to avoid drinking it. It can be found in drinks other than coffee and tea, such as cola, so they need to read ingredients labels carefully.

*Enquiry* | *Effect of coffee and tea*

1 Design and carry out an investigation to find out the effect of drinking coffee and tea on a human pulse rate. You could use datalogging equipment to compare the effect of caffeine on reaction times, for example, by dropping and catching a ruler from a given height. Do the experiment before and after a cup of coffee.
   How will you increase the reliability of your data?

2 Carry out a survey to find out how many cups of tea, coffee or cocoa people of different ages drink in a day.
   How will you ensure your data are fully representative?

3 Use your results from these two investigations to design a poster about caffeine as a drug.

**DID YOU KNOW?**

Holly plants also contain caffeine. The seeds, bark and leaves are all toxic, but the greatest concentration of caffeine occurs in the berries. If you grow holly in your garden, it is important to keep children from eating the berries.

# The digestive system

34 In your group, list as many hints for having a healthly digestive system as you can in 5 minutes.

35 Do the same thing again, this time listing things that are bad for the digestive system.

  Compile a class list of the things that are good and bad for the digestive system.

36 List the types of food we need to have in our diet to keep us healthy. Think back to your Year 7 work. What is each type for?

*Information processing*

## Energetic activities

The table below shows how much energy different activities use. Rank the activities from the most energetic to the least energetic, and make a graph to show this information in a visual way. Think about what type of graph you should draw – a pie graph, a bar chart or a line graph. Why?

**Energy used for a variety of activities**

| Activity | Gender | Age | Energy (kJ) used |
|---|---|---|---|
| sleeping | man | 40 | 7150 |
| | woman | 40 | 6400 |
| office work | man | 40 | 10500 |
| | woman | 40 | 9500 |
| car mechanic | man | 30 | 13000 |
| | woman | 30 | 12800 |
| builder | man | 30 | 15500 |
| | woman | 30 | 15000 |
| pregnancy | woman | 25 | 10000 |
| breastfeeding | woman | 25 | 12600 |
| playing | boy | 8 | 6700 |
| | girl | 8 | 6050 |

## Minerals and vitamins

As well as the major food types – carbohydrates, fats and proteins – the body also needs minerals and vitamins to keep healthy.

| Vitamin or mineral | Source | Function | Deficiency disease |
|---|---|---|---|
| A | • vegetables, butter, egg yolk, liver | • healthy skin<br>• helps vision in dim light | • lowered immunity<br>• poor night vision |
| D | • butter, egg yolk<br>• the skin synthesises it when exposed to sunlight | • regulates absorption of calcium and phosphate in food from the gut<br>• helps deposit these minerals in the bones | • poor bone formation (rickets)<br>• children have bowed legs and their bones break easily |
| E | • butter, wholemeal bread | • helps maintain healthy immune system | • nerve damage |
| K | • cabbage, spinach<br>• made by bacteria in the gut | • aids blood clotting | • wounds bleed for a long time |
| B1, B2, B12 | • wholemeal bread, yeast, liver | • general good health<br>• formation of red blood cells | • lack of B1 leads to beri-beri, a disease that inflames the muscles<br>• lack of B2 leads to pellagra, a skin disease<br>• lack of B12 leads to anaemia |
| C | • citrus fruit, milk, fresh vegetables | • repairs damaged tissue<br>• helps immunity | • scurvy – the skin flakes, gums bleed and wounds do not heal |
| Ca, Ph | • milk, cheese | • bones and teeth (see vitamin D) | • brittle bones and teeth |
| Fe | • liver, egg yolk | • healthy red blood cells | • anaemia |
| I, Na, K | • seafood, salt, leafy vegetables | • make the hormone thyroxine, which controls metabolism<br>• help nerves and muscles function | • swollen thyroid glands (goitre) |

*Evaluation* Diet

1 Review your diet this week. List the different minerals and vitamins you have eaten. Note down the ones you may be short of. What will you try to eat for the rest of the week to make sure you have enough of the necessary vitamins and minerals?

2 How does your analysis of your diet compare with a friend's? Do they eat a healthier diet than you?

3 Why does a 30-year-old woman require less calcium in her recommended daily intake than a 15-year-old girl?

4 Why are water and roughage (fibre) also necessary to keep healthy?

*Time to think* In your group, decide on a strategy that will help all of you to learn the facts in the vitamin and mineral table. Use that strategy. How effective was it for each of you?

*Information processing*  ## Vitamin C

Vitamin C is found in fresh fruit and vegetables.

**1** Name three specific foods that you would eat to give yourself vitamin C.

Vitamin C is needed to keep connective tissue healthy. It helps keep gums healthy, and cuts down the chance of microbes getting through the skin.

**2** What symptoms indicate someone is not getting enough vitamin C in their diet?

DCPIP is a chemical indicator that is used to test for vitamin C.

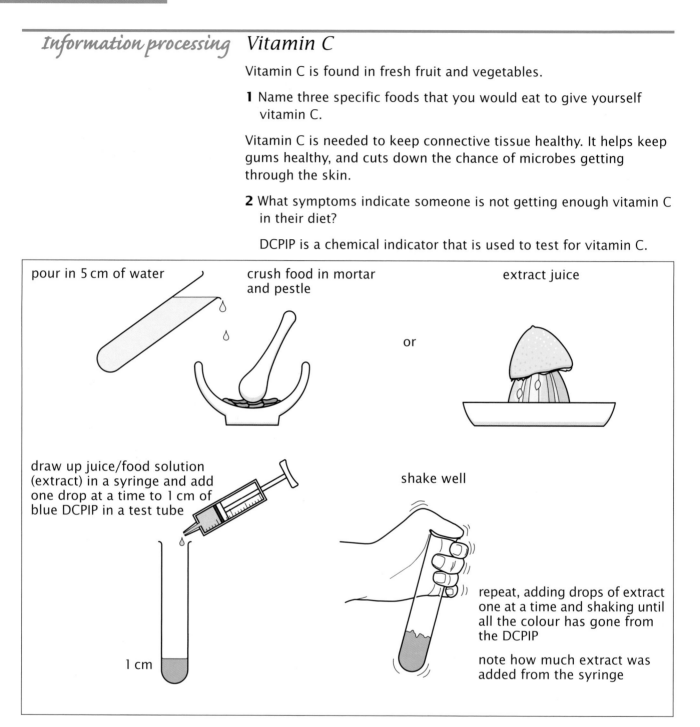

pour in 5 cm of water

crush food in mortar and pestle

extract juice

or

draw up juice/food solution (extract) in a syringe and add one drop at a time to 1 cm of blue DCPIP in a test tube

1 cm

shake well

repeat, adding drops of extract one at a time and shaking until all the colour has gone from the DCPIP

note how much extract was added from the syringe

**3** Make a list of the equipment you would need to carry out a vitamin C test.

**4** List the steps you would take.

### Planning an investigation

**5** Working in a group, plan an investigation to answer the following question:

Which contains the most vitamin C – freshly squeezed orange juice, concentrated orange squash or a carton of chilled orange juice?

**6** Write down your proposed method and draw a table to show how you would organise the data you would collect.

*Reasoning* ## Diets

A survey found the following data for the percentage of energy provided by fat in a typical diet in some countries, and the annual death rates for men in these countries.

| | Deaths per 100 000 men | % of total energy from fat |
|---|---|---|
| Finland | 403 | 48 |
| USA | 346 | 51 |
| Scotland | 343 | 47 |
| Australia | 297 | 52 |
| New Zealand | 273 | 37 |
| Canda | 270 | 41 |
| England and Wales | 259 | 45 |
| Norway | 213 | 41 |
| Czechoslovakia | 201 | 36 |
| Germany | 194 | 30 |
| Israel | 148 | 31 |
| Bulgaria | 72 | 31 |
| France | 66 | 29 |
| Romania | 61 | 27 |
| Spain | 50 | 31 |
| Hong Kong | 34 | 26 |
| Japan | 34 | 28 |

The figures show no correlation between diet and heart disease.

The figures show that the more fat you eat, the more likely you are to die of heart disease.

There is a correlation between percentage of fat eaten and death rate.

Dr Smythe          Dr Jones          Dr Singh

Discuss with a partner which doctor you agree with.

What other information would you want before you could make a better, more informed conclusion about heart disease and fat?

## Being 'out of balance'

To be healthy, all your body systems need to be in balance. Anorexia, bulimia and obesity are all disorders to do with undereating or overeating. They are caused by the digestive system being unbalanced by intake of food.

This in turn leads to an imbalance in what is absorbed into the blood system. Any imbalance in the blood affects all the other systems, particularly the heart.

**37** Look at these drawings and make some notes that describe the symptoms of each eating disorder.

REDUCED LIFE SPAN

- diabetes
- breast cancer in women
- shortness of breath
- high blood pressure
- polycystic ovaries
- gall bladder disease
- tiredness
- arthritis in back, hips, knees and ankles

LOW SELF-ESTEEM

- depression
- hormone imbalance
- dehydration
- loss of important minerals
- damage to oesophagus, kidneys and liver
- laxative use
- eating out of control (binges)
- vomiting

- perfectionist with low self-esteem
- periods stop
- may starve to death
- depression
- bones soften
- lowered immunity

*Creative thinking*  *Pregnancy advice*

Imagine your group has been asked to design a fact sheet for health visitors to give to couples intending to start a family.

Draft the facts you would want to include. You will need to read back over this chapter to find all the information related to pregnancy.

Make recommendations about daily food intake and substances to avoid. Explain to the reader why you are making these recommendations.

How would you make sure your leaflet was easy to understand, interesting and informative?

# The body's defence against pathogens

The diagram below should remind you of the many ways our bodies protect us from disease.

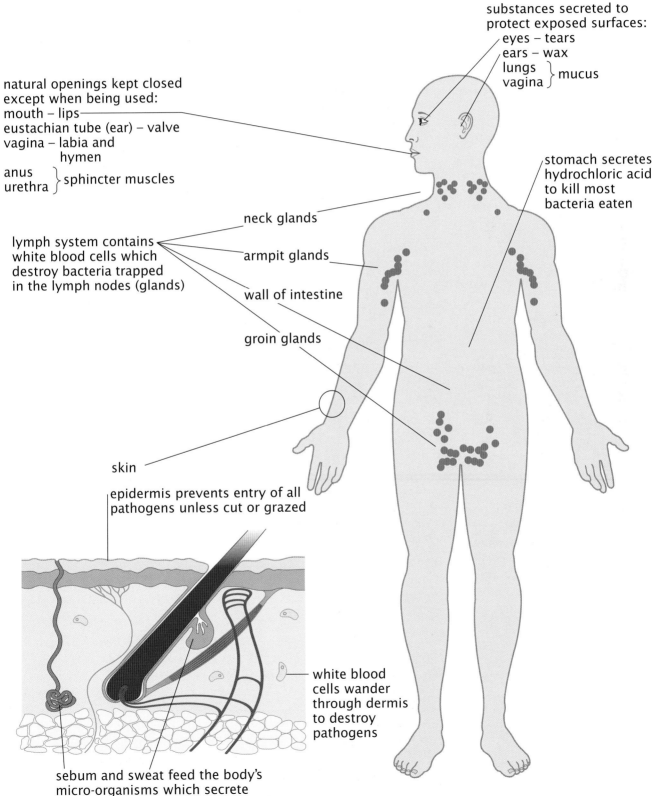

substances secreted to protect exposed surfaces:
eyes – tears
ears – wax
lungs
vagina } mucus

natural openings kept closed except when being used:
mouth – lips
eustachian tube (ear) – valve
vagina – labia and
          hymen
anus
urethra } sphincter muscles

stomach secretes hydrochloric acid to kill most bacteria eaten

neck glands

lymph system contains white blood cells which destroy bacteria trapped in the lymph nodes (glands)

armpit glands

wall of intestine

groin glands

skin

epidermis prevents entry of all pathogens unless cut or grazed

white blood cells wander through dermis to destroy pathogens

sebum and sweat feed the body's micro-organisms which secrete natural antibiotics on the epidermis

Think back to your previous work and see if you can answer these questions:

**38** Name some useful drugs and the diseases or infections they treat.
**39** What is an antiseptic?
**40** How would you treat a grazed knee?
**41** What is aspirin useful for?
**42** What might cause food poisoning?

---

*Creative thinking* *Immune system*

Use these notes to make a leaflet for a local gym called 'Habits that weaken your immune system'. Use visual methods such as diagrams, tables or lists to summarise some of the information. Many people find these visual presentations easier to remember.

Certain foods and environmental influences are damaging to the immune system, for example, too much sugary food, too much fat, excess alcohol, and smoking.

Overdosing on sugar
Eating or drinking 100 grams (8 tablespoons) of sugar, the equivalent of one 350 ml can of fizzy drink, reduces the ability of white blood cells to kill bacteria by 40%. The immune-suppressing effect of sugar starts less than 30 minutes after ingestion and may last for 5 hours. The ingestion of complex carbohydrates, or starches, has no effect on the immune system.

Excess alcohol
Harms the body's immune system in two ways:
1. It produces an overall nutritional deficiency, depriving the body of valuable immune-boosting nutrients.
2. Consumed in excess, alcohol, like sugar, can reduce the ability of white cells to kill bacteria. High doses of alcohol suppress the ability of the white blood cells to multiply. They inhibit the action of killer white cells on cancer cells, and lessen the ability of macrophages to produce tumour necrosis factors.
One drink (the equivalent of 350 ml of beer, 150 ml of wine, or 30 ml of hard liquor) does not appear to affect the immune system, but three or more drinks do. Damage to the immune system increases in proportion to the quantity of alcohol consumed. Amounts of alcohol that are enough to cause intoxication are also enough to suppress immunity.

Food allergens
Some people have a genetic allergic response to otherwise harmless substances (such as milk or wheat). After many encounters with food allergens, the gut wall bcomes damaged, enabling invaders and other potentially toxic substances in the food to get into the bloodstream and make the body feel generally unwell. This condition is known as 'the leaky gut syndrome'.

Too much fat
Obesity can lead to a depressed immune system. It can affect the ability of white blood cells to multiply, produce antibodies and rush to the site of an infection.

→ # *Cancer*

Cancer is the name given to a group of related diseases of cells. Cancer cells do not grow and multiply at a normal rate; they accelerate and grow out of control. All the extra cells can form into lumps called tumours. Tumours start to destroy normal cells around them. Tumours can be broken up by drug and radiation treatments, or removed by surgery. Sometimes they may break up on their own without treatment. Cancer cells can travel around the body in the lymph system, causing tumours all over the body. Cancer in children is rare, but the risks of getting cancer increase with age. Imagine a football stadium full of children – the probability is that only one will have cancer. These days, many cancers can be stopped and cured, and people who have had cancer can go on to lead normal, healthy lives.

We do not know why cells should 'go mad' and start multiplying into cancers, but we do know that smoking and alcohol increase the chances of getting cancer as you grow older.

43 What sort of graph would you expect to see to show a positive correlation between the number of cigarettes smoked on average per day and lung cancer?

→ # *Stress*

Most people are exposed to much higher levels of stress than they realise.

44 Which of these situations cause stress?

> You receive a prize at school.
> Your bike has a flat tyre.
> You go to a fun party that lasts until midnight but your parents do not know.
> Your cat gets sick.
> Your best friend comes to stay at your house for a week.
> You get a bad cough.
> You cannot do your science homework and it is too late to get help from a friend.
> You know your parents are planning a surprise birthday party for you.
> Your parents are getting divorced.

All of the above can cause stress, as stress is caused by many different kinds of things: happy things, sad things, allergies and other physical things. Many people carry enormous stress loads and they do not even realise it. To most of us though, stress is worry – being worried about being late for school, or about having enough pocket money to buy your friend a birthday present, or about your gran when the doctor says she may need an operation.

Your body has a much broader definition of stress than just worry. Your body thinks stress is anything that means change in your life or uncertainty. It doesn't matter if it is a 'good' change or a 'bad' change – they are both stressful. Catching a cold, breaking an arm, a skin infection and a sore back are all changes to your body. Very hot or very cold climates can be stressful. Very high altitude may be a stress. Toxins or poisons, like alcohol or nicotine, are stresses. Each of these factors threatens to cause changes in your body's internal environment.

Hormonal changes also cause stress to your body. Puberty is a very stressful time – a person's body is changing shape, sexual organs begin to function, and new hormones are released in large quantities.

Allergic reactions are a part of your body's natural defence mechanism. When confronted with a substance which your body considers toxic, your body will try to get rid of it by attacking or neutralising it. If it is something that you breathe in through your nose, you might get a runny nose and start sneezing. If it lands on your skin, you might develop blisters. If you inhale it, you'll get wheezy lungs. If you eat it, you may break out in itchy red lumps in your mouth and all over your body. Allergic reactions are a stress, requiring large changes in energy expenditure on the part of your body's defence system to fight off what the body perceives as a dangerous attack.

---

*Information processing*  ## Stress

1 Read the section on stress again. Make a list of all the negative things that can cause stress, and all the positive things that can cause stress. Check your list with a partner. Discuss any differences until you are sure you both know what might cause stress for some people.

2 What sort of physical problems are caused by stress?

3 Which organs of the body are affected by stress?

4 The number of people attending psychiatric clinics is much greater now than it was 50 years ago. Discuss what you think the reasons for this might be.

## Adrenaline

The body prepares itself for important action or activity with the 'stress response'.

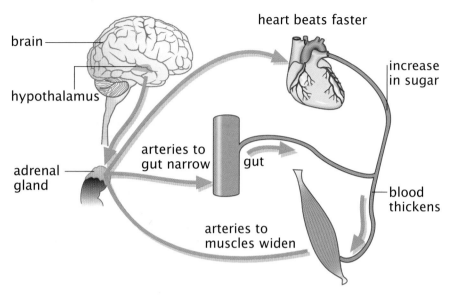

A chemical called **adrenaline** produces the stress response. Adrenaline is a **hormone**. A region in the brain called the **hypothalamus** controls its release by sending a message to the adrenal glands to release adrenaline into the bloodstream. The adrenal glands are on top of the kidneys.

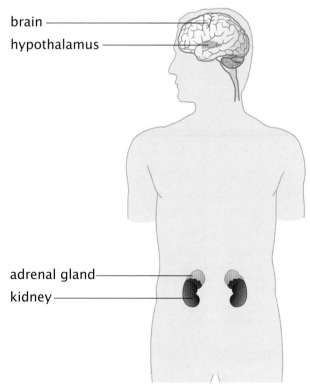

Location of the adrenal glands.

Adrenaline in the bloodstream very quickly causes the following short-lived changes in the body:

- the heart beats faster
- extra sugar is released into the blood
- the arteries to the muscles get wider
- blood thickens so that it will clot more easily.

45 In your group, discuss how you think each of these changes caused by adrenaline helps the body to prepare for action. Think about the last time you felt stressed. What caused the stress? How did you feel? List the ways in which your body responded to this stress.

46 Check that you know the answers to these questions:
Where is adrenaline made in the body?
Where is the hypothalamus?
What does it do?

*DID YOU KNOW?*

Adrenaline is sometimes called the 'fight or flight' hormone.

---

*Evaluation*  ## The effect of alcohol

One of the effects of stress is that the stomach can make too much hydrochloric acid. This can cause indigestion and heartburn. People suffering from stress sometimes claim that alcohol makes them feel happier or more relaxed. It can make them feel better, but it is likely to affect the stomach and the liver.

Nina, Su King and Karl did an experiment to investigate the effect alcohol might have on the lining of the stomach.

Here is part of their report:

We put six drops of dilute hydrochloric acid into five labelled test tubes. The hydrochloric acid had the same pH as stomach acid, pH 3.5. Here is a drawing of what we then did:

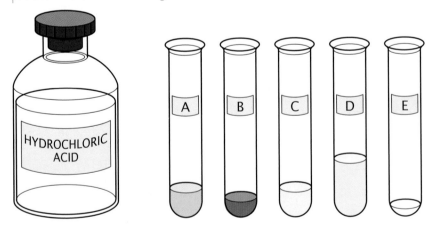

Test tube A contains 15 drops of lager, B 10 drops of whisky, C 15 drops of white wine, D 30 drops of water, and E contains only hydrochloric acid. This last tube is the control, so that this is a fair test. We then added 3 drops of Universal Indicator to each tube to find out the pH. We also found out the amount of alcohol in each alcoholic drink by looking at the labels on the cans or bottles, where it is given as a percentage. Here are our results:

| Type of drink | Lager | Whisky | White wine | Water | Hydrochloric acid |
|---|---|---|---|---|---|
| Percentage alcohol | 5% | 40% | 12% | 0% | 0% |
| pH | 3 | 2 | 2 | 3.5 | 3.5 |

**1** Why did the students put hydrochloric acid into each test tube?

**2** Why was the pH of the hydrochloric acid 3.5?

**3** Why did they say tube E was included?

**4** What is the purpose of tube D?

**5** Did they need both tubes D and E? Explain your answer.

**6** What do you conclude from their experiment about the effect of alcohol on the stomach?

**7** Some of these alcoholic drinks are likely to be more damaging than others; which ones and why? Use this drawing of the stomach to explain your answer.

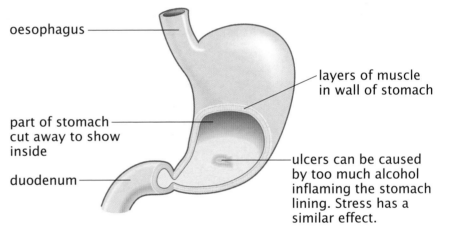

oesophagus

layers of muscle in wall of stomach

part of stomach cut away to show inside

duodenum

ulcers can be caused by too much alcohol inflaming the stomach lining. Stress has a similar effect.

**8** List at least three suggestions to improve this investigation. Explain why you think each suggestion would improve the investigation.

**9** Redesign the table so that they do not have to include drawings to show the treatments in each test tube.

*Research*

Find out what activities, courses and services there are in your school and local community that aim to help people manage stress. You might find out about evening classes in activities such as tai chi or yoga, or find out where there are counsellors for marriage guidance or dealing with bullying.

*Word play*

Lots of magazine articles and television programmes refer to people's 'lifestyle'.

In your group, discuss what you think 'lifestyle' means.

How would you describe your lifestyle? What similarities and what differences do you and your friends have between your lifestyles? How do you think you could improve your lifestyle?

## *Creative thinking* Fit and healthy

On your own, draw up a list of activities that you think are risky. Divide your list into two: unavoidable and avoidable. Now compare your list with other people's lists.

Design a 'fit and healthy' questionnaire for a health magazine to help readers see if they have 'risky' lifestyles. An example of the kind of question you might ask would be:

What type of milk do you drink?

**A** full cream
**B** skimmed
**C** semi-skimmed
**D** none

Recommend some lifestyle-changing action for readers who give particular answers or get particular scores.

## *Evaluation* Fit and healthy

Steve Redgrave is an Olympic gold medal winner. He won his medals for rowing. He is also a diabetic. Would you say he is fit and healthy?

- Are we healthier than our great-grandparents were?

What sort of information and evidence would you want to see to make your answer to this question 'objective', not just an uninformed opinion?

What do your parents think about this question? How are your ideas and theirs in response to this question similar and different?

### *Time to think*

Think back over the work you have done in this chapter. What have you found out about health and fitness that you did not know before?

Form the same group that you did at the start of the chapter and repeat the activity you did then:

- Agree and write down the five most important things that you must do to stay healthy.
- Agree and write down the five things that you think are the biggest dangers to health.

Have these changed or are they the same as at the start of the chapter?

# 3 Energy and electricity

**In this chapter you will learn:**

→ that energy conservation is a useful scientific accounting system when energy is transferred
→ to describe some energy transfers and transformations in familiar situations
→ about potential difference in electrical circuits
→ about the hazards of high-voltage circuits
→ how to compare the energy consumption of common electrical appliances
→ how electricity is generated from fuels, including the energy transfers involved
→ to recognise possible environmental effects of this

**You will also develop your skills in:**

→ identifying patterns and trends in measurement of voltage and using these to draw conclusions about the way voltage varies within a circuit
→ relating energy transfer devices in the laboratory to everyday appliances
→ extracting information from secondary sources
→ considering whether data are sufficient, and accounting for anomalies

→ → → WHAT DO YOU KNOW?

**Key words**
* fuels
* energy resources
* renewable
* non-renewable

You will have met the word energy many times already. Sometimes it will have been used scientifically and at other times it will have been used in everyday language.

**1** Write a sentence where the word energy is used in everyday language and another where it is used scientifically. Compare your sentences with at least three other pupils'.

**2** Make a two-column table. In one column write a list of **fuels** and in the other column give an example of where each fuel is used.

**3** We describe our **energy resources** as **renewable** or **non-renewable**.
   **a)** Write a list of energy resources and indicate for each one whether it is renewable or non-renewable.

**b)** What are the advantages and disadvantages of wind farms?

**c)** What do you think will be the main energy resource in the UK by 2010? Explain why you think this. Check if your ideas are similar or different to others'.

**4** Energy is an important idea you have already covered in Years 7 and 8 in the topics on food and digestion, and heating and cooling. In what other topics have you come across the concept of energy?

**5** On a piece of card, write a list of all the key words that you connect with energy. Cut out the key words and arrange them on a sheet of paper, to produce a concept map. Draw lines to link the words and write a connecting sentence.

*Word play*  Many scientific words are derived from Latin and Greek roots. They are often used as either prefixes or suffixes.

Here are some roots that you will meet in this chapter. How many different scientific words or phrases do you know that contain these roots as either a suffix or a prefix? Write a list of the words. Does this help you decide what each root means?

- therm
- kin
- trans
- gen
- hydro
- bio

# → *How is energy stored?*

**Key words**
* chemical energy
* kinetic energy
* thermal energy
* potential energy

Energy is an important concept in science – we need energy to live, to make things happen and to do things. It is very difficult to explain what energy is because you cannot see it. Because energy is an abstract concept, people have different ideas of it.

Energy can be stored in a number of ways. Some examples are:

- in chemical substances
- in moving objects
- in hot objects
- in an object lifted up high
- in a stretched or squashed object.

1 Think of an example for each of these ways of storing energy. Check your ideas with at least three other pupils.

The following terms are used by scientists when referring to energy:

- **chemical energy**
- **kinetic energy**
- **thermal energy**
- **potential energy**.

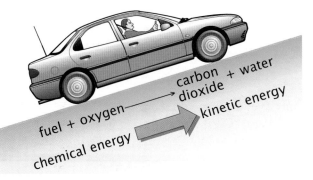

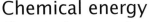

## Chemical energy

Chemical energy is the energy stored within the chemicals of a system. For example, when the fuel in a car reacts with the oxygen in the air, it transfers energy to the car so that it can do useful work, such as climb a hill. Fuels are the main sources of chemical energy. When we run up a flight of stairs, we are using chemical energy.

2 What is the source of our chemical energy?

## Kinetic energy

Kinetic energy is the name we use to describe the energy something has when it is moving. A skier will start at the top of a slope. As she moves down she moves faster and gains kinetic energy.

## Thermal energy

When a solid is heated, the particles that make up the solid gain energy and vibrate more. The material is gaining thermal energy, and its temperature rises.

## Potential energy

Potential energy is the name given to the energy something has because of its position. More precisely it is called gravitational potential energy. The car climbing to the top of the hill has gained gravitational potential energy. The energy has been transferred from the chemical energy in the fuel.

**EXTENSION**

**3** If the car were to roll back down the hill, what would happen to the potential energy?

## Elastic potential energy

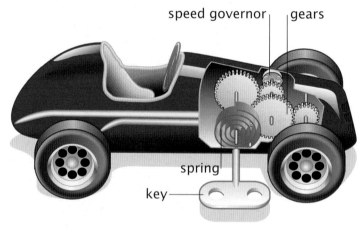

Another way in which energy can be stored is in a spring. The picture shows a toy which works from the energy stored in a spring. This energy is called elastic potential energy.

**4** Can you think of other examples of devices that make use of elastic potential energy? Write down the names of the devices and where they are used.

# Clockwork radio

Trevor Baylis OBE was born in Kilburn, London, in 1937. In 1991 he saw a television programme about AIDS in Africa. An AIDS worker commented that one way to help prevent the disease from spreading further would be to broadcast advice by radio, if only radios, and in particular batteries, were not so expensive. Baylis was inspired by what he saw and set about inventing a clockwork radio. In 1994 his first prototype was featured on BBC's *Tomorrow's World*. The radio ran for 14 minutes on just one wind-up. Finance expert Christopher Staines and South African entrepreneur Rory Stear acquired funding to make the radio, and the following year they set up BayGen Power Industries in Cape Town, South Africa, employing disabled workers to manufacture the Freeplay® wind-up radio. As well as the cost benefits, an environmental benefit of the clockwork radio is that there are no batteries to throw away; they can cause mercury poisoning.

Using springs to generate electricity was nothing new. What was so innovative was the fact that the electrical energy could be supplied over a long period of time rather than in a short burst. The radio gives 40 minutes of play from a 20-second wind-up.

Winding up the radio coils a spring

The spring is attached to a gearbox connected to a dynamo

When the spring is released, the gearbox allows the spring's energy to be slowly released to produce electricity

The dynamo produces 3 volts at 55–60 milliwatts

Wind-up radios are very popular where access to electricity is restricted and batteries are expensive. They are especially popular in South Africa where they are produced. Nelson Mandela was so impressed with the clockwork radio that he has helped to publicise it.

1 Why is the wind-up radio environmentally friendly?
2 What other 'free' sources of energy could be utilised to run a radio?

# Energy transfer

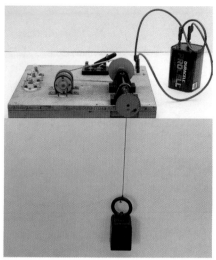

Sometimes books and question papers refer to energy **transfer** and sometimes to energy **transformation**. When energy is stored in one place and then a job is done, such as using an electric motor to lift a load, the energy has been *transferred* from the chemicals stored in the battery to the load which has been lifted to a higher position.

Sometimes people prefer to describe the process in terms of the types or forms of energy. In the example above, the energy is described as being *transformed* (or converted) from chemical energy (in the battery) to electrical energy (in the motor) and to gravitational potential energy (in the load).

It is important to understand that these are just alternative ways of describing the same process.

Look at the following pictures:

electrical energy → energy in the hot water, the kettle and the surroundings

In this example, energy is transferred by the electrical cord to the heating element, then to the water, the kettle and the surroundings.

energy stored in food → energy in the movement of the person + energy in lifting themselves up the stairs

In this example, energy is transferred from the food to the person.

# → *Energy transfer diagrams*

Energy transfer diagrams are a useful way of representing what happens in different situations. The first diagram here represents the kettle example. Note that the widths of the arrows are **proportional** to the relevant amounts of energy. These branching diagrams are also known as **Sankey diagrams**.

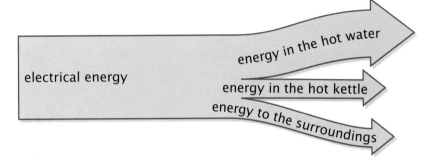

electrical energy

energy in the hot water

energy in the hot kettle

energy to the surroundings

This diagram represents the person climbing the stairs:

energy in food

energy in the movement of the person

energy in lifting themselves up the stairs

5 Describe the energy transfers in the two photogaphs below and draw an energy transfer diagram for each situation.

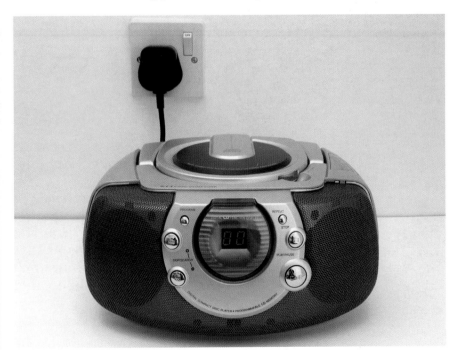

**6** Look at the experiments shown in the diagrams below. Each shows an energy transfer process.

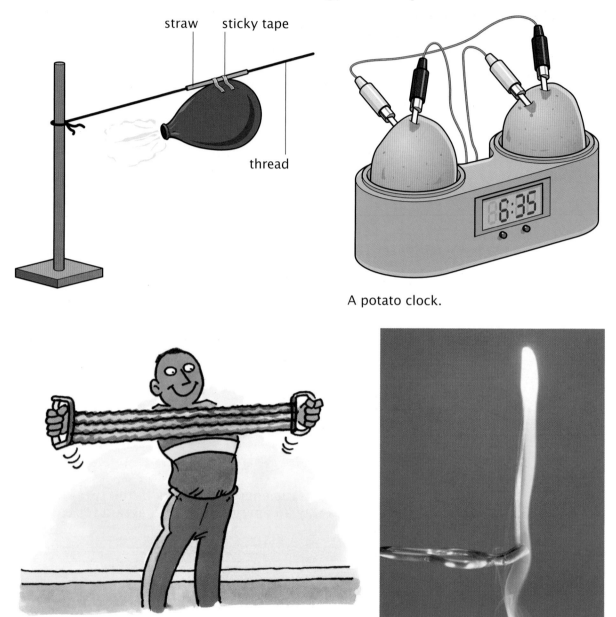

straw    sticky tape

thread

A potato clock.

Burning magnesium ribbon.

In your group, choose one of the experiments above and discuss:
a) What happened?
b) What made it happen?
c) Draw an energy transfer diagram and use it to explain the energy transfer that is taking place.
d) Get another group to check your diagram and explanation while you check theirs.

# → *Conservation of energy*

Although energy can be transferred from one place to another and stored in different forms, it cannot disappear altogether. The total amount of energy in the system remains constant. However, the energy can become less concentrated (more spread out) and so become less useful. Look at the energy transfer diagram for the kettle again. In this version of the Sankey diagram, the amounts of energy involved are also shown. Remember: we measure energy in units called **joules** (J).

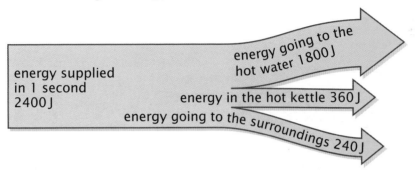

energy supplied in 1 second 2400 J

energy going to the hot water 1800 J

energy in the hot kettle 360 J

energy going to the surroundings 240 J

As you can see, the total energy going into the system is 2400 J and the total energy leaving is 1800 + 360 + 240 = 2400 J. The energy in the surroundings and the kettle is not useful – it is 'wasted' energy.

When energy is transferred, the total amount of energy before and after remains the same. This is called the principle of **conservation** of energy, and is an important scientific law. The energy that is spread out, usually as thermal energy, is wasted energy – it is not useful. When the energy is spread out in this way it is said to have been **dissipated**.

To explain the features of energy we sometimes use a comparison (or **analogy**). Suppose a source, for example, a rich aunt, gives one of her young relatives a £50 note. This could be used to buy a CD player. However, if the money were shared out amongst eight relatives, each would receive only £6.25. The total amount of money has not changed, but it has been moved from one person to a number of different people. They in turn may share their portion with yet more people. There would now be an even less useful amount for each person. Similarly, when energy is transferred, it ends up in a less concentrated form and so is less useful. In the case of energy, it usually ends up as low-level heating of our surroundings.

*Time to think*

In pairs, discuss what you understand about energy conservation and energy dissipation. Explain your ideas by drawing a diagram, using an example or constructing a model. Get another pair to check your work and give you feedback on how scientifically accurate it is, and whether it helps others understand these ideas.

# Energy and power

**Key words**
* power
* watt

Still thinking of our analogy between energy and money, suppose you have a part-time job packing toys into boxes. The pay is 50p per box, so if you were to pack 100 boxes how much money would you earn? Before you decided to do this job, there is another factor you would have to consider. You would also need to know how quickly you could pack a box.

7 If each box takes half an hour to pack, how many hours would you need to work to earn £50?
8 If you could pack a box in 6 minutes (that is 10 boxes an hour), how many hours would you have to work?

We have a similar situation with energy. We often need to know not just how much energy is transferred, but also how quickly this is done.

The energy transferred in every second is called **power**.

$$\text{power} = \frac{\text{energy transferred}}{\text{time taken}}$$

The unit of power is the **watt**.

A more powerful device can do a job more quickly than a less powerful one.

The unit of power is named after James Watt (1736–1819).

9 Look at the details in the table from the consumer magazine *Which?* showing a range of hairdryers.
   a) Which is the most powerful? How did you decide this?
   b) Do you think the most powerful hairdryer is necessarily the best?
   c) Is the most powerful hairdryer the most expensive?
   d) Which hairdryer uses the least energy during 20 minutes of use? How much energy does it use?

| Hairdryers | | | | | | |
|---|---|---|---|---|---|---|
| | **Babyliss** Salon Professional 1013 | **Boots** 1600 Coolshot | **Braun** Silencio PX 1600 | **Remington** Compact Turbo D2200 | **Revlon** Professional 1800 9003 | **Vidal Sassoon** Salon Professional VS-481 |
| Price (£) | 30 | 20 | 12 | 9 | 24 | 30 |
| Country of origin | China | China | Ireland | China | China | China |
| Weight (g) | 710 | 620 | 390 | 360 | 680 | 810 |
| Wattage (kW) | 1.2 | 1.6 | 1.6 | 1.4 | 1.8 | 1.3 |
| Drying time | ◐ | ◐ | ◑ | ◐ | ○ | ◐ |
| Quiet operation | ○ | ○ | ◑ | ◔ | ○ | ◑ |
| Ease of use switches/controls | ○ | ◐ | ● | ● | ○ | ○ |

key  best ◄─────────► worst
● ◐ ◔ ◑ ○

*Information processing* *Power ratings*

Here is a list of devices with different power-ratings:

| | |
|---|---|
| torch bulb | 2 W |
| electric fan heater | 1 kW |
| VW Passat 1.9 TDI | 97 kW |
| electricity power station | 2000 MW |
| Sun | 40 000 000 MW |

**1** Look at the information shown above. Can you think of a suitable way of representing this information in a chart? Don't forget that there are a mixture of units: W, kW and MW.

## Energy at a particle level

You will already have looked at the connection between thermal energy and temperature. When the temperature of a substance increases, the particles of the substance move on average more quickly. The diagram below is taken from Book 2. What does it show? Sometimes when we supply energy to a substance, the temperature does not increase. An example of this is when you melt a block of ice. The energy is used to overcome the forces between the particles in the rigid shape of the solid ice.

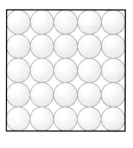
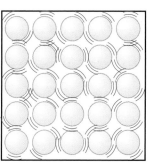

**10** A group of pupils are discussing energy and temperature. In your group discuss the statements made by the pupils. Who do you agree with? Who do you disagree with?

# Electricity

There are many situations where energy is transferred via electricity from one place to another. In a torch, the battery transfers energy to the electrons in a circuit, which carry it to the lamp where the energy is transformed to light and heat in the lamp. The lamp gives out light and gets hot.

11 Think of a device where the electricity transfers energy to:
   a) produce sound
   b) produce movement of air
   c) melt butter.

Different devices transfer different amounts of energy in a given time. For example, a light bulb may be rated 60 W. This means that it transfers energy at the rate of 60 J/s. Meters that measure energy transferred are called **joulemeters**.

A joulemeter measures how much energy is transferred.

12 You will find that many electrical appliances have a plate attached indicating their power rating. Other useful sources of power ratings are advertisements and *Which?*-type reviews. Produce a table including different household electrical appliances and the rates at which they transfer energy.

The table below shows some devices and their power ratings. To find out how much energy they transfer, we also need to know the length of time for which they are used. The third column in the table shows for how long they were used in a week.

| Device | Power rating (W) | Time used (per week) |
|--------|------------------|----------------------|
| toaster | 900 | 1 hour |
| kettle | 2400 | 80 minutes |

13 Copy the table above, and add two more columns. (You will need the other columns for Question 18.) You may wish to enter the results into a spreadsheet. Add further devices from your table from Question 12 and estimate how long they would be used during a week.

Consider the example of an electric fan heater. The power rating is 1 kW (1000 W). This means that:

in one second, 1000 J are transferred,
in one minute, 60 × 1000 J are transferred,
in one hour, 60 × 60 × 1000 J are transferred,
in 5 hours, the number of joules transferred is
   5 × 60 × 60 × 1000 = 18 000 000 J.

In practice, the joule is not a very convenient unit of energy to use for payment of electricity used. If the total energy

consumption was measured in joules, it would be a very large number over a period of several months.

Instead, electricity companies use another unit for calculating energy used. They call it the kilowatt-hour (kWh) or sometimes simply 'a unit'. So if a 1 kW electric fire is used for 5 hours the number of units of electricity used is 1 × 5 = 5 kWh.

**14** If a 7 kW electric shower is used for 30 minutes a day, how many units would it use in a week?

To find the cost of the units of electricity, use the following formula:

$$\text{total cost (in pence)} = \frac{\text{power (in kW)} \times \text{time (in hours)}}{\times \text{cost of a unit (in pence)}}$$

## Example of electricity bill and calculation

### PowerPro

#### Your electricity statement

Mr and Mrs S P Arking
51 Circuit Drive
Ampton
Wattshire
AM9 0HM

Name and address

Electricity readings in kWh

Note that the units used are calculated for a period of three months. The cost of each 'unit' is shown. The rate is different for the first 224 units consumed.

VAT is added at 5%. This is not the same rate as for other goods purchased.

This householder pays monthly by automatic direct debit payments of £50.50. Because they have paid too much, they are entitled to a refund and their monthly payments for the next year will be reassessed.

| Bill enquiries | Please ring full number given overleaf |
| | For other enquiries, please see overleaf |
| Our address | PO Box 2640, Jouletown |
| VAT registration number | 987 6543 21 |

Amount already in credit from previous payments

| Your customer reference number | 123 456 543 |
| | Please quote this if you contact us |

| | | |
|---|---|---|
| Bill date & tax point | **1 May 2004** | |
| Balance brought forward | 1 February 2004 | cr £99.58 |
| Present reading | **43304** taken on 29 April 2004 | |
| Previous reading | **42126** taken on 29 January 2004 | |
| Electricity used | 1178 units – 1 unit is 1 kilowatt hour (kWh) | |
| for first | 224 kWh at 9.000 pence per kWh | |
| for last | 954 kWh at 5.410 pence per kWh | |
| | Cost of electricity used | £71.77 |
| Dual Fuel Discount | 29 January 2004 to 29 April 2004 | |
| | 91 days at 3.9140 pence per day | cr £3.56 |
| | **Sub total excluding VAT** | £68.21 |
| | VAT at 5.0% | £3.41 |
| | **Total charges** | **£71.62** |
| Less balance b/fwd | (see above) | cr £99.58 |
| Less your payments | 7 DEC 03 to 7 MAR 04      cr £151.50 | |
| | **Total payments – thank you** | cr £151.50 |

### *Balance carried forward*   cr | £179.46

This is for information only. This balance will be refunded to you in the next 7 days.

**15** Looking at the electricity bill, how many kWh were consumed in this billing period? How is this calculated?
**16** How much does the householder pay for each unit?
**17** What is meant by 'dual fuel discount'?

18 Refer back to the table that you drew for Question 13 (page 84). This showed various devices and how long they were used for in a week. In the extra columns enter how long they would be used for in three months (13 weeks). Calculate the cost of using each device over the three-month period if electricity costs 7p a unit. You may wish to use a spreadsheet.

# ➡ *Power and efficiency*

**Key word**
∗ efficiency

Look back to page 81 where a Sankey diagram shows the transfer of energy in an electric kettle being used to heat some water. In this example, the energy being supplied by the electricity is 2400 J. The energy going to the hot water is 1800 J. The energy going to the kettle is 360 J. The energy going to the surroundings is 240 J.

The amount of useful energy is therefore only 1800 J. Scientists define **efficiency** as:

$$\frac{\text{useful energy}}{\text{total energy}} \times 100\%$$

In this example, the efficiency is:

$$\frac{1800}{2400} \times 100\% = 75\%$$

An electric kettle is rated 2000 W. It is filled with a litre of water. The water takes 3 minutes 15 seconds to boil. Some scientists have calculated that the amount of energy that needs to be transferred to the water to boil it is 36 000 J, however we know that the energy from the electrical energy does not all go to the water in the kettle.

19 How much energy does the electricity supply?
20 What happens to the rest of the electrical energy?
21 Calculate the efficiency in this example.
22 'Energy saving' campaigns suggest that the following actions will save energy. Try to explain why.

- Do not fill the kettle completely if you are only making one cup of tea.
- Keep the kettle element free of limescale.

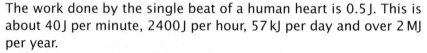

**DID YOU KNOW?**

The work done by the single beat of a human heart is 0.5 J. This is about 40 J per minute, 2400 J per hour, 57 kJ per day and over 2 MJ per year.

The energy content of the nuclear bomb dropped on Hiroshima, Japan, in the Second World War was 80 million MJ.

The energy output of a power station in one year is about 10 000 million MJ.

*Time to think*

This chapter has introduced a lot of new terms. Copy and complete each statement using the following key words: **power, million, efficiency, unit, joule, 4, energy, watt, 1000**.

**Definition**

- The scientific unit of energy is the _____.

- The scientific unit of power is the _____.

- The kilowatt-hour is sometimes used to measure _____.

- The formula: $\dfrac{\text{energy transferred}}{\text{time taken}}$ calculates _____.

- In SI units, kilo means multiply the basic unit by _____.

- The formula: $\dfrac{\text{useful energy}}{\text{total energy}} \times 100\%$ calculates _____.

- In SI units, mega means multiply the basic unit by _____.

- In household electricity bills, the consumption is measured in kilowatt-hours (kWh). This is often called a _____.

- When a 2 kW kettle is used for 2 hours, the number of units it will use is _____.

Now use these key words to modify and add to the concept map that you made at the start of this chapter.

# ➡ *Revision of current and voltage*

**Key words**
- \* ammeter
- \* voltage
- \* series
- \* parallel
- \* potential difference
- \* resistor
- \* resistance

Electric current is measured using an **ammeter**. **Voltage** gives the push that the current needs to get round the circuit. Look at the circuits shown below.

23 Which is a **series** circuit, and which is a **parallel** circuit? How do you recognise series and parallel circuits?

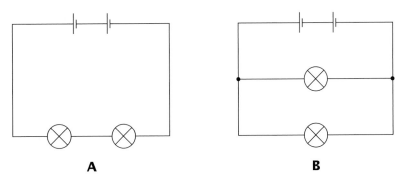

A                                          B

**24** In the circuit below, are the ammeters connected in series or in parallel?

**25** Is the voltmeter in series or in parallel?

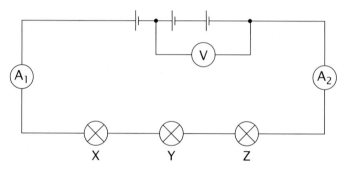

**26 a)** Ammeter $A_1$ reads 0.2 A. What does $A_2$ read?
  **b)** A voltmeter is connected across the first cell as shown above. It reads 1.5 V. It is then disconnected and reconnected across two cells as shown below. What will it read now?

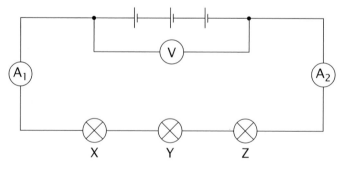

  **c)** The voltmeter is disconnected again and reconnected across the three cells as shown below. What will it read now?

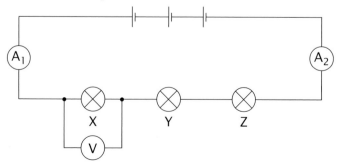

  **d)** The voltmeter is disconnected again and reconnected across lamp X as shown below. What will it read now?

**e)** The voltmeter is disconnected again and reconnected across lamp Y. What will it read now?

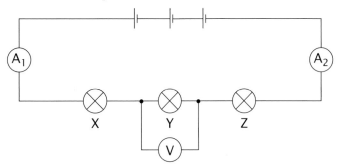

27 Check your answers with others in your group. Look back through the questions in this section and write out the rules that you needed to know about electric circuits to answer the questions.

Note that ammeters are connected in series with the lamps but voltmeters are connected in parallel. To measure the voltage of a cell or the voltage across a lamp, we connect the voltmeter across it in parallel. You do not need to break into the circuit to connect the voltmeter.

You will sometimes see the term **potential difference** (pd) used instead of voltage. Volts are a measure of the potential difference between two points in the circuit. The greater the voltage, the greater the 'push' of the electricity. The battery always has a potential difference, but unless there is a connection between the terminals of the battery, no current will flow and no energy will be transferred. The use of the word 'potential' here is similar to the way it is used in the term 'potential energy'.

28 **a)** Copy the circuit diagram below. The cells are each 1.5 V. Label the ammeter(s) A and the voltmeter(s) V.
   **b)** When the switch is open, is the lamp on or off?
   **c)** When the switch is open, what does meter 1 read? What does meter 2 read? What does meter 3 read?
   **d)** When the switch is closed, is the lamp on or off?
   **e)** When the switch is closed, what does meter 1 read? What does meter 2 read? What does meter 3 read?

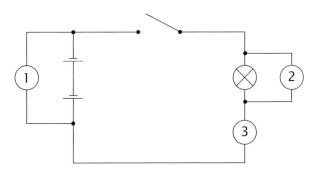

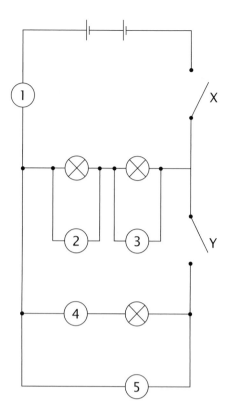

**29 a)** Copy the circuit diagram on the left. The cells are each 1.5 V. The lamps are identical.
  **b)** Label the ammeter(s) A and the voltmeter(s) V.
  **c)** When switch X is open, which lamps are on and which lamps are off?
  **d)** When switch X is closed and switch Y open, which lamps are on and which lamps are off?
  **e)** When switch X is open, what does meter 1 read? What does meter 2 read? What does meter 3 read?
  **f)** When switch X is closed and switch Y open, what does meter 2 read? What does meter 3 read? What does meter 5 read?
  **g)** When both the switches are closed, what does meter 2 read? What does meter 4 read? What does meter 5 read?

A **resistor** is an electrical component. It opposes the flow of electricity. The bigger the **resistance** of the resistor, the smaller the electric current that can flow through it. Resistance is measured in ohms. The symbol for ohm is the Greek letter Ω. In the same way that squeezing a hosepipe reduces the water that can flow, adding a resistor reduces the electric current in the circuit.

Resistors are usually quite small. Instead of printing the value, electrical engineers decided to put little bands of colour to represent the values.

  Hold your resistor with the tolerance band (usually gold) at the right hand end. In this example, the value in ohms is 560 ± 10%.

  The third band tells you how many zeros to add. Brown is one zero. If it was green, you would add five zeros.

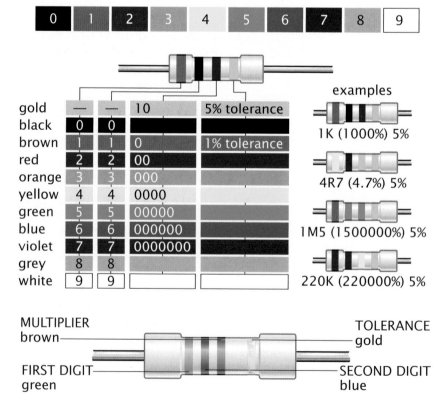

| | 0 | 1 | 2 | 3 | 4 | 5 | 6 | 7 | 8 | 9 |
|---|---|---|---|---|---|---|---|---|---|---|

| | | | | | examples |
|---|---|---|---|---|---|
| gold | — | — | 10 | 5% tolerance | |
| black | 0 | 0 | | | 1K (1000%) 5% |
| brown | 1 | 1 | 0 | 1% tolerance | |
| red | 2 | 2 | 00 | | 4R7 (4.7%) 5% |
| orange | 3 | 3 | 000 | | |
| yellow | 4 | 4 | 0000 | | 1M5 (1500000%) 5% |
| green | 5 | 5 | 00000 | | |
| blue | 6 | 6 | 000000 | | 220K (220000%) 5% |
| violet | 7 | 7 | 0000000 | | |
| grey | 8 | 8 | | | |
| white | 9 | 9 | | | |

MULTIPLIER
brown

FIRST DIGIT
green

TOLERANCE
gold

SECOND DIGIT
blue

*Evaluation*  ## Using a voltmeter

A group of pupils performed an experiment using resistors and a voltmeter. They were provided with a selection of resistors with resistances of 100 Ω, 220 Ω and 330 Ω, a 3 V battery, connecting wires and a digital voltmeter. They were also provided with a resistor whose value was not known. The resistors they were given were labelled as follows:

| | | |
|---|---|---|
| A = 100 Ω | C = 100 Ω | E = 220 Ω |
| B = 100 Ω | D = 220 Ω | F = 330 Ω |

X is the resistor with unknown resistance.

Below is Abi and Mark's experiment write-up.

We set up the four circuits shown in the diagrams.

For each circuit we measured the voltage across the battery, and the voltage across each resistor separately.

Our results are shown in the tables below.

Voltage across the battery in each case was 3 V.

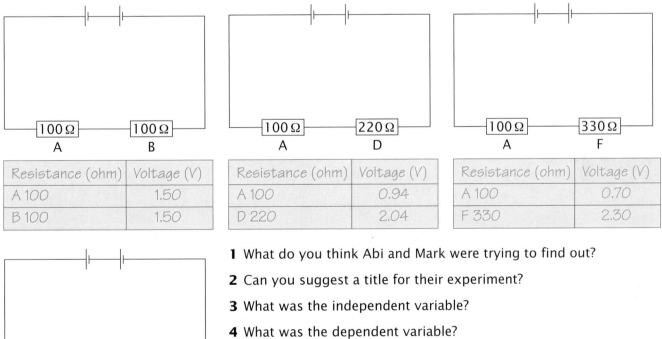

| Resistance (ohm) | Voltage (V) |
|---|---|
| A 100 | 1.50 |
| B 100 | 1.50 |

| Resistance (ohm) | Voltage (V) |
|---|---|
| A 100 | 0.94 |
| D 220 | 2.04 |

| Resistance (ohm) | Voltage (V) |
|---|---|
| A 100 | 0.70 |
| F 330 | 2.30 |

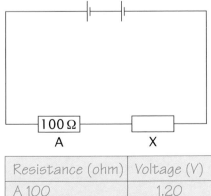

| Resistance (ohm) | Voltage (V) |
|---|---|
| A 100 | 1.20 |
| X | 1.80 |

**1** What do you think Abi and Mark were trying to find out?

**2** Can you suggest a title for their experiment?

**3** What was the independent variable?

**4** What was the dependent variable?

**5** What sort of relationship do their results suggest?

**6** Can the resistance of resistor of X be found from Abi and Mark's experiment?

# ➡ *Voltage and energy*

**Key word**
∗ electrons

The concrete and lorries analogy helps us to think about electricity. To understand voltage, we will refer to this model. Look at the following electric circuit.

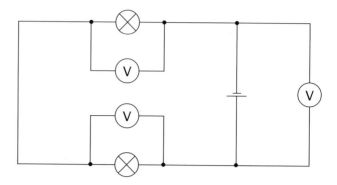

Charged particles move round the circuit. These charged particles are called **electrons**, and they are given energy by the cell. They transfer this energy to the lamp. If there are two identical lamps, the charged particles transfer half of their energy as they pass through the first lamp, and the other half as they pass through the second lamp. This is the energy that is radiated by the lamp. More particles passing through the lamp means that more energy is transferred.

In the electric circuit, the voltage of the cell is a measure of the amount of energy that the cell can transfer to the particles. The voltmeter reading across each lamp is a measure of the amount of energy that is transferred to that lamp by the particles passing through it.

In the concrete and lorries analogy, we will suppose that the firm has to maintain a continuous supply of concrete to two building sites at a steady rate. To do this, the lorries visit each site in turn and deposit half of their load of concrete at each site.

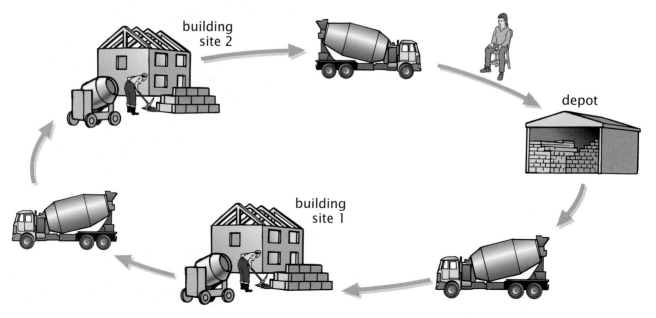

building site 2

depot

building site 1

**30** Copy and complete the table below.

| Electric circuit | Building circuit |
|---|---|
| battery | depot |
| lamps | |
| | lorries |
| wire | |
| ammeters measuring current flowing | person by side of road counting rate at which lorries pass |
| voltmeter measuring energy transferred by charged particles | site manager checking the amount of concrete left at each site by the lorry |

The example of lorries and concrete is just a model to help explain what happens in the electric circuit. A model has its limitations, and whilst it will help us to explain simple situations it is less useful for more complex ones. There are lots of different models that can help to explain this concept. In Book 1 we mentioned other models that may be used, such as water being pumped round plastic tubes, and cross-country runners.

**31** In pairs, think of your own model to explain our electric circuit. In your model you should explain what represents the potential difference or voltage and what represents the current. Think about your model and the model with the lorries. What are the advantages and disadvantages of your model? Compare your ideas with another group.

➡ # *Usefulness and hazards of high voltage*

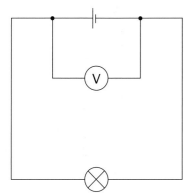

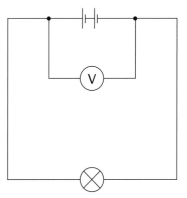

If you measure the potential difference across a single cell it will read about 1.5 V.

We know that in the circuit on the right, where a second cell has been added, the lamp will glow more brightly and the voltmeter reading will be twice as much. The circuit has twice the push for the electricity. The amount of energy being transferred by the bulb is more.

**32** What do you think would happen if the circuit were connected as shown below?

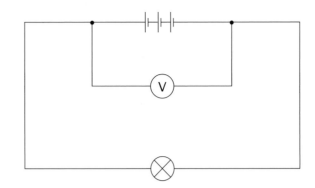

The voltage will read about 4.5 V. The bulb may shine very brightly – it may even 'blow'.

One of the effects of increasing the voltage is to increase the amount of energy transferred from the battery to the circuit components. High voltages allow more energy to be transferred by the electric current as it flows around the circuit.

If you touch both ends of a 1.5 V dry cell it will not harm you. The resistance of your skin is high enough to ensure that even with a 12 V car battery only a small current will flow through you should you touch its terminals.

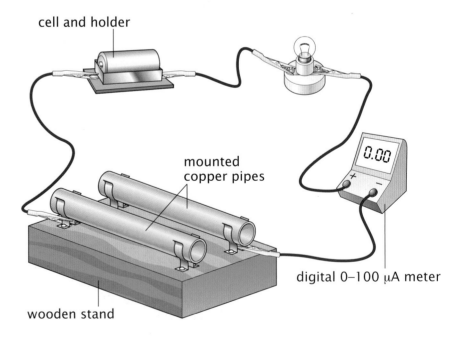

cell and holder

mounted copper pipes

digital 0–100 μA meter

wooden stand

This demonstration circuit shows the conditions needed for the human body to be a conductor: a volunteer gripping the two copper pipes will complete the circuit. An alternative demonstration you may have seen uses a digital multimeter to measure the resistance between your hands. Try getting someone to hold the leads of the multimeter and ask some questions that they might not want to answer truthfully!

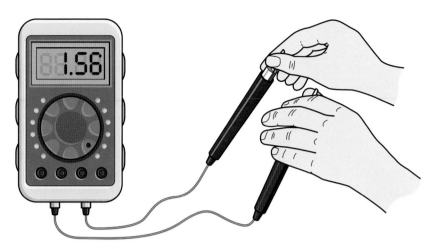

**33 a)** What sorts of things can happen to your skin when you become nervous?
  **b)** Do you think any of these changes will have any effect on the multimeter reading?
  **c)** Can you think how this may be the basis of equipment used by law enforcement agencies in some countries?

The size of a current depends on the resistance in the circuit, and the battery voltage.

## Resistance

In the experiment with the multimeter the resistance is the resistance of your body. This depends on a number of factors. The resistance between your little finger and thumb is different to that between the hand and foot. However, the main thing that influences your resistance is the amount of hard, dry skin on the surface and whether or not your skin is wet. Generally resistance of dry skin is quite high, but the resistance inside your body is very low. Wet skin means low resistance. Dry, hard skin may have a resistance of 10 kΩ whereas the resistance of wet, broken or contaminated skin could easily be as low as a few hundred ohms.

## Voltage

Whilst it is the current in your body that causes the electric shock, a greater voltage provides a bigger push and so higher voltages are potentially more dangerous. The voltage of the electric mains is 230 V which is potentially lethal. Every year in the UK about 100 people are killed by electric shocks. These are often received from household appliances such as electric lawn mowers, hedge trimmers and hairdryers.

  A shock current greater than about 50 thousandths of an amp (50 mA or 0.05 A) will probably start ventricular fibrillation. The ventricles are the chambers in the heart responsible for pumping blood out of the heart. When the heart is in ventricular fibrillation, the muscles of the

**SAFETY!**

**You should NEVER use electrical equipment, for example a hairdryer, in a bathroom where the damp air can make your skin wet.**

ventricles twitch irregularly and no blood is being pumped around the body. This is fatal if it is not corrected very quickly.

The nervous impulses from the brain to the muscles instructing the body to move are also electrical in nature. If a large current flows through the body it interferes with this nervous stimulation, and a person holding a live conductor is no longer able to let go. This is sometimes called the 'no let go' current. The value of this current depends on several factors, such as the contact area, the shape and size of the conductor and also the person's physiological characteristics. Typical values are about 10 mA for women, and a little greater for men.

**Effect of electric currents on the human body**

| Current (mA) | Effect |
| --- | --- |
| 1 | threshold of feeling, current just detectable |
| 1–2 | tingling sensation in the hands |
| 2–2.8 | sensation that the hands have gone to sleep |
| 2.8–3.5 | slight stiffening of the hand |
| 3.5–4.5 | considerable stiffening of lower arm muscles |
| 4.5–5.0 | feeling of cramp in the lower arm and slight trembling of the hands – this is accepted as the maximum harmless current |
| 5.0–15.0 | unpleasant cramping of the lower arm – limits of ability to 'let go' are reached |
| 15–20 | release is impossible; this level of current cannot be tolerated for more than 15 minutes |
| 20–40 | serious and very painful contraction of the muscles, breathing stops but will normally resume if current is interrupted |
| 50–200 | ventricular fibrillation (a state of the heart which leads directly to death if not treated) |
| over 200 | tissues and organs burn |

## *Creative thinking* Electricity

Produce a cartoon strip about electrical safety. Invent some electrical characters.

In your group, decide on the 'success criteria' for the task. Use these to give feedback to three other pupils. Be sure to recognise one or two good points and suggest one improvement each could make.

# ➡ *Transmitting electricity*

Mains electricity is produced at 25 000 V. It is then transformed (changed) to 275 000 V (or even higher). This is the voltage you find on the National Grid system. The very high voltages involved are extremely dangerous and potentially fatal to anyone touching the cables. To use the electricity in our homes the current is transformed back down to 230 V. Even the household mains electricity is very dangerous and potentially fatal. So why is electricity transmitted at such high voltages? It is mainly a question of economics. The experiment shown below helps to explain this. (For safety reasons, the voltages used in the experiment are much lower than would normally be used.)

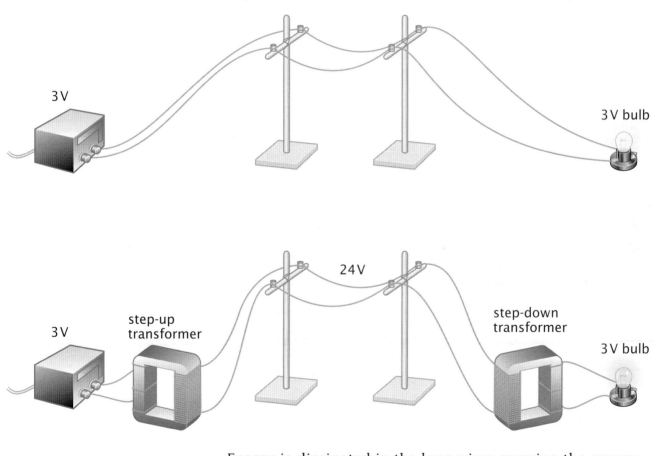

Energy is dissipated in the long wires carrying the energy to the distant village and so less energy is available to light the lamp in the village. With higher voltages, a given electric current can transfer more energy.

---

*Reasoning* *Transmitting electricity*

Write three or four questions to check whether other pupils have understood this passage on transmitting electricity.

---

# → *Electricity generation*

**Key words**
* magnetic field
* electromagnetic induction

In Book 2 you learnt about Oersted's experiment in which he showed that a conductor carrying an electric current produces a **magnetic field** around the conductor. Oersted's experiments were performed in 1820, and in 1831 Michael Faraday used this idea and succeeded in producing electric currents from magnetism. Today we call this **electromagnetic induction**, and it was this discovery that led to the development of the dynamo and modern methods of electricity generation.

Hans Christian Oersted firmly believed that all forces in nature must be linked. From this viewpoint, electric current should produce magnetic effects. As early as 1807, Oersted had announced that he was looking for a connection between magnetism and electricity. Oersted's inability to exhibit these effects did not deter him from believing that they existed. He continued to search obsessively, and in 1820 he discovered the magnetic effect of an electric current. However, when he discovered this effect it was more by chance than intention. He was demonstrating the heating effect of an electric current in a wire and had not cleared away the equipment from an earlier demonstration. On the table there was a compass. When the current flowed in a nearby straight wire it caused the compass needle to deflect.

The discovery of the reverse effect, the production of electric current by magnetism, originated in an intuitive belief of Michael Faraday that if an electric current produces magnetism there must be a way in which magnetism can produce an electric current. Like Oersted, Faraday was undeterred by his initial failure to demonstrate the effect. He was an outstanding experimentalist and he finally succeeded in 1831. The results were surprising: he discovered that an electric current was only produced when there was a changing magnetic field.

Faraday made a very important contribution to the development of the theory of electromagnetism by constructing a qualitative model of how electrical and magnetic forces act. He suggested electric fields and magnetic field lines to represent the effect. This is one of the most useful scientific models and it is still used today.

In this system, as you turn the handle faster you transfer more energy and the lamp glows more brightly.

## *Information processing*  *Power station*

The diagram below shows the main features of a coal-fired power station. The coal is delivered by rail and stored until it is needed. It is then transferred to the pulverising mills where it is ground into a fine powder. The powdered fuel is mixed with warm air and burnt. The furnace heats the boilers containing pure water, and this water is turned into steam. This high-pressure, high-temperature steam passes into the turbine. It strikes the blades making them rotate at 3000 revolutions per minute. This turbine turns the generator to produce the electricity. The transformer steps the voltage up from 25 000 V to 275 000 V and feeds the electricity into the National Grid. Meanwhile the steam is passed over a series of cold pipes in the condensers, where it is turned back into water. The warm water from the condenser passes through the cooling towers where it is cooled. From here the water is returned to the boiler.

On a sheet of paper, draw a block diagram to show the main features of the power station. Label each feature and use the information above to explain its function.

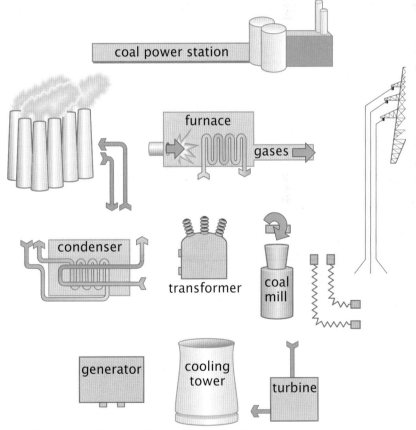

The features of a coal-fired power station.

## *Creative thinking*  *A world with no electricity*

Imagine you lived in a world in which there was no electricity. Write an article about how you think life would be different.

*Research* There is a lot of information now available about alternative ways of generating electricity. Some are listed below.

hydroelectric power stations (including pumped storage
   power stations)
tidal barrage power stations
solar power stations
wind farms
biogas
wave-generated
geothermal
nuclear power stations
combined heat and power (CHP)

Choose one of the methods mentioned above and produce your own leaflet about it.

## Clean low-carbon transport

'Clean low-carbon transport' is a term used in the Government's white paper called *Our Energy Future*, published in February 2003. Among the measures that have been taken to reduce carbon dioxide ($CO_2$) emissions is graduated Vehicle Excise Duty (VED) on all new cars. This charge is linked to the car's $CO_2$ emissions – the less the car pollutes (produces $CO_2$), the less VED you have to pay.

*Research* Find out about hybrid vehicles and LPG. How might the increased use of these lead to a cleaner environment?

A hybrid vehicle.

*Enquiry* *Solar energy*

The pictures below show two different devices that transfer energy from the Sun. Choose one of the devices to plan an investigation.

The questions to be investigated are:

What affects the temperature of water?
What affects the output from a solar cell?

Solar panels use radiation from the Sun to provide hot water.

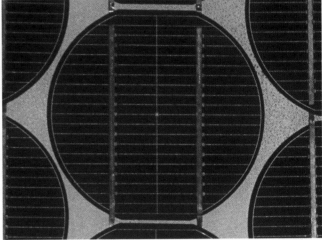

A solar cell uses energy from the Sun to provide electricity.

**1** There are a number of variables that you could change. Make a list of them.

**2** Plan which question you will investigate. Decide which variable you will change (the independent variable), and which variable you will observe (the dependent variable).

**3** Decide what equipment you will need.
Decide how you will collect and record the data.
How will you present the data?

*Time to think* Think back over the work you have done in this chapter.
What have you found out about energy and electricity that you didn't know before?
Repeat the activity you did at the start of the chapter where you wrote on a piece of card a list of all the key words that you connect with energy. Cut out the key words and arrange them on a sheet of paper to produce a new concept map. Remember to draw lines to link the words and write a connecting sentence.
Compare your concept map with the one you produced at the beginning of the chapter. How has it changed?

# 4 Forces and space

Forces and space  Forces and space  Forces and space  Forces and space

**In this chapter you will learn:**

➡ that gravity is a force of attraction between objects and that this force depends on their masses and how far apart they are
➡ that larger objects like the Earth have greater gravitational pull than smaller objects
➡ that gravity decreases the further an object moves away from the Earth's surface and this influences space travel
➡ to describe how weight is different on different planets
➡ what satellites are and how they are used
➡ how forces affect the movement of objects as they fall
➡ how streamlining reduces resistance to air and water and how this resistance increases with the speed of the object, and to relate this to the particle model

**You will also develop your skills in:**

➡ using a model of gravitational attraction to describe how stars, planets and satellites are kept in their orbits in relation to one another
➡ describing how ideas and evidence about the nature of the Solar System have changed over time
➡ researching secondary sources to find out about recent space exploration and how the Universe might have begun
➡ using data to compare gravitational forces and weights on different planets
➡ plotting and interpreting graphs about the movement of objects

## ➡ ➡ ➡ WHAT DO YOU KNOW?

1 Individually, decide which of the pupils on the next page are stating the truth as scientists see it, and which pupils have 'misconceptions' – wrong scientific ideas.

2 Now compare your answers with someone else in your group. If you disagree about any of the statements, find out which one of you is right.

3 What does the word 'force' mean?

**4** Which of these instruments measure mass, and which measure force?

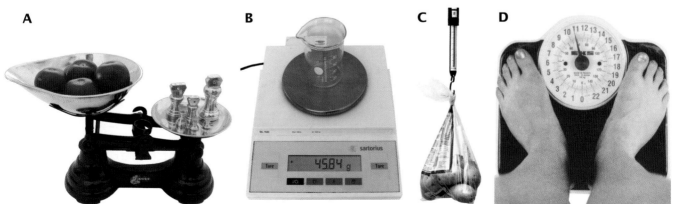

**A**

**B**

**C**

**D**

**5** Copy each of the drawings below and add arrows to indicate the forces that you think are acting on the objects. Are your drawings showing the same force direction as other people in your group? Mark each other's work.

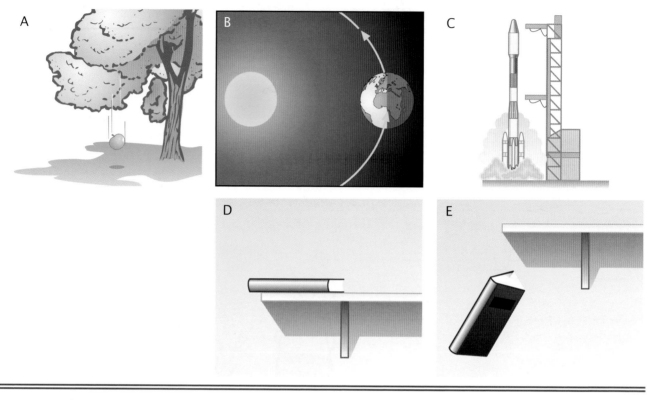

A    B    C

D    E

# → *Gravity*

The following words are commonly used when discussing gravity: mass, matter, weight, gravity, newton meter, force, orbit, arc, weightless.

1 Copy this paragraph into your book and complete the missing words using the words listed above. Take care – some words in the list may not be used at all; others may be used more than once.

In Book 1 we read about the unit of _____, the kilogram, and the unit of _____, the newton. The difference between mass and _____ was also explained. Mass is a measure of the amount of 'stuff' or _____ present in an object. It tells us about the number of particles that are in the object. Weight is a _____. It tells us about the pull of _____ on the object. Some things that appear _____ actually do have weight, and so qualify as matter. Air has weight, so it is a form of matter even though a cubic centimetre of air weighs less than a grain of sand. A helium balloon has weight, but is kept from falling by the _____ of the surrounding more dense air pushing up on it.

Astronauts in orbit around the Earth have _____, but they feel _____ and are falling along a curved _____. They are moving so quickly relative to the orbit of the Earth that the curved arc of their fall carries them all the way around the Earth in a circle. They feel weightless because their space capsule is falling along with them, and the floor therefore does not push up on their feet.

**DID YOU KNOW?**

Units were not standardised until fairly recently in history, so when the physicist Sir Isaac Newton gave the result of an experiment with a pendulum, he had to specify not just that the string was 37 inches long but that it was '37 London inches long'. The inch as defined in Yorkshire would have been a different length. The metric system of units was created in France during the time of Napoleon. The standard unit of mass is a lump of metal (a platinum–iridium alloy) kept at Sèvres near Paris, France.

## *Reasoning* *Definitions*

David has been asked to make a poster showing the differences between force, mass, weight and load. Decide in your group which definitions he should put under each heading.

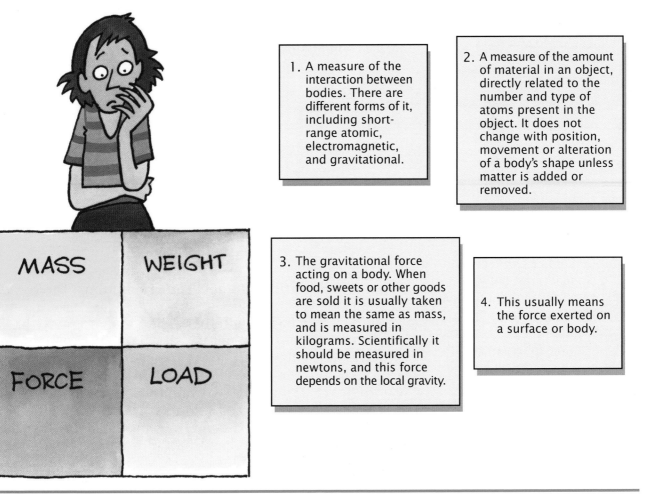

MASS    WEIGHT

FORCE    LOAD

1. A measure of the interaction between bodies. There are different forms of it, including short-range atomic, electromagnetic, and gravitational.

2. A measure of the amount of material in an object, directly related to the number and type of atoms present in the object. It does not change with position, movement or alteration of a body's shape unless matter is added or removed.

3. The gravitational force acting on a body. When food, sweets or other goods are sold it is usually taken to mean the same as mass, and is measured in kilograms. Scientifically it should be measured in newtons, and this force depends on the local gravity.

4. This usually means the force exerted on a surface or body.

**Key words**
* mass
* force
* gravity
* matter
* weight
* orbit
* newton meter

# → *A key scientific idea*

Any two massive objects (objects that have **mass**) have an attractive **force** between them. This attractive force is what we call **gravity**. If one object is big, like the Earth, the attractive force is large. If you drop an apple, it is attracted towards the Earth by the force of gravity. The Earth is attracted towards the apple by the same force, but because the Earth is so massive its movement towards the apple is so tiny it cannot be detected. The force of gravity on a mass of 1 kg on the surface of the Earth is about 9.8 newtons (N). To make calculations easier we can round this up to 10 N. Gravitational force pulls us towards the Earth; without it we would float about. As you travel away from the Earth, the pull of gravity gets less.

It was Newton who came to the conclusion that gravitational force exists between all objects or '**matter**'. Matter can be defined as anything that is affected by gravity, i.e., that has **weight** or would have weight if it were near the Earth or another planet or star. Gravity is responsible for holding the Moon in its **orbit** about the Earth and the planets in orbit around the Sun. The only reason the Moon does not fall to the Earth is because it is moving sideways.

2 Look at the graph below which shows how gravitational force changes with distance from the Earth. Describe in words the shape of the graph.

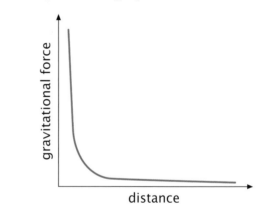

3 What is the relationship between gravitational force and distance?
4 Imagine a 6 kg bag of potatoes. The force of gravity on the Earth is about 10 N per kg, so what is the force of gravity on the bag of potatoes in newtons?
5 On the Moon, the force of gravity is only one-sixth that on the Earth. If you took the potatoes to the Moon (highly unlikely!) what would be their mass? What would be the gravitational force on the potatoes on the Moon? In other words, what would be the weight of the potatoes on the Moon in newtons?

---

*Enquiry* *Mars experiment*

If we took a **newton meter** to Mars we could easily measure the gravitational pull of Mars. Imagine the experiment is performed by a future visitor to Mars.

The mass hanger is suspended from the newton meter as shown in the diagram. A mass of 0.2 kg is added and the reading on the newton meter is noted. The experiment is repeated with further masses of 0.2 kg up to 1 kg. The results are shown in the table below the diagram.

**1** Plot a graph of mass against the gravitational pull of Mars.

**2** What is the shape of the graph?

**3** What is the pull of Mars on a mass of 1 kg?

**4** Predict what the reading would be for a mass of 0.5 kg.

**5** If the gravitational pull was 6 N, what would be the size of the mass?

**6** How does the gravitational pull of Mars compare to the gravitational pull of the Earth? Can you think why this may be so?

**7** On Jupiter, gravity is 2.7 times that of the Earth. What would be the weight of a 5 kg bag of potatoes on Jupiter?

| Mass (kg) | Weight (N) |
|-----------|------------|
| 0.2 | 0.75 |
| 0.4 | 1.49 |
| 0.6 | 2.24 |
| 0.8 | 2.98 |
| 1.0 | 3.73 |

---

# → *Gravity on different planets*

Our weight would vary from planet to planet because the gravity is different on each one.

**6** Look at the table below. Use a spreadsheet package to represent the data graphically. Add some formulae to automatically calculate your weight on each planet.

| Celestial body | Gravitational pull relative to Earth |
|----------------|--------------------------------------|
| Sun | 27.9 |
| Mercury | 0.38 |
| Venus | 0.91 |
| Earth | 1 |
| Moon | 0.17 |
| Mars | 0.38 |
| Jupiter | 2.54 |
| Saturn | 1.08 |
| Uranus | 0.90 |
| Neptune | 1.19 |
| Pluto | 0.07 |

Galileo (1564–1642).

Copernicus (1473–1543).

## Falling under gravity

Galileo (1564–1642) made two great contributions to the development of modern scientific thinking. The first was to recognise that the role of science was not to explain 'Why?' things happen.

Galileo asked a colleague why objects fall when they are released. His colleague replied that everyone knows that gravity makes objects fall. Galileo replied that he has not explained anything, just given it a name. This way of thinking simplified the work of scientists, who accepted without question that God caused a particular phenomenon to occur.

When Galileo heard of the invention of the telescope he designed and built one for himself. He was the first person to use a telescope for astronomical observations. He wrote a book which supported the suggestions of Copernicus, an astronomer who lived between 1473 and 1543. Copernicus understood that the Earth moved around the Sun, but this idea was revolutionary at the time – the Church believed that the Earth was the centre of the Universe, and that the Sun moved around the Earth. For this reason, Copernicus did not agree to have his work published until he was on his deathbed.

Galileo was able to observe through his telescope Jupiter and its moons, and saw that it was a miniature model of the Solar System. He saw that Venus showed phases similar to those of the Moon, as would be expected under the Copernican system. The Church saw this as heresy. It was seen to contradict not only the teaching of Aristotle, a Greek philosopher who lived between 384 and 322 BC, but also the authority of the Church.

In 1616 Galileo was warned to stop teaching that the Copernican heliocentric system (in which the Sun is the centre of the Solar System) was correct. The Church saw him as a threat. The Inquisition tried Galileo when he was 68, and his book was placed on the 'Index' of forbidden books. It remained there until 1824. Galileo was sentenced to house arrest for the remainder of his life for daring to support Copernicus' theory, although he recanted when faced with the death sentence, saying publicly that he thought Copernicus was wrong.

I, Galileo, aged 70 years, arraigned personally before this tribunal, having before my eyes and touching the Holy Gospels, do abandon the false opinion that the Sun is the centre of the world and immovable and that the Earth is not the centre of the world and moves.

I have been pronounced by the Holy Office to be vehemently suspected of heresy (for these views). I will never again say or assert, verbally or in writing, anything that might furnish a similar suspicion regarding me.

Ironically he used his time under house arrest to develop his understanding of mechanics so that he could hypothesise why the planets would not fall into the Sun if they were not held up by their 'natural place'. This was an example of his second major contribution to science: using maths to describe natural phenomena, then performing experiments to see if the mathematical description agrees with what happens in reality. Nowadays we think of science as a cycle of theory and experiment. The theory allows you to design new experiments to test new predictions.

Galileo's book on mechanics.

Galileo compared the motion of a heavy object and a light one. He described mathematically how far an object fell in a given time, and was then able to verify experimentally that this description was correct. He demonstrated that a heavy object and a light object both fall at the same rate. If his results had disagreed with his theory he would have had to think of a new theory.

This was very different to the qualitative science of Aristotle, where explanations did not need to be tested. Aristotle theorised that solid objects fell because they were composed of 'Earthy' material, whose natural place was at the centre of the Universe.

Galileo recognised that you had to design experiments to minimise the effect of other variables not under investigation, such as the effect of air resistance when studying falling objects. He demonstrated that all objects fall at the same rate, whatever their size and mass, if their air resistance is the same.

Aristotle (384–322 BC).

*Evaluation* Gravity

Do these two cartoons show scientific explanations? In your group, discuss what you think and why.

*Reasoning* *A conundrum*

Galileo made up a dialogue between two characters, 'Simplicio', who is a bit simple, and 'Salviati', a 'know it all', to explain his theory about objects falling at the same rate. Salviati asks Simplicio to think of two stones, one heavier than the other. He asks which stone Simplicio thinks falls faster and when he says the heavy one Salviati gives him a conundrum (mental puzzle) like this:

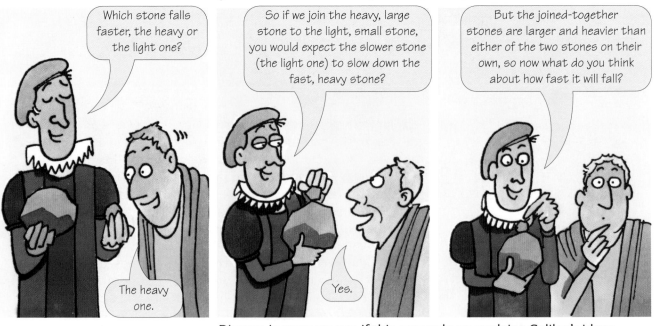

Discuss in your groups if this conundrum explains Galileo's ideas clearly to Simplicio. Continue the cartoon and add some more dialogue between Simplicio and Salviati that would help Simplicio see why he was wrong to think that heavy objects fall faster than light objects.

# → *Sir Isaac Newton*

Newton (1642–1727) was born the year Galileo died. He is famous for his ideas about mechanics and planetary motion. Newton showed that the entire Universe obeyed the same laws of nature, as published in 1687 in his *Mathematical Principles of Natural Philosophy* (or *The Principia* as it became more commonly known). He proved that the mechanics that determined how bodies fall on Earth also explained the periodic motions of the planets. His first law of motion says that an object will continue to move at a steady pace in a straight line when no forces are acting on it. This is why this deep space probe sent out into space by NASA is now moving away from Earth unassisted by rockets at a constant velocity and will keep on going.

*Time to think*

Work with a partner.

1 Using the information in this chapter so far, create a celebrity timeline listing the names of the people famous for their thoughts on space and movement.

2 Read the sections on gravity again, noting down any words you are not sure of. Ask a friend to explain them to you. Produce a list of words that neither of you are sure about. Use a dictionary to look up the words in your list, and check that you both now understand them all.

3 What instrument did Galileo construct? How did he use it in a way that it had never been used before?

4 Galileo made two major contributions to the way scientists think. Write a sentence to explain each contribution.

5 Galileo performed experiments on the rate at which objects fall. Rather than measure the time to drop vertically, he allowed them to roll down a ramp. Why was this?

6 Galileo also recognised the importance of careful planning of his experiments. Can you give an example of this?

7 Find out about Aristotle's model of the Solar System. Compare it with that of Galileo. Make some notes on the evidence for and against the two models.

*DID YOU KNOW?*

The centre of gravity of an object is the point inside an object where there is as much mass on one side as the other. In a balance beam this would be called the pivot or fulcrum. Men and women have different centres of gravity.

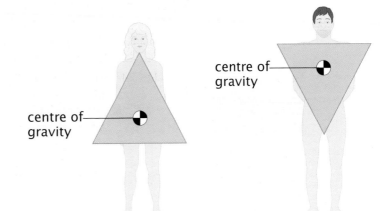

centre of gravity

centre of gravity

Test this out at home. Stand with your toes touching a wall. Put one foot behind the other and walk three paces away from the wall. Ask someone to put a stool between you and the wall. Lean over and put the top of your head against the wall so that your legs make an angle of about 45 degrees with the floor.

Grip the edges of the stool, pick it up and hold it against your chest. Now try to stand up. Get other people to try this, including adults.

What do you expect the difference between men and women to be?

# → *Weightlessness*

**Key words**
* weightless
* free fall
* inertia

Most people think that out in space you would be **weightless**. There would be no nearby massive objects pulling on you. You would be too far from the Earth or the Sun for them to have any effect, and too far away from any other star. According to Newton's law there is gravitational pull between you and the spacecraft, but both you and the spacecraft have very small masses compared with large bodies like planets. The attraction between you and the spacecraft is therefore far too small to pull you back in. In fact, astronauts are not weightless in space. At the orbit of

the Space Shuttle, 200 miles from the surface of the Earth, the force of the Earth's gravity is not very different from what it is on the ground. The sense of weightlessness comes about because the shuttle is in **free fall** around the Earth. The shuttle is 'falling' through its orbit and being pulled around the Earth by the Earth's gravity. You experience the same sensation of weightlessness when you are on a roller coaster or amusement park ride. You are weightless for a few seconds, when the roller coaster is in free fall. This does not mean that weightless objects do not have any mass, and if a massive object should bump into them it would still be damaging because of its mass. Similarly, you could hold a very heavy box in space because it is apparently weightless, but to push it away from you would still be difficult. To get it moving you still have to shift the same mass. The property of matter that causes it to resist changes in speed or direction is called **inertia**.

Spaceman easily holding a heavy box.

Man on Earth having difficulty picking up the same box.

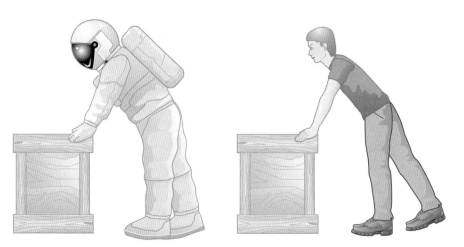

Both the spaceman and the man on Earth having difficulty pushing the box along the floor.

*Reasoning* ## Living in space

**1** Imagine trying to pour a liquid into a cup and drinking it inside a spacecraft in outer space. What would happen?

**2** Why are astronauts joined to their spacecraft with lifelines?

*Research*

Produce a poster to show the milestones of space exploration. Use the library and the internet. These questions will also help you in your research:

**1** Who was the third man to land on the Moon and in what year did he land?
**2** Why is the Englishwoman Helen Sharman famous, and what did she do?
**3** What is meant by 'escape velocity'?
**4** Who or what is Shoemaker Levy?
**5** How are astronomers finding out about Jupiter?

# → Experimenting in space

**Key words**
* NASA
* friction
* light year

Some experiments simply can't be done on Earth. That's why the National Aeronautics and Space Administration (**NASA**) is building the International Space Station, a full-time low-gravity research lab out in space. It's also why NASA schedules space shuttle missions dedicated to scientific research. In the USA last year 14.5 billion dollars was given to NASA. One mission was the space shuttle Columbia, which carried plans and equipment for over 80 scientific experiments. One investigation was into the behaviour of flames.

On Earth, flames have a teardrop shape caused by hot air rising in a gravitational field. On board a spaceship, flames break apart into little balls that move around like UFOs. They burn using almost no fuel. Researchers would like to replicate this in petrol-saving car engines. Scientists hope to learn how the little balls of flame burn and what keeps them lit. The human brain is also the subject of investigation. An astronaut just arriving in orbit finds there is no 'up' or 'down.' If you drop something, it doesn't fall. The brain adapts by building a 'mental model' that tells the body how to interpret this unusual environment, and the astronaut successfully adapts to it. No one knows how the brain constructs such models, but neuroscientists want to find out because many believe model building is the key to everyday human learning. Unfortunately, the space shuttle Columbia broke up and was destroyed on re-entry into the Earth's atmosphere. There is a lot of information about this on the internet.

Space shuttles get hot on re-entry because of the **friction** they experience on entering the Earth's atmosphere at very high speeds. Special ceramic tiles are used on the outside

of the spacecraft to protect it from the heat. The angle of entry into the atmosphere is also crucial. It is important that the angle of entry is not too steep, or the spacecraft will overheat. It must also not be too shallow, otherwise the spacecraft will bounce back out into space.

In the case of Columbia, NASA scientists think that a piece of fuel-tank insulation that fell off at launch may have damaged one or more of the heat-resistant ceramic tiles. Temperatures on the left side of the shuttle rose significantly before it burst into flames, and this could have caused more tiles to fall off.

The space shuttle Columbia.

## Falling foam "caused shuttle disaster"

A DRAMATIC experiment appears to have confirmed the leading theory for the Columbia space shuttle disaster: that it was fatally damaged by a falling piece of foam insulation during its launch on January 16.

NASA investigators say that the debris from the orbiter's fuel tank could have punched a hole in a critical heat shield. ... The results appear to remove any doubt that the foam, which struck the leading edge of Columbia's wing in the first seconds of launch, was ultimately responsible for its disintegration over Texas ...

From *The Times* 9th July 2003

7 What causes space shuttles to get hot on re-entry?

8 What types of energy does a shuttle have as it re-enters the Earth's atmosphere?

*Reasoning* ## Counting the cost

Form a group of four. Two of you will present an argument for continuing space research and two of you will argue that it is a waste of money. Agree how long you will have to research and prepare your arguments, then have a debate. What did your group conclude? Did you reach the same conclusion as other groups in your class?

**DID YOU KNOW?**

Because astronomical distances are so enormous, special units are used to measure them. The Astronomical Unit (AU) is the average distance of the Earth from the Sun. It is about 150 million km. The parsec is another unit of distance. It is even bigger than the AU: 1 parsec is about 200 000 AU or 30 000 000 000 000 km. The third unit used is the **light year**. This is how far a ray of light will travel in a year. As light travels at about 300 000 km/s, it would travel about 9 461 000 000 000 km in a year.

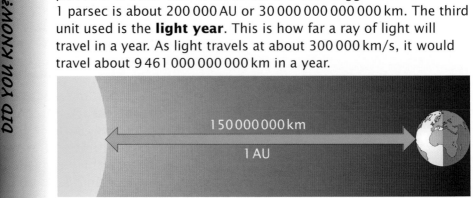

150 000 000 km

1 AU

# → The Big Bang theory – Ideas about how the Universe began

**EXTENSION**

**Key words**
* Big Bang
* cosmos
* radiation
* absolute zero
* steady state theory

## Countdown

In the beginning there was nothing. It was a 'nothing' so profound it defies human comprehension. We may think of the emptiest parts of the Universe today – out in the cold realms between the distant galaxies – as 'nothing regions'. But even they contain a sprinkling of atoms, and the faint radiation of dim shafts of light passing through. More fundamentally, the emptiest regions today are supported by the invisible structure of space, and respond to the inaudible clock of time. A long, long time ago, there was no matter, and no radiation. More importantly space didn't exist; time did not flow. Our story begins 'once upon a time' – when there was no space, and there was no time.

From *Big Bang* by Heather Couper and Nigel Henbest, Dorling Kindersley 1997.

All civilisations have had their theories about how the Universe began. The **Big Bang** model is one modern theory to explain the origin and evolution of our Universe. It is based on a large amount of evidence. This evidence is now so overwhelming that most people believe that this theory is correct. It says that between 12 and 14 billion years ago the Universe came into existence at a specific moment in time, starting with an enormous explosion. Both time and space were created in this huge blast. Just after the Big Bang, all the material in the Universe was packed into a tiny volume. The Universe has since expanded from this hot, extremely dense state into the vast and much cooler **cosmos** of today. We can still see remnants of this hot dense matter, which some scientists call 'cosmic background **radiation**'. Arno Penzias and Robert Wilson discovered this in the 1960s. It is visible as microwave radiation, and is visible to microwave detectors as a uniform glow across the entire sky. These radio waves warm space to a few degrees above **absolute zero**.

Edwin Hubble (1889–1953).

It was in the 1920s that the American astronomer Edwin Hubble found that galaxies were moving away from us, and the further away they were the faster they were receding. He concluded that the whole Universe appears to be expanding. He thought that at one stage the galaxies must all have started from a single point.

One question that many scientists ask is: 'Will the Universe continue to expand?'. There seem to be two possibilities. Either it will continue to expand forever, or it will stop expanding and the Universe's own gravity will begin to pull it all back together. This has been called 'The Big Crunch'. It is something that we needn't worry about, because if it happens it will be a long time in the future!

There are some scientists who do not believe in the Big Bang theory at all. Most of them prefer the idea that the Universe always has been and always will be – this is known as the **steady state theory**.

*DID YOU KNOW?*

A star is made of a mass of gas and particles that collapse together under their own gravity and pull towards each other. As the matter falls inwards, it speeds up and heats up so that eventually the star glows red. As it goes on collapsing inwards it gets smaller and hotter. Nuclear fusion begins, and the star glows yellow (shines). It becomes stable as the gravitational forces collapsing inwards are balanced by the outward pressure of nuclear fusion.

*Creative thinking* ## Starburst

Giant stars are thought to be stars that have run out of hydrogen – it has all been converted by nuclear fusion into helium – so the interior of the star collapses and the huge rise in temperature expands the outer layers of the star so that it becomes cooler and redder. The star may then start to shrink again under the pull of gravity, and become a white dwarf star. If it goes on shrinking, the matter becomes so dense that not even light can escape the pull of gravity. This is called a black hole.

Write a science fiction episode for a TV programme called Starburst where our star, the Sun, begins to change because of cosmic forces.

A red dwarf star.     The formation of a nova.     A supernova.

## Modelling the Big Bang

An analogy based on baking a fruitcake may help to explain the Big Bang theory. Think of the Universe as a fruitcake mix of raisins, currants and cherries in a cake mixture. The mixture is poured into a cake tin, which it does not completely fill. The cake is put into the oven to bake. Imagine you are a raisin inside the cake. As it bakes, the cake rises and all the other bits of fruit move further and further away from you. No matter where in the cake you are, everything around is moving away at the same rate.

9   In this analogy, what could the cake mixture be compared to? What is the fruit supposed to represent?

10  Think about the cake baking. It suggests that there are two possible answers to what may happen to the Universe in the future. What are they?

11  There is one more possibility. What might this be?

### Research

1   Use either the internet or other sources to produce a short biography of one of the scientists who have contributed to our knowledge of astronomy and space. Imagine you have to write a short biography for the back cover of a book they have written. You could select one of these scientists:

Ptolemy, Copernicus, Kepler, Galileo, Newton, Hawking

Find out when they were born, where they lived, what they discovered, plus at least one other interesting fact about them.

**EXTENSION**

2   Research and write an article for a teenage magazine about the life cycle of a star. You need to mention the Big Bang theory, the expanding Universe, red giants, black holes and white dwarfs.

# → *Satellites*

**Key words**
* satellite
* axis
* geostationary

We call an object orbiting a planet a **satellite**. Some are natural, like our Moon. Others are man-made. These are artificial satellites that have been put into space by us.

Today we have many different uses for satellites. There are communications satellites, spy or military satellites, navigation satellites, weather satellites, science research satellites and many others.

In 1959 the Soviet satellite Lunik III photographed the far side of the Moon, which we cannot see from Earth.

The world's first man-made satellite was Sputnik 1, launched by Russia in October 1957. The science fiction author Arthur C Clarke had first suggested using artificial satellites for communication as early as 1945. He called the communications satellites 'Extra Terrestrial Relays.' In an article in *Wireless World* he calculated that satellites placed in a high orbit of 36 000 km would take exactly one day to go around the Earth. This is exactly the same time as it takes for the Earth to spin a full turn on its **axis**. Satellites in these positions would appear stationary from the ground – they would always be above the same point on the Earth. Such an orbit is called a **geostationary** orbit. Clarke concluded that a minimum of three satellites, capable of receiving and transmitting radio signals and stationed 120 degrees apart, would give almost total global coverage.

**12** Can you think of any other examples where science fiction has become reality?

It was 1965 before the world's first commercial communication satellite was launched. It was called Early Bird. It didn't have a battery, so it only worked when its solar panels were in the Sun. Ask your grandparents or someone else you know who can remember the 1960s about their memories of satellites. A lot of 1960s pop tunes were inspired by space research.

*Word play* Think of some rhyming lyrics about the twenty-first century space age. You could make up a tune as well.

Polar satellites are satellites that travel over both of the poles. As the Earth turns on its axis, the satellite passes over a different area of the planet with each orbit.

Some satellites have equatorial orbits. These satellites are placed a lot further out than polar satellites. As predicted by Clarke, if they are placed at 36 000 km, then the satellite will take 24 hours to make one orbit. Such satellites are geostationary and are useful for communication.

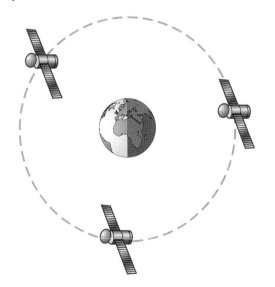

Navigation satellites can tell you where you are on Earth, as well as the local time. Receivers are increasingly being installed in cars to help people find routes. They are also useful for emergency workers, such as police, so they can get to an emergency faster. Planes and ships have navigation systems to tell them where they are – these are called Global Positioning Systems (GPS). The GPS is a very accurate system, locating your position to within a few metres. GPS satellites are spaced in orbits so that a receiver anywhere on Earth can always receive signals from at least four satellites. They give global coverage. Four satellites are needed in each of six different orbits, so 24 GPS satellites are required in all.

*Evaluation* **GPS**

Make a list of the advantages and disadvantages of using GPS compared with a map for finding your way by car from London to Edinburgh.

Spy satellites are widely used today to collect information about battlefields and possible military targets. They can take very detailed pictures on which it is possible to pick out individual people on the ground. Other military satellites monitor the Earth for signs of hostile activity, such as the launch of a missile or a nuclear explosion. These defence satellites are able to monitor large sections of the Earth's surface and usually have a polar orbit.

Weather satellites help us to forecast the weather. They look at air movements and cloud cover, monitoring storms and hurricanes. Weather satellite information contributes to the improved accuracy of our weather forecasts and we now not only know what weather to expect tomorrow but also in two days' time or even a week. Weather satellites also act as remote dataloggers. They can take readings of temperature, pressure and humidity.

Satellites also help scientists to study the Earth's surface. They can monitor the growth of crops and the size of the polar ice caps. They can also be used to identify the location of resources such as ores and coal.

Satellites detect these things by analysing light and other radiation which is reflected and emitted from surface features. Each feature (for example, a building, an ocean or a forest) has a different signature of reflected and emitted radiation.

Other satellites are used to look away from the Earth to study space. An example is the Hubble Space Telescope. This is able to observe distant galaxies without any interference from the Earth's atmosphere.

An image from a weather satellite.

## *Information processing* Artificial satellites

Read the information about artificial satellites on the previous page. Summarise the information in a table. Choose suitable headings for the columns and rows.

**EXTENSION**  Use the internet or other resources to find out further facts about satellites, and add them to your table.

## *Reasoning* Motion of satellites

**Key words**
* circular motion
* tension

To understand the motion of satellites, we need to think about **circular motion**. This is an experiment you can try outdoors.

Imagine a rubber bung on a string is released at point A.

**1** Where does the bung go after its release? Why? Discuss this with your neighbour and make a sketch to explain your reasoning.

In the same way that the **tension** in the string is providing the force for the bung to move along a circular path, so the Earth provides the gravitational force to maintain the motion of the Moon.
   Newton described a 'thought' experiment to explain the motion of satellites. Imagine firing a cannon ball from a cannon. The bigger the charge firing the cannon the faster the cannon ball would go, so the further it would travel before it fell to the Earth. If it were travelling fast enough it would fall to the Earth at the same rate as the Earth curved away, so the cannon ball would keep going round the Earth and eventually return to where it started.

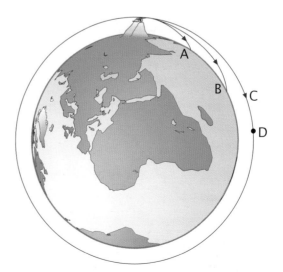

**2** In real life, there are other factors that would need to be taken into account. Can you think of any?

## Model movement

This cartoon shows an investigation being done by a Year 9 class.

1 Why doesn't the ball fall out of the bucket?

2 Sam says this is a good model of how a satellite moves. Think about the ways this model is a good representation of reality and how it differs from reality. Decide in your group if Sam is right.

# → Rockets

**Key words**
* thrust force
* trajectory

The picture shows a water rocket. You may have seen one. It consists of a plastic 1.5-litre drinks bottle about a quarter filled with water, then connected to a foot pump. As air is pumped in the pressure builds up and the tube connecting the pump to the bottle comes off. Water is ejected from the bottle. There is a reaction force on the bottle. As well as this **thrust force** acting on the bottle, there is another force acting on the bottle. This is its weight. To get off the ground the force acting upwards must be greater than the weight of the water rocket.

water rocket

balloon rocket

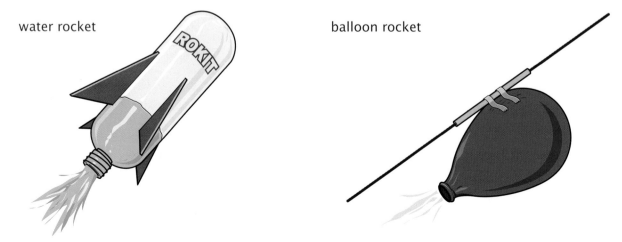

Another simple rocket is the balloon rocket, also shown in the picture.

**13** Explain how a balloon rocket works.

To lift a rocket into space, a lot of energy must be supplied. Look at the information for the giant Saturn rocket.

The Saturn rocket.

> The Saturn rocket was a three stage vehicle. Its total mass was 3 038 500 kg. It was 110 m high and 10 m in diameter.
>
> The first stage weighed 2.3 million kg. It travelled at 8600 km/h for 2.5 minutes.
>
> The second stage weighed 0.5 million kg. It travelled at 24 600 km/h.
>
> The third stage travelled at 39 400 km/h.

As the rocket travels further away from the pull of the Earth's gravity, the force on the rocket from the Earth becomes less. It will now become more affected by other objects in the Solar System. A German scientist, Wernher von Braun, was the first to successfully develop modern liquid-fuelled rockets. During the Second World War, von Braun and fellow German scientists produced a rocket to carry out long-range bombardment of English cities. On 3rd October 1942, a V2 rocket was launched from a launch pad on a Baltic island and followed its programmed **trajectory** to land perfectly on-target 193 km away. On the way it had risen nearly 100 km, rising beyond the Earth's atmosphere. This date may be considered to mark the beginning of the space age.

**14** A rocket needs to carry all its fuel. It cannot use ordinary air to 'burn' its fuel. Why not?

# → *Measuring speed*

In Book 1 we covered some work on speed. To measure the speed of something we need to take two measurements: the distance travelled and the time taken. Speed is measured in metres per second, m/s, in science but a car speedometer will usually show miles per hour, mph. Other units of speed are km/hour. The speed shown on a car speedometer gives us the instantaneous speed – the speed we are travelling at the instant we look at the speedometer. This is not the same as the average speed, which is found using the following equation:

$$\text{average speed} = \frac{\text{total distance travelled}}{\text{total time taken}}$$

## *Information processing* Looking for patterns

Look at the information provided in the table. The data show information on a number of races at a recent international athletics meeting.

| Men (M)/ Women (W) | Race distance (m) | Race time (min:s) | Race time (s) | Last lap distance (m) | Last lap time (s) | Race speed (m/s) | Last lap speed (m/s) | Type of race |
|---|---|---|---|---|---|---|---|---|
| W | 3000 | 8:26.53 | 506.53 | 400 | 59.95 | 5.92 | 6.67 | flat final |
| M | 800 | 1:44.55 | 104.55 | 400 | 52.83 | 7.65 | 7.57 | flat heat |
| M | 110 | 12.99 | 12.99 | | | 8.47 | | hurdles |
| W | 400 | 48.65 | 48.65 | | | 8.22 | | flat final |
| M | 800 | 1:43.45 | 103.45 | 400 | 53.91 | 7.73 | 7.42 | flat final |
| W | 800 | 1:56.10 | 116.10 | 400 | 59.67 | 6.89 | 6.70 | flat final |
| M | 10 000 | 27:21.30 | 1641.30 | 400 | 65.02 | 6.09 | 6.15 | flat final |
| M | 200 | 19.76 | 19.76 | | | 10.12 | | flat final |
| W | 200 | 21.33 | 21.33 | | | 9.38 | | flat final |
| M | 1500 | 3:40.89 | 220.89 | 400 | 52.62 | 6.79 | 7.60 | flat heat |
| M | 3000 | 8:05.51 | 485.51 | 400 | 57.63 | 6.18 | 6.94 | steeple final |
| W | 10 000 | 31:05.21 | 1865.21 | 400 | 66.38 | 5.36 | 6.03 | flat final |
| W | 100 | 12.38 | 12.38 | | | 8.08 | | hurdles final |
| M | 1500 | 3:38.09 | 218.09 | 400 | 53.64 | 6.88 | 7.46 | flat semi-final |
| M | 1500 | 3:35.96 | 215.96 | | | 6.95 | | flat final |

**1** Do runners run faster or slower at the end of the race? Is there a pattern in the results?

**2** What types of races are run at a faster speed?

**3** Do men always run faster than women?

This table gives information on some fast cars.

| Car | Acceleration (0–100km/h) (seconds) | Top speed (km/h) | Mass (kg) |
|---|---|---|---|
| Callaway Sledgehammer Corvette | 3.9 | 408 | 1665 |
| 2001 Lotec Sirius | 3.7 | 400 | 1280 |
| 1998 Ferrari F50 GT | 3.3 | 380 | 909 |
| 2003 Lamborghini Gallardo | 4.0 | 308 | 1614 |
| 2003 Alfa Romeo 147 GTA | 6.3 | 246 | 1355 |

**4** Use a spreadsheet program to produce a suitable chart of the data.

**5** Is the fastest car the one with the greatest acceleration?

**6** Is there any relationship between the mass of the car and its acceleration?

*Enquiry* *Measuring the speed of a trolley down a slope*

This experiment uses light gates to measure the speed of a trolley running down a runway. You may have seen a similar experiment.

When the card attached to the trolley breaks the infrared beam of the timing gate the timer starts recording. As the card leaves the gate the timer stops. The software displays and records the time and can show the speed of the object if the length of the card is known. In an experiment using this equipment, the trolley was released from different places farther up the runway to see how this affected the speed. The results obtained by one group are shown below:

| Distance from light gate (cm) | Speed (cm/s) |
| --- | --- |
| 10 | 5 |
| 20 | 10 |
| 30 | |
| 40 | 20 |
| 50 | 25 |
| 60 | 29 |
| 70 | 31 |

1 What were the key variables in this experiment? What were the independent and the dependent variables? What variables were kept constant?

2 Use the results from the table above to plot a graph of speed against distance from the light gate.

3 One of the readings in the table is missing. How would you make a good estimate of the missing reading? Write your own estimate. Compare your answer with those of at least three other people. Did they use the same method? Did they get the same answer?

4 Describe the shape of the graph you have plotted. Why does it change shape the way it does? What relationship does it illustrate?

**5** In the experiment described on the previous page the pupils kept the slope constant and altered the position of launch of the trolley. Another group of pupils did some new experiments with the same apparatus. They kept the point of release unchanged, but increased the angle of the slope.

**a)** Write a series of instructions for these new experiments.

**b)** What do you predict would happen in such an experiment? Can you give a reason for this?

**c)** What would their graph look like? Sketch it.

**d)** How can you see if your prediction is correct?

# → *Interpreting graphs*

**Key words**
* speed
* velocity
* acceleration

The graph below shows the actual distance-time graph for a car making a journey. Discuss the shape of the curve with a partner and write a paragraph about the motion of the car using words such as: speeding up, stops, slows down, goes at a steady speed.

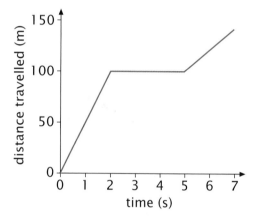

Lots of people use the words **speed** and **velocity** without realising they have two different meanings. Speed and **acceleration** are two other scientific concepts that people often wrongly assume mean the same thing. Scientists must define them clearly to use them as part of their models about the Universe.

Think about a model train going at a steady speed around a track. It is travelling at 15 cm/s. Imagine a second train on a parallel track travelling in the opposite direction, also at 15 cm/s.

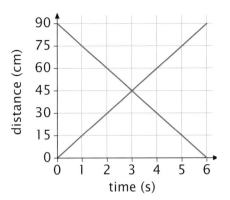

When they pass one another in front of you, one train is moving from your right to your left and the other is going from left to right. The trains have the same speeds but different velocities. If the one going to the left has a velocity of +15 cm/s, the one going to the right has a velocity of –15 cm/s. Whilst speed gives us information about how fast something is travelling, velocity also gives us information about the direction of travel.

In Book 1 we referred to the use of a motion sensor to plot a graph on a computer screen as you move towards or away from the sensor. As well as plotting a distance-time graph, the equipment can be set up to plot a velocity-time graph. The first graph shows the motion of a pupil walking at a slow steady speed towards the sensor. The second graph shows the equivalent velocity-time graph for the motion.

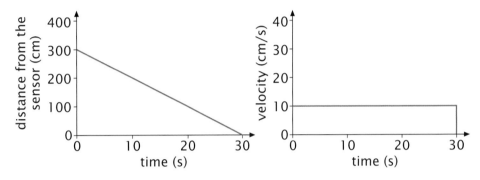

15 How far away is the pupil at the start?
16 How far does he travel in 5 s?
17 What was his average velocity?

## Air-cushioned vehicles – hovercraft

Hovercraft are vehicles that depend on the low resistance of air compared to, for example, water. The vehicles 'float' on a cushion of air. You may have made a model hovercraft or seen a linear air track or magnetic pucks floating on a cushion of carbon dioxide from 'dry ice'.

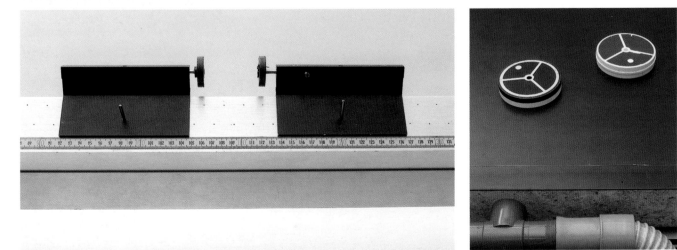

A linear air track.

You may have played air hockey with similar disks.

In diagrams of moving objects you are often asked to show the direction of the forces acting on the object. It is important that you do not confuse the direction of motion of the object with that of the force acting on it.

**18** Look at the objects shown below. Copy the drawings and add arrows to show the directions and relative sizes of the forces acting on them.

*Research*

Use the internet to find out when and where the last Concorde made its last official flight. What happened to it after that?

Record how you carried out your internet search in a series of instructions so that someone else could replicate your search and check your facts. Get a friend to try out the instructions.

*Time to think*

Think back over all the work you have done in this chapter.

What facts have you found most interesting? Why?

Which topics do you think will be hard to revise? How can you make your revision of these topics more effective?

List all the sets of scientific concepts in this chapter that many people might get confused, for example, mass and weight. Explain their differences to someone else, and see if they found your explanations helpful.

# 5 Patterns of reactivity

**In this chapter you will learn:**

➜ to establish and use a reactivity series for metals
➜ to represent chemical reactions by word and symbol equations
➜ that although metals react in a similar way with oxygen, water and acids, some react more readily than others

**You will also develop your skills in:**

➜ making predictions using the reactivity series
➜ presenting data in a way that enables patterns to be described
➜ identifying and controlling variables in an investigation of the reactivity of different metals

➡ ➡ ➡ WHAT DO YOU KNOW?

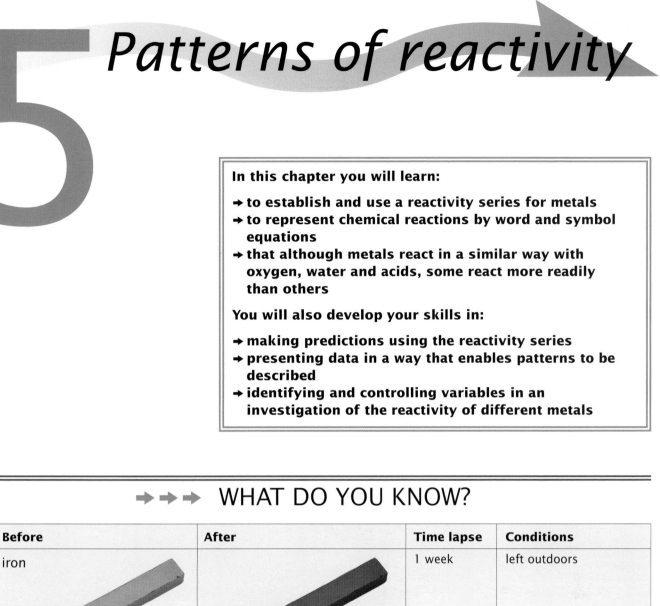

| Before | After | Time lapse | Conditions |
| --- | --- | --- | --- |
| iron | | 1 week | left outdoors |
| gold | | over 2000 years | buried underground |
| lead | | 6 months | left outdoors |

| Before | After | Time lapse | Conditions |
|--------|-------|-----------|------------|
| silver | | 2 years | left indoors, uncleaned |
| copper | | 1 year | left outdoors |
| potassium | | 2 seconds | left indoors |
| sodium | | 4 seconds | left indoors |

1 Look at the photographs and explain what has happened to each object. Try to use the words tarnish and corrode in your answer.

2 Look again at the photographs of potassium and sodium.
   a) Describe one piece of evidence that shows that these two elements could be metals.
   b) Describe one piece of evidence that shows that these two elements could be non-metals.
   c) i) Which group of the periodic table are these two elements in?
      ii) From their position in the periodic table, are the two elements metals or non-metals?
   d) Freshly cut sodium reacts with oxygen in the air. Write a word equation for this reaction.

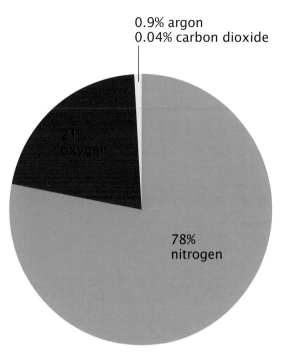

0.9% argon
0.04% carbon dioxide

21% oxygen

78% nitrogen

Composition of dry air.

**3** The above pie chart is taken from Book 2. Using your knowledge of the reactivity of the different substances in moist air, predict which substances could cause the tarnishing and corrosion of metals.

**4** What makes copper go green?

In your group, look at the above cartoon and discuss the three pupils' answers.
**a)** Decide if each answer:

- is definitely correct
- could be correct
- is definitely wrong.

Give a reason for each decision.
**b)** If you have decided that an answer 'could be correct', you will need some more evidence to make a definite decision. Discuss what sort of evidence you would need.

5 List the seven metals in the table in order of their increasing reactivity. Use the evidence in the table.

6 Freshly cut calcium also reacts with oxygen in the air.
   a) Write a word equation for this reaction.
   b) Copy and complete the symbol equation for this reaction with the help of the combining power pictures below:

   $Ca + O_2 \rightarrow$

# ➡ *Reacting metals with water*

**Key word**
✱ tarnish

Some metals react with water. Other metals **tarnish** in damp air. When metals tarnish in air they are reacting with the oxygen <u>and</u> water.

Potassium is a metal that reacts vigorously with water.

Copper is a metal that does not seem to react at all with water.

This is how potassium is stored.

1 Which metals, apart from potassium, would you expect to react vigorously with water?
2 List all of the evidence that you might see if a chemical reaction occurs between a reactive metal and water. Share your ideas with others in your group.
3 Why are metals such as potassium and sodium stored under oil?

4 This is part of a pupil's results table for an experiment investigating the reactions of some metals with water:

| Metal | Observations | Test on the gas | Test on the remaining solution |
|---|---|---|---|
| Lithium | The metal floated, giving off bubbles of gas. It eventually disappeared. | The gas popped when ignited | The remaining solution turned Universal Indicator dark blue (pH 14) |

 a) Which piece of evidence under 'Observations' might be unexpected for a metal?
 b) Which gas is formed in the reaction?
 c) Where has the lithium gone? Has it really disappeared?
 d) i) What type of substance has a pH of 14 in solution?
  ii) Can you give the chemical name of one example of this type of substance?
 f) Give a word equation for the reaction of lithium with water.

# Uses of the periodic table

**Key words**
* compounds
* combining power
* bond

One feature of the periodic table is the arrangement of the elements into vertical groups. This feature means that it is very useful for predicting how the elements will behave.

**Group 1**
lithium
sodium
potassium
rubidium
caesium

5 What is the link between the order of the group 1 metals in the periodic table and their reactivity with water?

**Group 2**
beryllium
magnesium
calcium
strontium
barium

6 Predict which group 2 metal is the most reactive with water.

Another important use of the periodic table is to help with the writing of formulae. Generally, the **compounds** that elements in the same vertical group form the with other elements all have the same simple ratios of atoms. This is because they have the same **combining power**.

The table below shows some of the metals in group 1 and the formulae of some of their compounds. The group 1 metals sodium (Na) and rubidium (Rb) are not listed in the table.

| Metal | Metal chloride | Metal oxide | Metal sulphate |
|---|---|---|---|
| lithium (Li) | LiCl | $Li_2O$ | $Li_2SO_4$ |
| potassium (K) | KCl | $K_2O$ | $K_2SO_4$ |
| caesium (Cs) | CsCl | $Cs_2O$ | $Cs_2SO_4$ |

Note that the three group 1 metals all have one 'hand' to form a **bond**.

7 For the three group 1 metals shown in the table, what is the ratio of:
   a) metal to chlorine in the metal chlorides
   b) metal to oxygen in the oxides
   c) metal to sulphate ($SO_4$) in the sulphates?
8 Write the formula of:
   a) sodium chloride
   b) rubidium oxide
   c) sodium sulphate.

The periodic table is also helpful when writing word and symbol equations. Generally, all elements in the same vertical group have very similar equations for their reactions with a given substance. The equations for the reactions of two group 1 metals with water are shown below:

sodium + water → sodium hydroxide + hydrogen

$$2Na + 2H_2O \rightarrow 2NaOH + H_2$$

rubidium + water → rubidium hydroxide + hydrogen

$$2Rb + 2H_2O \rightarrow 2RbOH + H_2$$

9 Write a word equation for the reaction of:
   a) potassium with water
   b) caesium with water.
10 Write a balanced symbol equation for the reaction of:
   a) potassium with water
   b) caesium with water.

## Summary

Using the evidence looked at so far, the metals can be placed in a 'league table' with the most reactive at the top:

| Metal | Reaction with water | Time to tarnish |
|---|---|---|
| potassium | explosive | 2 seconds |
| sodium | vigorous | 4 seconds |
| lithium | quite fast | 8 seconds |
| magnesium | slow | some hours |
| iron, zinc, copper | very slow | days or months |
| silver | does not react | months |
| gold | does not react | does not tarnish |

The evidence we have does not enable us to put the metals copper, iron and zinc in order. We need more evidence to be able to compare them. This can be obtained by looking at the reactions of metals with acids.

# ➡ *Reacting metals with acids*

**Key words**
* variables
* activity series

11 In Chapter 1 you saw that most metals react with acids.
  a) What is the gas formed?
  b) What is happening to the magnesium in the beaker?
  c) Write a word equation for the reaction of magnesium with hydrochloric acid.
  d) Write a general word equation for the reaction of metals with acids.
  e) Write a symbol equation for the reaction using these combining power pictures:

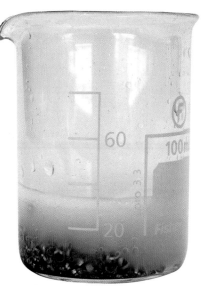

Magnesium reacting with hydrochloric acid.

## Planning

Plan an investigation to find out the correct order of reactivity of the following metals with sulphuric acid: copper, iron, magnesium and zinc.

Key parts of your plan will be:

- deciding what you are going to measure to determine the order of reactivity
- deciding which **variables** must be kept the same to make it a fair test.

## Summary

Adding evidence from the reactions of metals with acids, our league table now looks like this:

| Metal | Reaction with water | Time to tarnish | Reaction with dilute acid | |
|---|---|---|---|---|
| potassium | explosive | 2 seconds | react explosively | |
| sodium | vigorous | 4 seconds | | |
| lithium | quite fast | 8 seconds | | |
| magnesium | slow | some hours | dissolve, giving off hydrogen gas | more slowly |
| zinc | very slow | days or months | | |
| iron | | | | |
| copper | | | | |
| silver | does not react | months | no reaction | |
| gold | does not react | does not tarnish | | |

This is called the **activity series** for metals.

*Time to think*

With a partner, write a paragraph to explain what is meant by the activity series. Compare your explanation with another pair's explanation. Together form a group explanation about the activity series for metals.

## Quality of evidence

**Key words**
* quantitative
* qualitative
* valid
* accurate
* reliable

When we investigate a question in science we need to look carefully at the nature of the evidence. In the above table, the length of time that the silver takes to tarnish is an approximate value, whereas the time taken for the sodium to tarnish has been accurately measured with a stopwatch. Evidence that involves measurement is called **quantitative**. Evidence that does not involve measurement is described as **qualitative** – it uses descriptions such as 'quite fast' or 'fairly fast'.

**1 a)** Which of the evidence in the above table is quantitative?
  **b)** Which of the evidence is qualitative?

Key words used in describing the quality of evidence are **valid**, **accurate** and **reliable**. Their scientific meanings are similar to their meanings in everyday use, as shown below.

2 James, Kath and Susan spent a rainy afternoon at Susan's house, playing darts and chatting. James suggested that they should decide who was the best player by throwing six darts at the 'bull's eye'. The results are shown below:

James

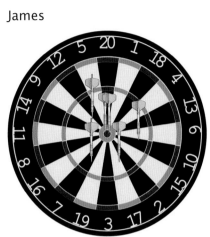

Kath

Susan

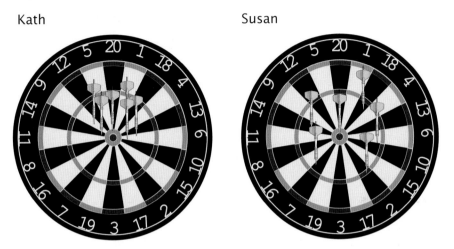

**a)** James declared that he was the best player. Was his evidence valid?

**b)** Who had the most accurate set of throws?

**c)** Who had the most reliable set of throws?

**d)** Who had the least reliable set of throws?

**e)** Who was reliable but not very accurate?

**f)** Do you think that the sample size was large enough to make a decision about who was the best darts player? Discuss your ideas with others in your group.

*Evaluation* ## Order of reactivity

In an investigation into the question 'What is the order of reactivity of the metals copper, iron, magnesium and zinc?', groups of pupils followed these instructions:

- Take some sieved grains of copper metal.
- Add some dilute hydrochloric acid.
- Measure the volume of hydrogen gas produced after a time.
- Repeat the experiment for the other metals.

Clara and John planned and carried out their investigation and wrote the following report:

Method
- 1.00 g of metal grains were weighed out each time using an electronic balance.
- 20 cm³ of dilute acid were measured each time using a conical flask.

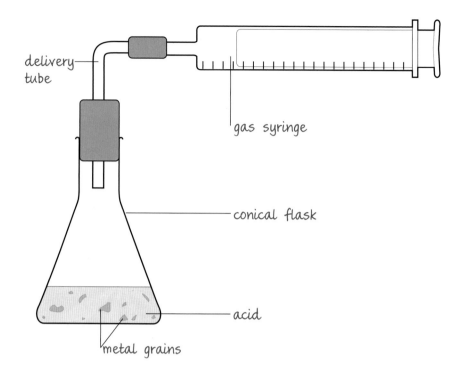

- The metal was added to the acid, a rubber bung with a gas syringe was fitted as shown in the diagram and a stopwatch was started.
- After 1.0 min, the volume of hydrogen gas was measured.
- This was repeated two more times for each metal.

Results

| Metal | Volume of gas produced in 1.0 min ($cm^3$) | | | |
|---|---|---|---|---|
| | Exp 1 | Exp 2 | Exp 3 | Mean |
| copper | 0 | 0 | 0 | 0 |
| iron | 7 | 17 | 6 | 10 |
| magnesium | 42 | 47 | 37 | 42 |
| zinc | 9 | 10 | 8 | 9 |

Conclusion   We think that the order of reactivity of the four metals starting with the most reactive is: magnesium, iron, zinc, copper. However we were unsure about the positions of iron and zinc because iron may have given an anomalous result. We need more measurements to decide this.

1 Clara and John thought carefully about their plan.
   **a)** What should they do to make the final result for each metal more reliable?
   **b)** Which are the dependent and independent variables in this experiment?
   **c)** What did they do to make it a fair test?

**2** The results of Clara and John's experiment were not as accurate as those of other groups.
   **a)** Which part of their method had the worst effect on accuracy?
   **b)** What would you do to improve this part of the method?

**3** Which metal has the most reliable set of results?

**4 a)** Which single result from the table would you say was definitely anomalous (odd)?
   **b)** Suggest a possible cause of this result.
   **c)** How has this result affected the conclusion?

**5** Is Clara and John's conclusion:
   **a)** accurate from the viewpoint of the 'correct' answer?
   **b)** valid from the viewpoint of the evidence used?
   Explain your answers.

# → *Reacting metals with oxygen*

Pure oxygen is a very dangerous substance because almost any material will readily burn in it.

**DID YOU KNOW?**

The first fatal accident in the NASA space programme happened in 1967, when three astronauts were testing an Apollo command module on the ground. The sealed spacecraft contained an atmosphere of pure oxygen, and a short circuit in some electrical wiring started a fierce fire, killing all three men. Following an inquiry, the cabin atmosphere was changed to a mixture of nitrogen and oxygen.

*Enquiry* *Predicting*

You have seen how the periodic table can be very useful for predicting reactions and equations. The activity series can also be used to make predictions.

**1** Predict two metals that will burn fiercely in oxygen.

**2** Predict two metals that might not burn in oxygen. Compare your answers with other people in your group.

The word equations for the burning of some metals in oxygen were looked at in Book 1.

**3** Predict the word equations for the burning of the following metals in oxygen:
   **a)** magnesium
   **b)** sodium
   **c)** zinc.

**4** Write balanced symbol equations for the burning of the following metals in oxygen, using the information given in the particle pictures below:

**a)** magnesium **b)** barium **c)** calcium.

**5** Scientists are always looking for patterns in evidence and links between ideas.

**a)** Can you see a pattern in your three symbol equations from Question 4?

**b)** Can you see a link between this pattern and the periodic table?

**6** Look back at your explanations about the activity series and check that they still fit with the latest patterns that you have found.

# → *Displacement reactions of metals*

Tug-of-war – guess who wins!

**Key word**

* displacement reaction

So far we have seen that some metals are more reactive than others in their reactions with water, dilute acids and oxygen. In this section we will find out if one metal can win a tug-of-war against another metal in a compound. For example, can magnesium take away the sulphate from copper sulphate to form magnesium sulphate and copper? This is called a **displacement reaction** – the copper has been displaced from the copper sulphate.

magnesium ribbon

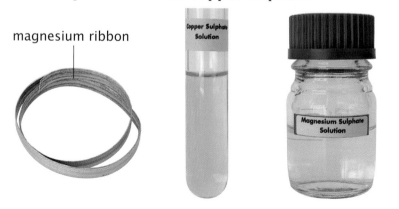

**12** Write a word equation for the reaction described above.

*Enquiry* *Planning*

## Can the activity series predict which displacement reactions will occur?

In order to test this question, you need to plan a series of reactions. You might be given the following materials:

solids: copper, iron, magnesium and zinc

solutions: copper sulphate, iron sulphate, magnesium sulphate and zinc sulphate

1 **Prediction:** From the above list, predict which metal will displace all of the other metals from solutions of their compounds. Give a reason for your choice.

2 **Choosing equipment:** How many test tubes would you need to carry out *all* of the different combinations of possible reactions?

3 **Presenting evidence:** Design a simple results table that would show which combinations produced a displacement reaction.

The table below shows some observations made by a pupil for some displacement reactions.

| Test | Metal | Metal compound | Observations |
|---|---|---|---|
| 1 | zinc | copper sulphate | blue solution went colourless; brown coating formed on the silver-coloured zinc |
| 2 | iron | zinc sulphate | iron stayed shiny and silvery |
| 3 | magnesium | iron sulphate | grey coating on the silver-coloured magnesium |

1 In which of the pupil's tests did a displacement reaction occur?

2 What pattern do the above results show?

3 Is there enough evidence to be confident about your answer to Question 2?

4 Write word equations for the combinations that did react.

5 Write balanced symbol equations for the combinations that did react, using the information given below:

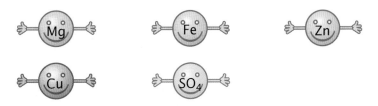

6 Name a metal that is <u>not</u> in the above table that you think will:
a) be displaced from its compounds by copper
b) displace copper from copper sulphate.
Explain your answers and compare your ideas with others in your group.

## Activity series

| |
|---|
| potassium |
| sodium |
| lithium |
| calcium |
| magnesium |
| aluminium |
| zinc |
| iron |
| lead |
| copper |
| silver |
| gold |

Look at the activity series on the left. Note that it includes more metals than we have looked at so far.

**13** Decide if a reaction will occur between the following pairs of substances:
   **a)** lead and silver nitrate solution
   **b)** zinc and iron oxide
   **c)** magnesium and sodium sulphate solution.
**14** Write word equations for the reactions identified in Question 13.
**15** Write symbol equations for the reactions identified in Question 13, using the information given below.

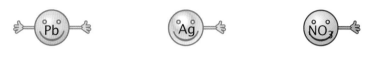

**16** Tin is a metal which reacts slowly with warm, dilute acid. It displaces lead from lead nitrate solution.
   **a)** What is the likely position of tin in the activity series?
   **b)** Give an example of a reaction that would confirm your answer. Explain your choice.

**Key word**
✱ Thermit reaction

Displacement reactions are used to separate some metals from their compounds. These reactions can also be useful in other ways.

   The photograph shows a displacement reaction where so much heat energy is released that the displaced iron is molten. It runs out of the container and into the gap between two sections of rail, welding them together. This is called the **Thermit reaction** and the reaction mixture contains powdered iron oxide and aluminium.

**17 a)** Write a word equation for the above Thermit reaction.
   **b)** Suggest an alternative metal to aluminium that would still displace iron from its oxide and be reactive enough to release enough heat energy to melt the iron. Explain your choice.

Welding railway lines using the Thermit reaction.

**18** An AA cell has a voltage of 1.5 V. The electrical energy is obtained from a chemical reaction inside the cell. Different chemical reactions produce different voltages. The following table gives values for some different cells made by dipping two different metals into a dilute acid. For any pair of metals, one is the positive terminal and the other is the negative terminal.

| Metal 1 (+) | Metal 2 (–) | Voltage (V) |
| --- | --- | --- |
| copper | iron | 0.78 |
| copper | zinc | 1.10 |
| zinc | magnesium | 1.60 |
| silver | copper | 0.46 |
| silver | zinc | 1.56 |

a) Reorganise the table so that it shows a pattern.
b) Try to identify a pattern based on:
   i) the combinations of metals that give a high voltage
   ii) which metal is the positive in the pair.
c) Which list in science has a strong link with the above patterns?
d) Predict a pair of metals that will give a higher voltage than any pair in the above table.

*Time to think*

Divide a sheet of paper into quarters. In each part write one of the following headings:

- Reaction with oxygen
- Reaction with acid
- Displacement reactions
- Activity series

Check back through the work you have done so far and make notes under each heading. Compare your notes with others in your group. Add to or improve your notes so that you have a good summary.

## The metals of antiquity

The first metal that humans used was gold, in about 6000 BC. Over the next 7000 years only six more metals were discovered: copper, silver, lead, tin, iron and mercury. These metals were used by the ancient Egyptians, Greeks, and Romans, and are known as the seven metals of **antiquity**.

Most metals can only be obtained by extracting them from rocks containing a compound of the metal (a metal **ore**). However, five of the above metals can be found in their **native state** as the pure metal. These are gold, copper, silver, iron (in meteorites) and mercury.

| | |
|---|---|
| 6000 BC | gold |
| 4000 BC | copper, silver |
| 3500 BC | lead |
| 1800 BC | tin |
| 1500 BC | iron |
| 750 BC | mercury |
| 1400 AD | zinc |
| 1500 | platinum |
| 1735 | cobalt |
| 1751 | nickel |
| 1783 | tungsten |
| 1791 | titanium |
| 1807 | potassium, sodium |
| 1808 | barium, calcium, magnesium |
| 1827 | aluminium |
| 1898 | radium |
| 1940 | plutonium |

discovery dates of some metals

Gold nuggets are easily panned from the gravel beds of streams. Stone Age people discovered that these nuggets could be hammered into shape to make jewellery and ornaments, but not tools. This is because gold is too soft.

Panning for gold.

Silver was discovered later than gold. It slowly tarnishes, forming a black coating due to the effect of sulphur or hydrogen sulphide. Silver is slightly harder than gold but it is still too soft to make tools with.

Copper is harder than silver but it can still be hammered into shape. It was the first metal used to make tools such as knives and arrowheads. However, there were two problems:

1 When copper is hammered, it becomes brittle and breaks easily. The answer was to **anneal** the copper – heat it and let it slowly cool down.
2 There was not enough native copper available. However, copper is found in many ores. The answer was to obtain more copper by **smelting** – extracting the metal from its ores by heating it with charcoal. This was first done in Asia in about 4000 BC. A high temperature of approximately 800 °C is needed, as found in a pottery kiln.

Tin is not found in its native state. It is extracted from its ores by smelting. Tin was used to make bronze, by melting it with copper.

Mercury is found in its native state in volcanic areas. It is also easily extracted from its ores by smelting at relatively low temperatures, and is easily separated from the impurities. Mercury had limited uses but people were fascinated by its appearance. The chemical symbol for mercury is Hg, which comes from the Greek word *hydrargyros*, meaning liquid silver.

Lead is not found in its native state, but its main ore galena (lead sulphide) is common. The ancient Egyptians used this black material as eye make-up. The smelting process for lead is relatively easy because the temperature needed (600 °C) can be reached in a simple wood fire. Since lead melts at 327 °C, it is easily separated from any

The ancient Egyptians used galena, the main ore of lead, as eye make-up.

solid impurities. It can be filtered and poured off. Lead is too soft to use for tools. It was mainly used for containers and piping for water.

Iron is only found in very small amounts in its native state in meteorites. The ancient Egyptians called it 'black copper from heaven'. Meteoric iron was five times more expensive than gold, and it was used to make jewellery. It is difficult to extract iron from its ores by smelting because a very high temperature is needed (at least 1200 °C). Also, the iron formed contains impurities from the rocks ('slag') and this is difficult to separate off.

1 Why are nuggets of gold easily identified in the gravel beds of streams but nuggets of silver are not?
2 What is the name of the black compound that coats silver when it has come into contact with sulphur?
3 Why is lead easily separated from solid impurities in a smelting furnace?
4 The most common ore of mercury is a red rock called cinnabar (mercury sulphide). Mercury can be extracted by simply roasting cinnabar in air, but a poisonous gas is released.

$$HgS + O_2 \rightarrow \underline{\hspace{1cm}} + \underline{\hspace{1cm}}$$

   a) Write a balanced symbol equation for the reaction.
   b) What is the poisonous gas that is formed?
5 There are large differences in the amount of energy needed to extract the seven metals of antiquity from their ores. Some are even found in their native state.
   a) Name a metal found in its native state.
   b) Name a metal that needs only a little energy to extract it from its ores.
   c) Name a metal that needs a lot of energy to extract it from its ores.
   d) What is the relationship between the energy needed to extract a metal from its ores and the position of the metal in the activity series?
   e) From the information about mercury, where would you place it in the activity series (page 142)?
   f) Why is gold found only in its native state?
   g) Bronze is an alloy of copper. Why did the Bronze Age come before the Iron Age in the history of mankind?
6 In a group, make a game, PowerPoint presentation or poster that would help other people learn more about these metals.

# → *Alloys*

**Key words**
* alloy
* steel
* bronze
* casting
* quenching

An **alloy** is a metallic material composed of a mixture of two or more elements. All the elements are usually metals, but the non-metal carbon is an essential component of the alloy **steel**.

**Bronze** is an alloy of copper and tin. The earliest samples were found in an area which is now Iraq, and date from 3000 BC. It was made by mixing copper and tin ores together before smelting. Bronze is much harder than copper, and bronze objects are made by **casting**. In this process the molten mixture of copper and tin is poured into a mould (cast).

Steel is an alloy of iron and carbon. Modern steels also contain small amounts of other elements such as nickel and tungsten. As the furnaces used to make copper and bronze were improved, the operating temperatures increased. They eventually reached the minimum temperature needed to obtain iron from its ores (1200 °C). Iron smelting started around 1500 BC in an area now occupied by modern Turkey. Depending on the conditions, the product is either pure iron or steel. Steel is harder than iron and it can be made even harder by **quenching** – plunging the hot steel into water.

The new technology of steel-making spread slowly from Turkey. It had reached China by 600 BC and Britain by 100 BC. The ancient metal-workers developed

This bronze axehead dates back to the Bronze Age, 5000 years ago.

Iron pillar, Delhi, India.

extraordinary skills. In Roman times the best steel was imported from India, and shown on the previous page is an iron pillar dating from 400 AD still standing in Delhi, India, with virtually no signs of corrosion.

Arab metal-workers produced the famous Damascus swords that were renowned for their hardness, strength and sharpness.

A Damascus sword.

*Research*

Use the internet, CD-ROMs and reference books to find out about some modern alloys.

- What are they made from?
- What are their properties?
- What are they used for?
- What have they replaced?

Use the information you have found to produce a poster or leaflet on 'Modern alloys'.

*Word play*

Copy and complete this word puzzle.

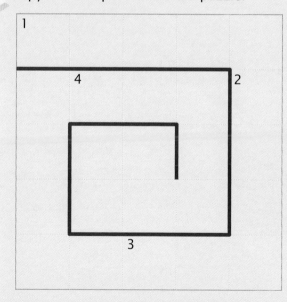

**1** To extract a metal from its ore
**2** Steel is an example of an _____.
**3** A process to reduce metal brittleness
**4** A metal first discovered in 1827

Now make up your own word puzzle about metals and their reactions. Swap your puzzle with a partner and see if you can do each other's.

*Time to think*

In the *Thinking Through Science* books you have seen that scientists try to make sense of the world around them in various ways, for example:

- sorting – arranging observations, ideas or things into groups with different characteristics. For example, different types of chemical reactions and different types of forces.
- listing – arranging things in order according to a chosen characteristic. For example, listing metals in order of their reactivity.

Working in groups:

1 think of one other example of sorting, and note down the characteristics that identify each group
2 think of one other example of listing, and note down the characteristic the items are ordered by.

Share your ideas with others in your group. With another group of pupils, take turns to study your examples. The other group should list the characteristics they think you chose and compare them with your answers. Can they add any extra items to your list?

3 'The periodic table could be described as a combination of sorting and listing'. Discuss this statement and explain what it means, giving some examples.

# Environment

6

**In this chapter you will learn:**

→ **the causes and effects of acid rain and how they can be reduced**
→ **about factors that might affect the pH of rainwater**
→ **how the appearance of landforms and/or buildings may change over time, and the factors that cause chemical weathering**
→ **how fertilisers affect plant growth and the optimum environment for growing plants**
→ **how pests affect plant growth and the effect of pesticides on the food chain**
→ **about the role of the leaf and roots in photosynthesis**

**You will also develop your skills in:**

→ **using secondary sources to investigate which factors affect the pH of rainwater**
→ **evaluating strengths and weaknesses in the evidence obtained**
→ **representing a sequence of reactions using flow diagrams, equations and concept maps**

---

## → → → WHAT DO YOU KNOW?

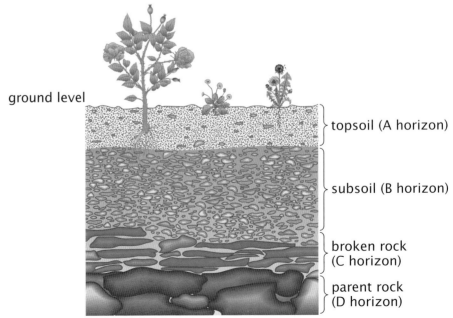

ground level

topsoil (A horizon)

subsoil (B horizon)

broken rock (C horizon)

parent rock (D horizon)

A soil profile.

1 Soil is a mixture of different minerals, water and living or decaying matter. Three types of soil are loam, clay and sand. One of the easiest ways to identify a soil is to take some in your hand, wet it thoroughly and rub it between your fingers. Try to match up the descriptions with the correct soil type (loam, clay or sand).

| Description | Type |
|---|---|
| it 'polishes', i.e. makes a shiny smooth coating on your fingers, and is greyish-brown in colour | |
| very gritty and a pale colour | |
| crumbly and dark, but not especially gritty, smooth or shiny | |

2 The table below contains information on different soil types: clay, chalk, peat, loam and sandy.

| Soil type | Advantages | Disadvantages | How to improve |
|---|---|---|---|
| A | • usually very fertile – lots of nutrients | • poor drainage, heavy to work<br>• rock hard when dry, very sticky when wet | • add organic matter and maybe gravel |
| B | • easy to work and easily improved | • free draining so dries out quickly<br>• relatively infertile | • add organic matter and use fertilisers |
| C | • good drainage (usually), while being moisture-retentive<br>• moderate fertility | • shallow and stony<br>• not suitable for rhododendrons and other lime-haters | • add organic matter |
| D | • lots of organic matter | • wet and acidic | • may need drainage<br>• add concentrated fertiliser and possibly lime |
| E | • easy to work<br>• good drainage<br>• good fertility<br>• plants love it | | • further enrich by recycling garden plants as compost<br>• use fertilisers |

a) In pairs, discuss how these soils are similar and how they are different.

b) Match the soils (A, B, C, D and E) with the soil types (clay, chalk, peat, loam and sandy). Give reasons based on the information in the table to justify your matching.

c) Why do clay and organic soils hold nutrients better than sandy soils?

d) Do you think it is possible to increase the nutrient-holding capacity of a sandy soil? Suggest how this may be done.

e) Suggest a disadvantage of soil E.

3 Chalky soils can look like many other soils – it is the presence of chalk or limestone that characterises this soil type. A pupil suggests that the use of acid would help to show the presence of chalk or limestone.

a) How would the use of acid help to identify a chalky soil?

b) Provide a word equation for the reaction that is taking place.

c) What other rock types would react with acid in a similar way?

Different plants grow best under different conditions. One factor that must be considered when choosing plants for crops or for the garden is the level of acidity in the soil. Soil testing kits are often used by gardeners to measure soil pH.

This table gives the ideal soil pH for a range of plants.

| Plant type | Optimum soil pH |
|---|---|
| azalea, rhododendron, camellia, mountain laurel | 5.0–5.5 |
| most shrubs and shade trees | 6.0 |
| fescue, Bermuda grass, Saint Augustine grass | 6.0–6.5 |
| centipede grass | 5.5 |
| rose | 6.5 |
| berries and most fruit trees, except blueberries | 6.0–6.5 |
| most vegetable and field crops | 6.0–6.5 |

**4** What type of soil pH does each of these plant types prefer – acidic, alkaline or neutral?

**5** Suggest a method to find the soil pH. Remember that soil testing kits contain an indicator.

A farmer tested his soil and found that the soil pH was 3.5. He added lime to the soil to raise the pH.

**6** What type of chemical is lime? What type of reaction is taking place when lime is added to the acidic soil?

**7** Pupils were discussing the pH scale and one group suggested adding sodium hydroxide to neutralise acidic soil. Why is this not a sensible idea?

**8** The soil of a houseplant was tested and found to have a pH of 8.5. *Gardeners' World* magazine recommends a slightly acidic soil for this plant. Which of these household reagents would you suggest to remedy the problem? Explain your reasons.

| Household reagent | pH |
|---|---|
| fruit juice | 4 |
| ammonia-based cleaning fluid | 11 |
| toothpaste | 8 |
| lemonade | 5 |
| milk of magnesia | 9 |

# ➡ *What happens to building materials over time?*

**Key words**
* weathering
* physical weathering
* chemical weathering
* biological
* acid rain

Soil contains rock fragments that have been broken down very slowly over many many years. Rocks may seem very hard but they are softened and break down as they are attacked by frost and rain. This is called **weathering**.

**Physical weathering** breaks down the rock into smaller pieces of the same type of rock. In **chemical weathering** the chemical composition of the rock is changed to produce a new mineral. **Biological** action causes both physical and chemical weathering. Roots growing through cracks in rocks widen the cracks as the roots extend deeper into the rocks. Acids from plants such as lichens can dissolve rocks and break them down into fragments. The actions of humans have also contributed to weathering, particularly through the impact of **acid rain**.

1 Study these photographs of a Cornish cottage built from granite, and a house in the Cotswolds built from limestone/dolomite.

Granite cottage.

Limestone house.

a) Which of the two buildings is more at risk from chemical weathering? Agree two or three points in your group, write them down and compare them with other groups.

b) Decide which type of weathering has affected the Cornish building. Give reasons for your choice.

c) What evidence is there from the photographs that biological weathering has occurred? Classify the nature of the biological weathering as either physical or chemical.

d) This photograph shows weathering on a family home in southern Spain.

Suggest why differences in climate between the UK and Spain would result in different types of weathering. Use the climate data in the tables below to support your answer.

| Average monthly temperature (°C) | | | | | | | | | | | | |
|---|---|---|---|---|---|---|---|---|---|---|---|---|
| | **Jan** | **Feb** | **Mar** | **Apr** | **May** | **Jun** | **Jul** | **Aug** | **Sept** | **Oct** | **Nov** | **Dec** |
| **Madrid** | 9 | 11 | 15 | 19 | 22 | 27 | 31 | 32 | 25 | 18 | 13 | 9 |
| **London** | 3.9 | 4.2 | 5.7 | 8.5 | 11.9 | 15.2 | 17.0 | 16.6 | 14.2 | 10.3 | 6.6 | 4.8 |

| Average monthly rainfall (mm) | | | | | | | | | | | | |
|---|---|---|---|---|---|---|---|---|---|---|---|---|
| | **Jan** | **Feb** | **Mar** | **Apr** | **May** | **Jun** | **Jul** | **Aug** | **Sept** | **Oct** | **Nov** | **Dec** |
| **Madrid** | 45.1 | 43.2 | 36.8 | 45.4 | 39.7 | 25.2 | 9.4 | 10.0 | 29.3 | 46.4 | 63.9 | 47.0 |
| **London** | 48.9 | 38.8 | 39.3 | 41.4 | 47.0 | 48.3 | 59.0 | 59.6 | 52.4 | 65.2 | 59.3 | 51.2 |

*Creative thinking* *School survey*

Take some photographs or make drawings of local buildings, showing examples of weathering. Build up a class record and use this to make a display or PowerPoint presentation to inform others about weathering.

# How pure is rainwater?

➡

**Key words**
* solvent
* environment
* pollutants
* photosynthesis
* respiration

Pure water consists of only water molecules – nothing is dissolved in it. Water is an excellent **solvent**. It will dissolve many chemicals, including gases such as oxygen and carbon dioxide from the air. Some of these gases will be naturally occurring but others will be manufactured. Some of these pose a significant threat to our **environment** – they are **pollutants**.

Plants play an important role in maintaining the balance of carbon dioxide and oxygen in the atmosphere. The plant process which results in the removal of carbon dioxide from the atmosphere, and the release of oxygen to it is called **photosynthesis**.

$$\text{carbon dioxide} + \text{water} \xrightarrow[\text{chlorophyll}]{\text{light}} \text{glucose} + \text{oxygen}$$

$$6\,CO_2(g) + 6H_2O(l) \rightarrow C_6H_{12}O_6(s) + 6O_2(g)$$

Carbon dioxide is released into the atmosphere by a combination of natural and manufacturing processes.

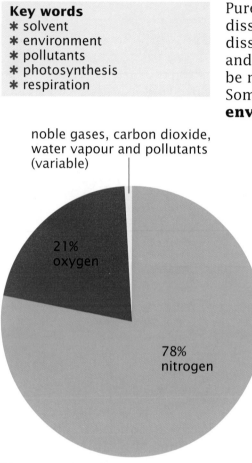

noble gases, carbon dioxide, water vapour and pollutants (variable)

21% oxygen

78% nitrogen

The gases found in air.

Another process that plants perform is **respiration**, which releases the energy stored in glucose molecules so that it can be used for growth.

$$\text{glucose} + \text{oxygen} \rightarrow \text{carbon dioxide} + \text{water} + \text{energy}$$

$$C_6H_{12}O_6(s) + 6O_2(g) \rightarrow 6CO_2(g) + 6H_2O(l) + \text{energy}$$

Animals also respire. During respiration in both plants and animals, carbon dioxide is released into the atmosphere.

2 What do plants use the process of respiration for?
3 Look at the equations for photosynthesis and respiration. How are they similar and how are they different?

A chemical reaction takes place between water molecules and carbon dioxide in the air to produce a weak acid called carbonic acid ($H_2CO_3$). This makes rainwater slightly acidic.

4 Write the word and symbol equation for this reaction. Try to include the appropriate state symbols (s, g, l).

*Reasoning* *Carbon dioxide*

**Key words**
* fossil fuels
* carbon cycle

A group of students are surprised at the low level of carbon dioxide in the atmosphere.

Sophie comments, 'What about the burning of **fossil fuels**? All fossil fuels and many other fuels contain carbon. As these fuels are used they are releasing more and more carbon dioxide into the atmosphere.'

Lily adds, '... and don't forget respiration. Both animals and plants respire.'

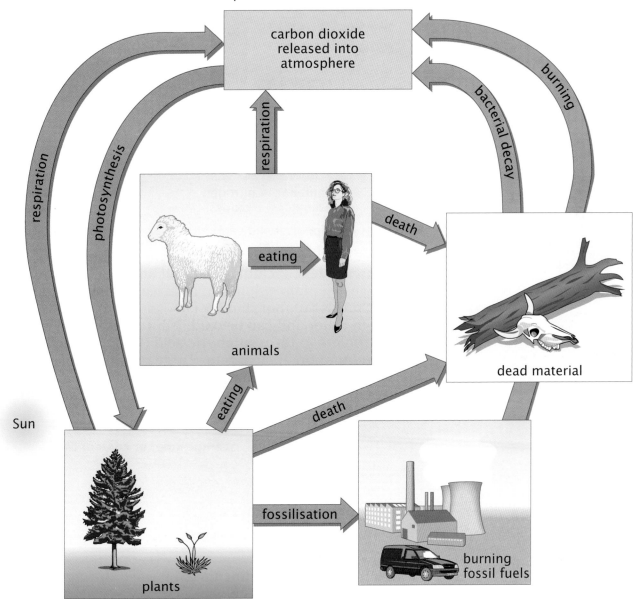

The carbon cycle.

**1** Write an explanation of how the balance of carbon dioxide and oxygen is maintained in the atmosphere.

**2** Suggest two ways in which humans have an impact on the **carbon cycle**. Compare your ideas with those of at least three other pupils.

# What causes acid rain?

**Key words**
* pollution
* heavy metals

Analysis of acid levels in the atmosphere shows that the pH level can be as low as 4. This low pH is due to both natural and manufacturing processes. Throughout the world, emissions of the gases sulphur dioxide and nitrogen oxides contribute to the international problem of acid rain **pollution**.

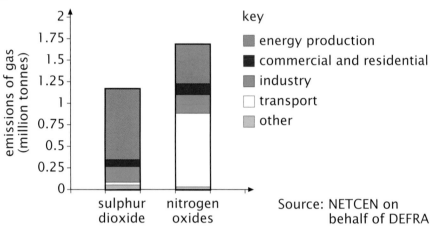

key
■ energy production
■ commercial and residential
■ industry
□ transport
□ other

Source: NETCEN on behalf of DEFRA

Emissions of sulphur dioxide and nitrogen oxides in the UK in 2002.

Sulphur dioxide emissions arise during combustion of fossil fuels. Fossil fuels, including coal, oil and to a lesser extent natural gas, contain sulphur in different forms. Oxidation of sulphur forms sulphur dioxide ($SO_2$), a colourless gas. It is soluble in water and can be oxidised further within airborne water droplets to form sulphuric acid ($H_2SO_4$), which falls as acid precipitation or 'acid rain'. Large quantities of sulphur dioxide are released naturally when volcanoes erupt.

This table compares the sulphur levels of different fossil fuels in the UK.

| Fuel | Average sulphur content (%) |
|---|---|
| UK coal | 1.6 |
| imported coal | 0.8–1.0 |
| oil | 2.9 |
| natural gas | trace |

5 Explain how sulphur dioxide is released during the combustion of fossil fuels.
6 Produce a flow chart showing how the sulphur contained naturally in fossil fuels is converted into sulphuric acid which falls as acid rain.
7 Which of the fossil fuels listed would you recommend as the most environmentally friendly? Give reasons for your choice.

The problem of acid rain is not a recent development, but we are much more aware of the damage caused by acid rain nowadays.

The Acropolis of Athens.

The Taj Mahal, India.

The Colosseum, Rome.

This famous structure was built over 2000 years ago. The damage that has been done to the Acropolis is largely due to the pollution caused by cars and other vehicles in Athens – the most polluted city in Europe. Car engines burn petrol as a fuel and release acidic gases such as sulphur dioxide into the atmosphere.

Many other countries have also noticed an acceleration of damage to their cultural heritage. The Taj Mahal in India, the Colosseum in Rome and monuments in Krakow, Poland are all deteriorating. In Sweden, medieval stained glass windows are thought to have been affected by acid rain.

Buildings have always been subject to attack by weathering – the effects of rain, wind, Sun and frost. Acid rain can accelerate the rate of this damage. In addition to damage to buildings, bridges and vehicles above ground, structural damage can also occur to underground pipes, cables and foundations submerged in acidic waters.

Acid rain also affects living things. Acid rain falling into lakes or ponds can change the pH of the water. This directly affects the animals and plants living there. It also lowers the pH of surrounding soil, which releases aluminium and **heavy metals** such as zinc and copper into the water. These metals can poison aquatic animals and plants.

In 1970, emissions of nitrogen oxides from road transport in the UK were 0.769 million tonnes. By 1990, they had risen to over 1.31 million tonnes. Since then, emissions from transport have been declining thanks to improvements in vehicle technology, such as the use of catalytic converters and cleaner fuels. In 1999, transport emissions were 0.714 million tonnes, lower than in 1970.

8 Present these data as a pie chart or bar chart that might be used in an advertising campaign for a new car.

**9** This question is about the sources of nitrogen oxides.

- Nitrogen from the air burns when temperatures are high enough.

- Nitrogen oxide is produced in motor vehicle engines and power station furnaces.

- Burning nitrogen in air forms various nitrogen oxides.

**a)** Starting with these three facts, write a sequence for the formation of nitric acid from nitrogen in the atmosphere.

**b)** Present the data as a flow chart and suggest the sequence of word equations for the formation of nitric acid from nitrogen gas.

*Evaluation* **Which materials are most affected by acid rain?**

In an investigation about acid rain a pupil produced the following report:

Method
Place pieces of different building materials in 10 ml of 1 M sulphuric acid. Leave them in a warm room until the next lesson.

Results

| Material | Observations | |
|---|---|---|
| | Before treatment | After 7 days |
| iron | shiny dark grey solid | iron broken up, some rusting |
| aluminium | light grey solid | little change, some bubbles |
| wood | light brown solid | material darkened, some flaking |
| zinc flashing | shiny grey solid | very little solid left |
| glass | transparent, clear solid | no effect |
| rubber seals | flexible brown solid | slight darkening |
| stainless steel | shiny silver solid | no effect |
| copper pipe | shiny brown solid | no effect |
| plastic guttering | opaque white solid | no effect |

Conclusions
My results show that some materials are more likely to be attacked by acid rain than others. Overall, metals are more likely to be attacked by acid.

**1** Summarise the data for the metals in the table. Is there a pattern in the data?

**2** Suggest some improvements to the pupil's system of recording observations.

**3** In her conclusion the pupil states that: 'Overall, metals are more likely to be attacked by acid.' Do you think the results give enough evidence to say this?

**4** How useful are the data for answering the question set – very useful, of limited use or not useful? Justify your choice.

**5** In order to make the investigation more convincing, suggest which other materials you would test.

**6** Would you change any other part of the method and, if so, why?

**7** A 5-year research program in the UK has suggested that if sulphur dioxide emissions were reduced by 30%, savings over 30 years could be as high as £9.5 billion. Suggest how these savings would be made. Think about savings in repairs to damaged buildings and in the use of alternative sources of energy.

**DID YOU KNOW?**

In 1856, Robert Angus Smith – the scientist who first used the term acid rain – wrote:

'It has often been observed that the stones and bricks of buildings crumble more readily in large towns where much coal is burnt. ... I was led to attribute this effect to the slow but constant action of acid rain.'

## Acid rain

Factories during the Industrial Revolution.

The problem of acid rain probably originated during the 1730s at the height of the Industrial Revolution. This was a time when there were huge technological leaps as many new machines were invented. Most of these machines used coal as a fuel.

However, it was only in the 1950s and 60s that ideas about acid rain and its damaging effects started to be noticed.

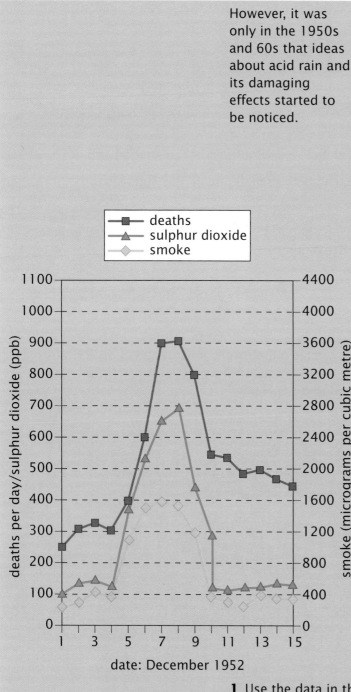

date: December 1952

During the winter of 1952 an area of high pressure settled over London. The wind dropped and the air grew damp; a thick fog began to form. The cold weather meant that many coal fires were burnt which produced sulphur dioxide, smoke and dust. The Great London Smog lasted for five days and led to around 4000 more deaths than usual. As a result of the high death rate, the Clean Air Acts of 1956 and 1968 were passed. This prevented the burning of smoky fuels in certain areas.

1 Use the data in the graph to work out the daily number of deaths from 1st to 15th December 1952.
2 During which period was the rate of fatalities at its highest?
3 What was the smoke concentration on:
   a) 1st December
   b) 5th December
   c) 8th December
   d) 13th December?
4 Explain the relationship between the levels of sulphur dioxide and smoke and the number of deaths during this period.
5 How would you explain the term 'smog'? From which words is it derived?

Since 1952, industry has moved out of central London and the burning of coal has slowly diminished. However, the use of motor vehicles has increased and has become one of the main sources of air pollution. In 1990 changes to the Clean Air Act set rules which aimed to cut the release of sulphur dioxide from power plants down to 10 million tonnes per year by 1st January 2000. However, sulphur dioxide is released from other places where fuels are burnt. From 12th to 15th December 1991 a mass of stagnant winter air again settled over London, trapping beneath it a hazardous mixture of fumes and particles. It was estimated that this smog caused around 160 more deaths than normal for the time of year.

| Pollutant | Source of pollutant (percentage) | | |
|---|---|---|---|
| | **Power stations** | **Road traffic** | **Other sources** |
| sulphur dioxide | 72 | 2 | |
| nitrogen oxides | 28 | | 21 |
| smoke particles | 7 | 46 | |
| carbon monoxide | 1 | 90 | 9 |

**6 a)** Calculate the missing percentages in the above table.
   **b)** Suggest why the carbon monoxide levels from road traffic sources are much higher than from power stations. Think about the type of combustion taking place.
   **c)** Suggest why the sulphur dioxide levels from road traffic are low.
   **d)** What effect might the level of smoke particles have on the growth of plants in urban areas?
   **e)** Suggest one other source of each pollutant. Share your answers with a partner. Then work in teams of four. Agree your final list and share your answers with the whole class.

### Emissions of exhaust fumes for road vehicles (per vehicle kilometre)

| Vehicle | Carbon monoxide | Hydro-carbons | Oxides of nitrogen | Particulate matter | Carbon dioxide |
|---|---|---|---|---|---|
| petrol car without a catalytic converter (control)* | 100 | 100 | 100 | – | 100 |
| petrol car with a catalyst | 42 | 19 | 23 | – | 100 |
| diesel car without a catalyst | 2 | 3 | 31 | 100 | 85 |

* Petrol cars without catalysts have been given a relative value of 100 for comparison purposes.

**7** Despite much debate over which car fuel is cleaner, petrol or diesel, weighing up the advantages and disadvantages is not always clear-cut. Compare the advantages and disadvantages of each type of fuel.

# → *How can the pollution problems caused by acid rain be solved?*

**Key words**
* catalytic converters
* catalyst
* leached

## Reduce levels of nitrogen oxides

About 80% of the air is nitrogen. When fuels are burnt, the high temperatures cause some of this nitrogen to react with oxygen also in the air to produce nitrogen oxides. Since nitrogen is not present in fuels, altering the fuels does not help to reduce levels of nitrogen oxides. These are some of the ways levels of nitrogen oxides can be reduced:

### In power stations
* eliminate excess air by using the minimum amount of air needed for combustion
* lower the combustion temperature.

10 How will these two strategies help to reduce the level of nitrogen oxides produced?

### In cars
* change the air:fuel ratio, which reduces the amount of oxygen available to make nitrogen oxides
* recirculate exhaust fumes, which lowers oxygen content and lowers burning temperature, thus producing less nitrogen oxides
* **catalytic converters** in exhaust systems in cars change carbon monoxide to carbon dioxide, nitrogen oxides to nitrogen, and hydrocarbons to water and carbon dioxide. The **catalyst** used is a precious metal such as platinum.

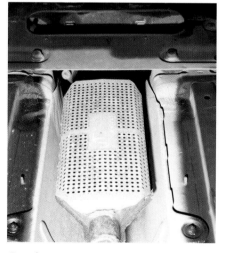

Catalytic converter in a car.

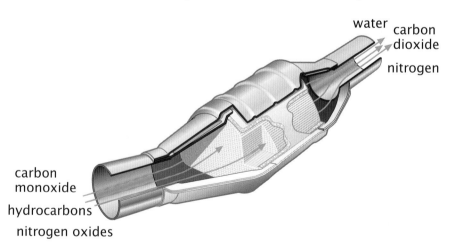

Section through a catalytic converter.

11 In your group, produce a table including one advantage and one disadvantage of each method of reducing production of nitrogen oxides. Compare your table with other groups'.

## Reduce levels of sulphur dioxide

These are some ways we can reduce levels of sulphur dioxide in the air:

- burn less fossil fuel (substitute fuel sources need to be found)
- switch to low sulphur fuels, such as petrol labelled ULS, which stands for ultra low sulphur fuel. Coal with less than 1% sulphur is not as readily available and is much more expensive than regular coal
- fuel desulphurisation – this process takes place before combustion, but it is expensive and is still being developed
- sulphur reduction during combustion by the addition of lime to coal during combustion
- flue gas removal – as gases are released from the chimney, a mixture of finely-ground limestone and water is sprayed onto the gases.

12 Two of the methods for the removal of sulphur dioxide listed above use lime (CaO) and limestone ($CaCO_3$).
  a) What type of reaction is taking place?
  b) Can you name the salt produced in each reaction?

## Treat damaged areas

In many cases, the damage already caused has to be treated or action is needed to restore conditions in the environment. Two of the most commonly used methods are:

- fertilising damaged conifer forests with calcium, magnesium, potassium, zinc and manganese, the elements **leached** out of soil by the action of acid rain
- spreading lime on affected lakes and forests – this is expensive.

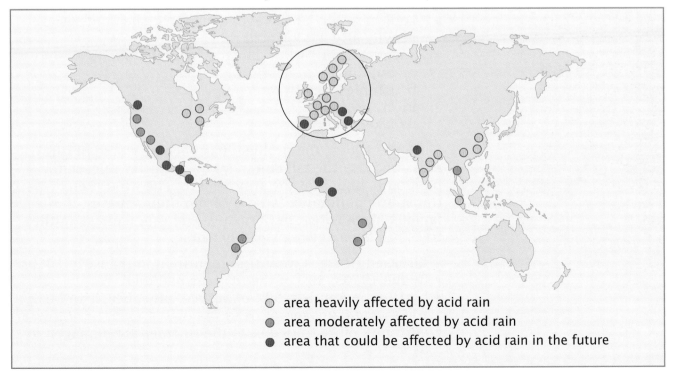

○ area heavily affected by acid rain
◑ area moderately affected by acid rain
● area that could be affected by acid rain in the future

The map on the previous page shows the areas that are currently affected by acid rain (heavily or moderately), and areas that could be affected by acid rain in the future. Most damage is done downwind of the sources of heavy emissions of sulphur dioxide and nitrogen oxides.

13 Use an atlas to identify which parts of the world are heavily affected by acid rain.
14 Decide whether these areas are built-up areas, industrial cities or rural/forest areas. Present the data as a table.
15 Decide which methods of prevention are most likely to be successful in these areas.
16 Suggest how the areas in light green on the map below could be affected by acid rain in the future.

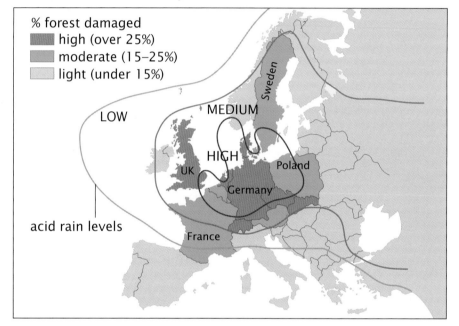

% forest damaged
high (over 25%)
moderate (15–25%)
light (under 15%)

17 Look carefully at the above map. Which countries are heavily affected by acid rain?
18 Suggest what sort of damage is being done to:
   a) buildings
   b) peoples' health
   c) crops
   d) lakes and rivers.

Since the 1960s, the problem has become worse in rural areas because the tall chimneys on factories release the pollutants high into the atmosphere. The wind then transports pollutants far away from their sources. In the famous Black Forest in Germany, acid rain damage to the trees has been getting steadily worse:

• diseased fir trees were first identified in the early 1960s
• by the 1970s, 30% of the fir trees had died
• by 1984, more than 50% of spruce, pine, beech and oak trees were damaged or dead
• currently more than 90% of the fir trees are damaged or dead.

This is one of the most dramatic examples of acid rain damage to trees.

19 Two of the most seriously affected areas receive large amounts of acid rain which is transported from other parts of Europe. Suggest the most likely source of acid rain for each of the following areas:
   a) southern Scandinavia
   b) industrial parts of central and western Europe.
   How do you think it is transported such long distances?

---

*Enquiry* ## Acid rain investigation

1 A group of students were trying to decide on a title for their acid rain investigation. Jonathan wanted to use the title: 'Is acid rain dangerous?'.
   Can you suggest an improvement to this question? Rewrite his title as a question that can be investigated scientifically.

2 After the class had completed Question 19 above, some groups were interested to find out why the pH of rainwater might vary from place to place, with time of year or with changes in the weather conditions. They decided that the following factors might affect the pH of rainwater:

   - location
   - wind direction.

   In your group, discuss what other factors should be considered.

3 Daisy said they should decide on the size of the sample. Farhad suggested that the method of data collection would affect how much data was available for their analysis. What do you think of Daisy and Farhad's suggestions?

4 Suzy suggested that in order to find an answer to their question they could:

   - collect data by testing rainwater samples
   - use secondary sources such as databases, CD-ROMs or the internet.

   Give one advantage and one disadvantage of each method.

5 Use the sources of data available to you to investigate the following questions:

   - Is there a link between rainwater acidity and volume of rainwater?
   - Is rainwater more acidic when the wind blows from the east?
   - Is there a link between acidity of the rainwater and the season?

*Enquiry* *Analysing data*

Here are research data from three different groups.

### Group 1

This group analysed rainfall data collected in one particular day at 42 different locations across Great Britain and Ireland.

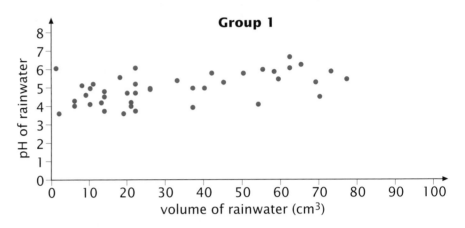

1 The pupils have presented their data as a scatter graph.
   a) Is there a correlation between the volume of rainwater and the pH?
   b) What additional data would you need to find a more meaningful pattern?
   c) How else could these data be presented?

### Group 2 and Group 3

Two groups collected data on rainfall and pH levels in their local area. They carried out their study during April.

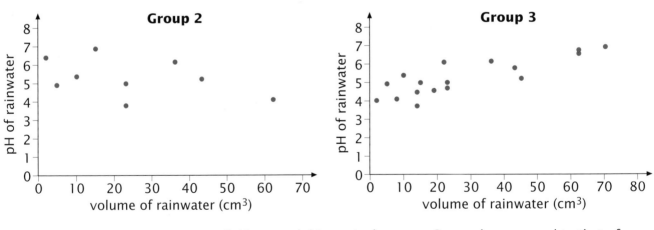

2 How much bigger is the group 3 sample compared to that of group 2?

3 Both groups stated: 'When there was lower rainfall, the pH is higher. It is less acidic.' Do you agree with this statement?

4 Group 3 were concerned that a small sample might provide misleading results. Which group has the more reliable evidence?

5 What advice would you give both groups when presenting this data as a scatter graph?

# → *How does acid rain affect fish and other aquatic organisms?*

**Key words**
* biodiversity
* toxic
* tolerance

In Norway, scientists started seeing an increase in the number of dead fish in lakes and rivers at the beginning of the twentieth century. Currently, at least 20% of Norwegian lakes have no fish.

Acid rain causes a variety of effects that harm or kill individual fish and reduce fish population numbers. In some cases, acid rain completely eliminates some fish species from certain bodies of water and results in decreased **biodiversity**. As acid rain flows through soils, aluminium is released from the soil into the lakes and streams, resulting in a lower pH and a higher aluminium level. Both low pH and increased aluminium levels are directly **toxic** to fish and cause them chronic stress. This may not kill individual fish, but leads to lower body weight and smaller size, making the fish less able to compete for food and space and more susceptible to disease.

Some types of plants and animals are able to tolerate acidic waters. Others, however, are acid-sensitive and will die as the pH falls. Generally, the young of most species are more sensitive to environmental conditions than adults. At a pH of 5, most fish eggs cannot hatch. At lower pH levels, some adult fish die. The table below shows that not all organisms can tolerate the same amount of acid; for example, frogs can tolerate water that is more acidic (has lower pH) than can trout. Frogs are said to have a lower pH **tolerance** than trout.

| Organism | Lowest pH tolerance |
|---|---|
| frog | 4.0 |
| perch | 4.5 |
| trout | 5.0 |
| bass | 5.5 |
| mayfly nymph | 5.5 |
| snail | 6.0 |

20 Explain why smaller, lighter organisms might be less competitive.
21 One student suggested 'Being smaller and lighter could be an advantage'. Do you agree?
22 Suggest how the food web on the following page would be affected if the pH level dropped below 5.

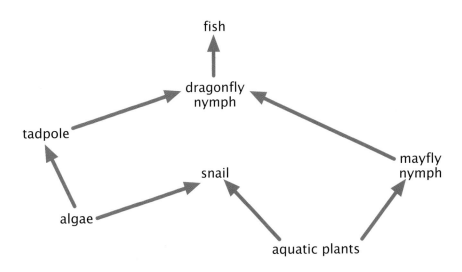

## What is happening to the environment?

It is vital that we learn lessons from the past and protect both ourselves and our environment from further harm. There are national air quality and water quality monitoring systems in place to inform us of pollution levels. The five main pollutants are:

- sulphur dioxide
- nitrogen dioxide
- ozone
- carbon monoxide
- smoke particles.

Information on each of these pollutants is gathered every hour from over 110 automatic monitoring sites around the UK. Levels of the five main air pollutants that can cause immediate health effects are given a numerical index. The index is given during weather reports to give a warning to those people who are more likely to be at risk from pollution because they have respiratory problems such as asthma and bronchitis. The pollution index has a scale from 1 to 10:

| Pollution band and numerical index | Health effect |
|---|---|
| 1–3 (low) | effects are unlikely to be noticed, even by people who know they are sensitive* to air pollutants |
| 4–6 (moderate) | mild effects are unlikely to require action, but sensitive people may notice them |
| 7–9 (high) | <ul><li>sensitive people may notice significant effects, and may have to act to reduce or avoid them (for example, by reducing time spent outdoors)</li><li>asthmatics should find that their inhaler reverses the effects of pollution on their lungs</li></ul> |
| 10 (very high) | the effects of high levels of pollution on sensitive people may worsen when pollution becomes very high |

*Sensitive individuals are people who suffer from heart and lung diseases, including asthma, particularly if they are elderly.

Air pollution levels vary from area to area and from day to day. Levels of pollution can be influenced by a number of things, including:

- local landscape features and surroundings
- local and regional sources of pollution
- seasonal variations and prevailing weather conditions.

**23** Classify the following locations and weather conditions according to the level of pollution they are likely to be associated with. Grade them as:
A – low
B – moderate
C – high
D – very high

| Location/weather condition |
| --- |
| Cities and towns in deep valleys |
| In winter, in cold, still, foggy weather, particularly vehicle pollutants in large cities |
| Smoke control area or areas with high levels of gas or electricity used for heating |
| Busy roads with heavy traffic next to high buildings and busy road junctions |
| Residential roads with light traffic |
| Windy or wet weather at any time of year |
| In summer, during sunny, still, weather, particularly ozone in suburban and rural areas |
| Rural areas away from major roads and factories (for most pollutants except ozone) |
| Cities/towns on hills |
| High levels of solid fuel (for example, coal and wood) used for heating in the local area |

Check your grades with others and be prepared to give reasons for your decisions.

## Biological indicators: signs of pollution

**Key word**
* biological indicators

**Biological indicators** are useful for assessing levels of pollution.

1 Black spot is a mould that grows on roses. This mould cannot grow if there is sulphur dioxide in the air.
2 Lichens are plants that are sensitive to sulphur dioxide. Each type has a different tolerance to sulphur dioxide levels. By observing the type of lichens growing locally, environmental scientists can monitor the level of sulphur dioxide pollution.
3 Mosses are sensitive to air pollution and have disappeared from many metropolitan and industrial areas over the last century.

Shrubby lichens are highly intolerant of pollution.

Leafy lichens show medium tolerance.

Some lichens can tolerate higher pollution levels.

24 Describe the type of lichen profile you would expect to find in:

- a town park
- trees along a busy main road
- a village orchard.

Think about the type and abundance of lichen you might find.

25 How would the data in the table on page 167 (pH tolerances) allow scientists to judge the water quality of a freshwater lake?

*Time to think*

1 Imagine that the British Government wanted to make major reductions in the levels of acid rain. What should they do to achieve this aim?

2 Imagine that you had to plan a research project to investigate some aspect of acid rain – how it forms, the damage it does, etc. List your ideas. Discuss the questions you would ask and the steps you would take to carry out the research.

3 Role playing. In your group, each take the role of an 'interested party' (for example, a Friends of the Earth supporter, coal miner, factory owner, fisherman, farmer, environmental scientist or forester) in a group discussion on acid rain. Give each person 3 minutes to state their case about acid rain. Spend some time not only deciding on your main points, but also collecting evidence to challenge others. Present your arguments for or against laws to control acid rain. After all the presentations, debate the various ideas.

# ➡ *Green machine*

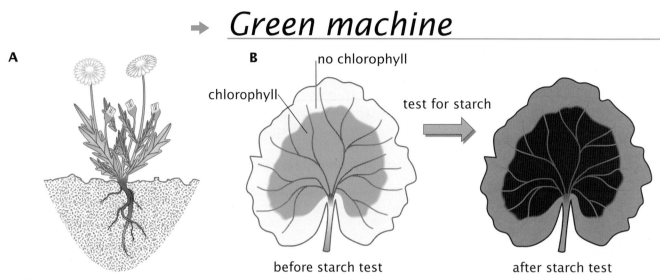

**A**

**B**
no chlorophyll
chlorophyll
test for starch
before starch test — after starch test

Each plant part has specific jobs to do.

26 Use the information in the pictures above to explain your ideas about plant nutrition in a poster, a concept map or summary notes. Share your ideas with another group, checking their accuracy and finding suitable questions to ask to move your ideas forward.

27 How is plant nutrition similar to and different from human nutrition?

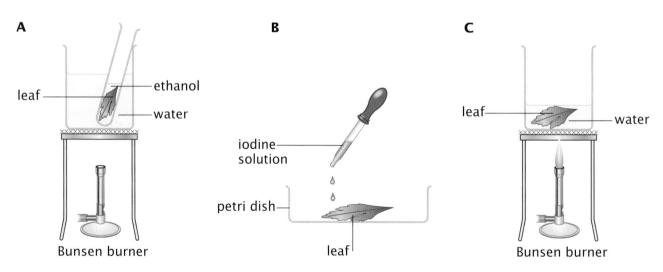

**A**
leaf — ethanol — water
Bunsen burner

**B**
iodine solution
petri dish — leaf

**C**
leaf — water
Bunsen burner

Some of the stages in testing a leaf for starch.

28 The pictures above show some of the stages of a starch test on a leaf.
a) Why do we need to put the leaf in boiling water before testing for starch?
b) Rearrange the stages of the starch test above to give the correct order for the test.
c) Which chemical do we use to test for starch?

**d)** What would you expect to happen if this chemical was poured onto:

- starch
- a leaf that had been kept in the light and then boiled in alcohol
- a leaf that had been kept in the dark and then boiled in alcohol
- a piece of potato
- a crushed seed?

**29** Leaves from four different plants were tested for starch. The leaves and their starch test results are shown below.

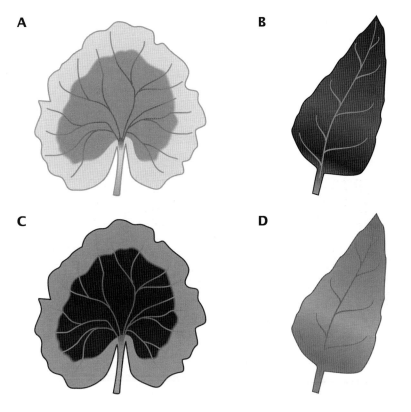

When Sally wrote up this experiment, she wrote the conclusion as:

*Leaves A and D were from plants in the dark while B and C came from plants in the light.*

Her teacher commented:

*More detailed conclusion needed.*

**a)** Rewrite Sally's conclusion in more detail. Compare what you have written with others in your group.

**b)** What happens in the leaves?

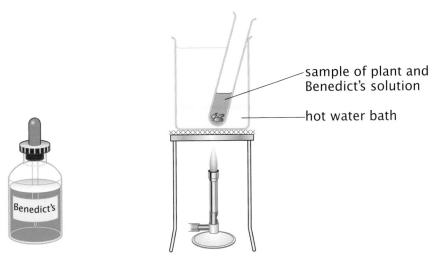

sample of plant and Benedict's solution

hot water bath

Benedict's

Most plants make glucose when they photosynthesise, which they convert into starch. Some plants like garlic, grass and cereal crops only produce sugar. Both glucose and starch are carbohydrates.

Plants are very useful organisms for humans. All of the products pictured here came from plants. Some of them provide us with food. Others provide materials for us to use.

**30** Make a table or diagram to show the different uses we make of plant products. Add two different examples of products to each group.

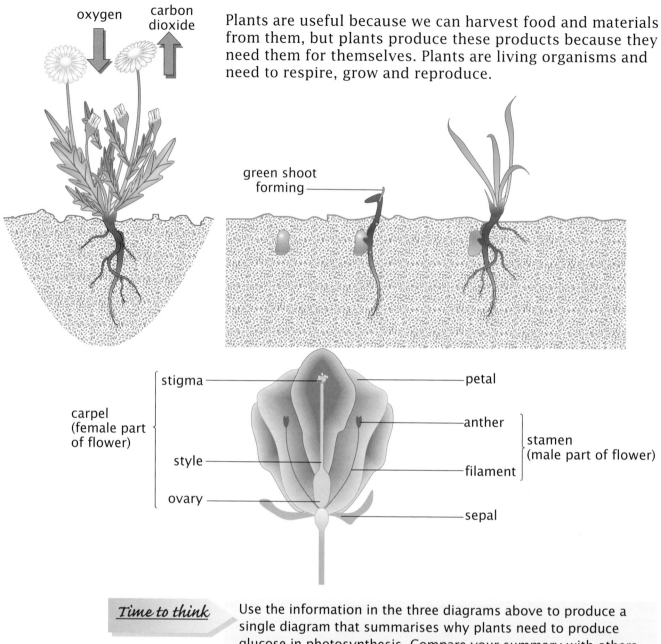

oxygen    carbon dioxide

Plants are useful because we can harvest food and materials from them, but plants produce these products because they need them for themselves. Plants are living organisms and need to respire, grow and reproduce.

green shoot forming

stigma — petal

carpel (female part of flower)

style — filament

anther

stamen (male part of flower)

ovary — sepal

*Time to think*

Use the information in the three diagrams above to produce a single diagram that summarises why plants need to produce glucose in photosynthesis. Compare your summary with others in your group. 'Traffic light' each other's work:

Green dot = includes ideas you had not thought of/ideas put together clearly.
Amber dot = good attempt.
Red dot = some ideas missing/incorrect/muddled.

Talk to one another about your assessment, and if you got an amber or red dot try to improve your summary.

Plants make glucose when they photosynthesise. Plants can use this glucose when they respire. In most plants, excess glucose is converted to starch because starch stores better than glucose. In a few plants, for example, olives, the glucose is turned into oil. Glucose can also be converted into cellulose and protein, which are both important for making new cells.

# The story of wheat

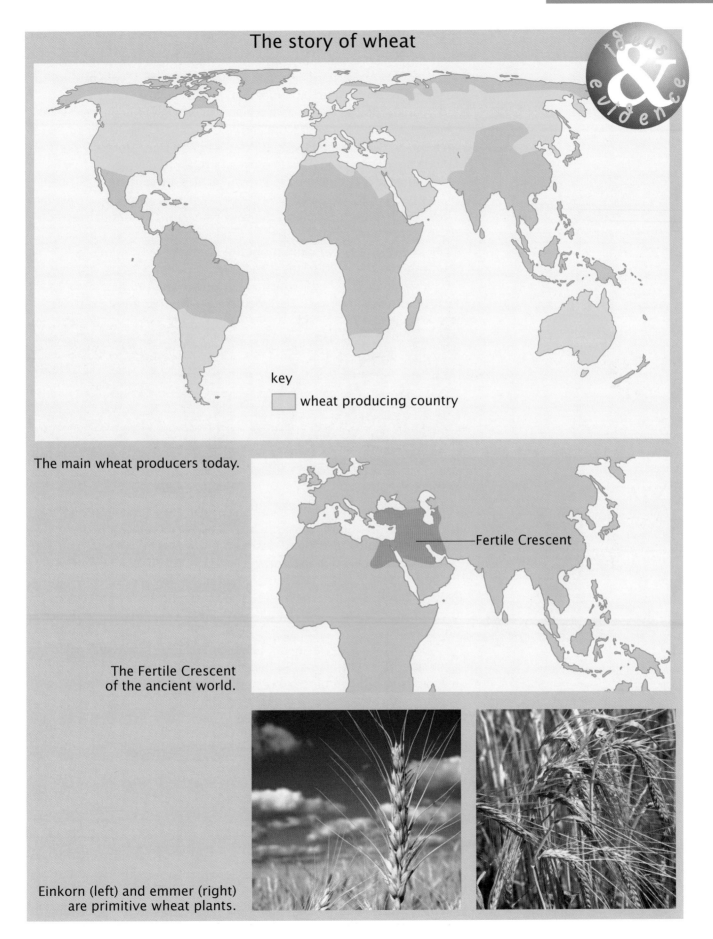

key

☐ wheat producing country

The main wheat producers today.

Fertile Crescent

The Fertile Crescent of the ancient world.

Einkorn (left) and emmer (right) are primitive wheat plants.

Wheat has been cultivated by humans as a valuable food source for over 9000 years. Greek and Roman writings show that wheat was their main cereal crop. The seeds or grains of wheat were ground to make flour. Some grains of wheat have also been found preserved in Egyptian tombs. The main advances in wheat cultivation took place in a region known as the Fertile Crescent which today includes part of Israel, Egypt, Turkey, Iraq and Iran. Much of this land is now desert, but it was once a rich farming region.

The first wheat plants were known as einkorn and emmer. These plants had long thin stalks which were easily broken in bad weather. They also had quite small seeds, so the ancient farmers needed to grow a very large crop in order to produce enough wheat for food. They began wheat breeding programs to improve both the stalk strength and the yield of the wheat plants. Today we have much better varieties of wheat, which are stronger and produce high yields. Some varieties are also resistant to drought and to disease.

Durum wheat.

Bread wheat.

One type of modern wheat is durum wheat. It has been produced by intensive breeding. Durum wheat has large grains. It is grown to provide the flour for making pasta and biscuits. In some parts of the world it is called macaroni wheat. It cannot be used to make bread because it has a low gluten content. Bread wheat has a high gluten content. Gluten makes the dough elastic and helps to trap the carbon dioxide bubbles that yeast produces. This makes bread light and airy.

Today some countries grow wheat on a large scale with vast expanses of wheat plants. To harvest the grain, farmers use large machines called combine harvesters to collect the seeds. The wheat seeds are stored in grain stores before they are shipped to mills and factories to make flour.

1 What evidence do we have that wheat has been cultivated for thousands of years?
2 Suggest why ancient people began to cultivate wheat.
3 How have breeding programs improved wheat plants?
4 What is meant by plant yield?
5 Why is bread wheat better than durum wheat for making bread?
6 In which parts of the world is wheat mainly cultivated today?

*Research*   Use the internet and books to find out about how and where cotton is grown, harvested and processed into material or thread these days.

# Plant drugs and poisons

In ancient times, plants were the main source of **medicines**. By trial and error, people found out which plants helped with particular illnesses. The plants that worked were usually grown in special gardens and used by the local people to treat various diseases. In the Middle Ages, details of medicinal plants were recorded in books called 'Herbals'.

Ginseng has been prized in China for over 5000 years. People take its powdered root because they believe that it can aid recovery from many illnesses and promote general wellbeing. Today, ginseng is sold commercially all over the world.

In South America, the bark of cinchona trees is used to treat malaria. The bark produces quinine which can help control malaria. Quinine is also used to flavour tonic water.

Foxglove leaves contain the chemical digitalis, which is used to treat some heart conditions. In small doses it can help the heart beat more slowly and strongly. However, in large doses it produces heart palpitations and dizziness. While the deadly nightshade plant is poisonous, it can also be used to produce the drug atropine. This drug is used in eye surgery and to treat some stomach complaints.

Castor oil plants have been grown for health reasons since the days of the Egyptians. The oil from these plants is used to purify the digestive system. Castor oil plant beans also contain the lethal **poison** ricin. Eating just a single bean from this plant would kill an adult.

Jojoba and aloe vera plants are grown to obtain their oils. These oils keep skin soft and supple and they also have healing properties.

*Creative thinking*  *The importance of plants*

Make a poster, pamphlet or PowerPoint presentation about the importance of plants to humans.

## van Helmont

It was thought at one time that plants used materials from the soil to grow. We now know that plants only use a tiny amount of material from the soil to grow. Most of the plant is made using the materials produced by photosynthesis. One of the key pieces of research that led to this idea was carried out by van Helmont in the seventeenth century.

Jean Baptiste van Helmont was born in Brussels in 1579. He is recognised as the discoverer of carbon dioxide. Like many scientists of his time, he was interested in various aspects of science, but chemistry was his main interest. He did a lot of work on gases. The most important investigation he carried out about plant nutrition was to take a young willow tree growing in a pot and weigh it and the soil in which the tree grew.

Over the next 5 years he added nothing to the soil other than water. At the end of this time he found that the tree and its pot of soil had gained 164 lb (about 74.5 kg). He weighed the soil and found that it had only lost a few ounces (less than 100 g). He reasoned that the tree's food could not have come from the soil. van Helmont went on to suggest that the increase in the weight of the tree came from its taking in water.

Today we know that plants take in carbon dioxide through their leaves and water through their roots. These two substances react together during photosynthesis to produce glucose.

1 Write two or three questions that would test whether someone understood the importance of van Helmont's work to our understanding of photosynthesis.
2 Try out each other's questions and decide which questions are the best.

*Evaluation* ## Mung bean experiment

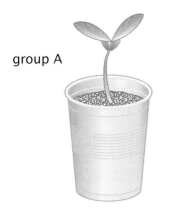

group A

Mung beans germinate and grow quite quickly. Three groups of students decided to carry out their own version of van Helmont's experiment.

Group A planted one mung bean in a plastic cup of moist soil. They weighed the cup of soil and bean and found that it weighed 175 g. Each day they lightly sprayed the soil surface with water. After 10 days the bean had sprouted, and when they weighed it again, it weighed 175 g.

group B

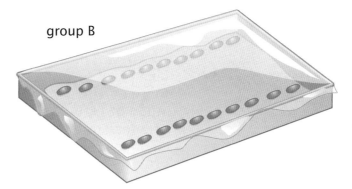

Group B decided to grow 20 mung beans. They soaked their seeds and placed them on wet paper towel in a plastic dish. They covered the top of the dish with cling film. They weighed the dish and contents and found that it weighed 50 g. They left the seeds to grow and at the end of ten days they reweighed the dish and contents. It now weighed 55 g.

group C

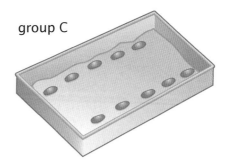

Group C decided to grow 10 mung bean seeds. They soaked the seeds then placed them on a moist paper towel in a small plastic dish. The dish and contents weighed 45 g. Every day they lightly sprayed the paper towel with water. By the tenth day, nine of the beans had germinated and grown. They reweighed the dish and contents and found that it now weighed 48 g.

**1** Why do you think group A's pot of soil and bean had not increased in weight after 10 days?

**2** Which groups carried out a fair test? Explain what they did to make the test fair.

**3** Which group's investigation was most similar to van Helmont's experiment? Explain why you think this.

# Looking inside leaves

**Key words**
* photosynthesis
* chlorophyll
* chloroplasts
* biofuels
* non-renewable fuels
* palisade

It takes 8 minutes for light to travel from the Sun to the Earth's surface, but green plants need only a few seconds to capture that light and store it. This process is called **photosynthesis**, and it takes place in plants and some types of bacteria. In plants, leaves are the main site of photosynthesis. **Chlorophyll** is the green pigment that helps plants make glucose. It is found in many of the leaf cells in little sacs called **chloroplasts**. Chloroplasts are energy transfer systems. They change light energy into chemical energy locked in glucose molecules. As a process, photosynthesis contains some of the fastest reactions that we know. The most important events in photosynthesis take place in just a fraction of a second. Understanding of these events is important and this is why the Center for Study of Early Events in Photosynthesis was set up at Arizona State University in the USA, in 1988. About twenty chemists, biochemists and botanists are working there on projects to find out more about the beginning of the photosynthetic process. One of the reasons so much research is being carried out in this area is that knowledge of photosynthesis is essential if we want to improve food production and find alternative energy sources in the future.

**31** Which organisms photosynthesise?
**32** Why are green plants called energy transfer systems?
**33** Why is it important for scientists to study photosynthesis?

Another research group looking at the potential of photosynthesis is based in Lincolnshire, UK. Here they are comparing the amount of energy that has been used to plant, grow and harvest crops (input) with the energy that you can get back from crops (output). The two main crops they have worked on so far are wheat and oil seed rape. Bioethanol can be produced from wheat, and biodiesel from oil seed rape. Both are good fuels.

The scientists have estimated that for wheat, 1 gigajoule of bioethanol energy is produced for every 0.9 gigajoules of support energy that is put in. For oil seed rape, 1 gigajoule of biodiesel energy is produced for every 0.561 gigajoules of support energy that is put in. Their calculations assume that the farm will be situated within 60 miles (100 kilometres) of fertiliser suppliers, and includes energy expenditure on fertiliser production as well as the energy that went into farming the crops. These estimates are even higher if the farmers cut and bale the straw left from the wheat crop and take this to a factory or power station for burning. In the case of oil seed rape, the residue plant can be used as fertiliser for other crops, again decreasing overall energy use.

Advances in the manufacture of nitrogen fertilisers have reduced its energy costs from 65–75 MJ/kg in the 1970s to 30 MJ/kg in most modern plants. Crop yields have increased by 30–40% over the same time period. We are now moving into an age where **biofuels** could become essential in overcoming the problems associated with depletion of **non-renewable fuels**.

**34** How energy efficient is production of bioethanol from wheat, and production of biodiesel from oil seed rape? What can be done to increase their energy efficiency?

**35** How big is a gigajoule?

**36** How might the introduction of pest-resistant crops increase the energy efficiency of bioethanol or biodiesel production?

**37** Why is it likely that we will see more biofuels being used in 20 years' time than are used today?

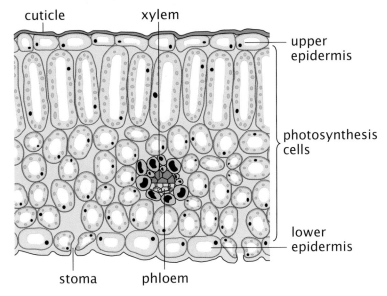

Section through a leaf.

The main photosynthetic layer in the leaf is the layer just below the upper surface. It is called the **palisade** layer.

**38** How are the cells in the palisade layers adapted for photosynthesis?

**39** Which two substances do plants use to make glucose?

**40** Which other product is produced in photosynthesis?

**41** Write a word equation for photosynthesis.

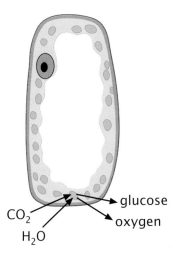

A chloroplast.

*Information processing* *Underwater photosynthesis*

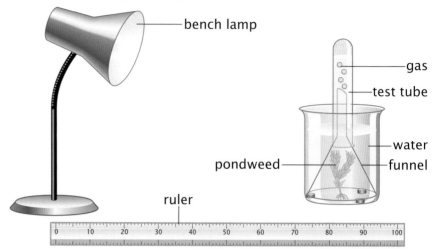

Photosynthesis results in an increase in biomass, but this takes some time to measure. Testing for glucose or starch destroys the leaf, so to see photosynthesis in action Canadian pondweed is often used in laboratories. It is used because it is an aquatic plant and the oxygen it produces in photosynthesis can actually be seen leaving the plant. The oxygen diffuses out of the chloroplasts into the leaf, pushing bubbles out of tiny pores (the stomata, single stoma) into the water. The amount of gas or the rate that the bubbles are produced gives us some indication of how quickly photosynthesis is taking place.

In one experiment, scientists looked at the relationship between the rate of photosynthesis and light intensity. The table below shows their results.

| Light intensity (distance from lamp) | Number of bubbles per minute |
|---|---|
| 200 cm | 2 |
| 150 cm | 4 |
| 100 cm | 9 |
| 75 cm | 11 |
| 50 cm | 16 |
| 25 cm | 19 |

**1** Plot these data on a graph.

**2** Which is the dependent (input) variable?

**3** Which variables would be controlled (the fixed variables)?

**4** Why has light intensity been measured in centimetres?

**5** Predict the rate of photosynthesis (in bubbles per minute) when the lamp was:
   **a)** 55 cm away
   **b)** 70 cm away
   **c)** 250 cm away.

**6** How far away was the lamp if the photosynthesis rate was 14 bubbles per minute?

**7** If you collected the gas produced by the photosynthesising leaves, how would you check that it contained oxygen?

The same experiment was carried out again but the water had extra carbon dioxide pumped into it. These are the new set of results.

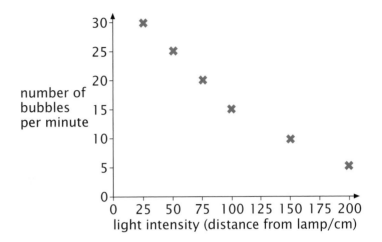

**8** What do these results suggest about the role of carbon dioxide in photosynthesis?

## The discovery of oxygen

Joseph Priestley was born near Leeds in 1733 and is recognised as the discoverer of oxygen. This is how he described his experimental findings: 'I have discovered an air five or six times as good as common air'. He continued with his experiments to show that the gas he had isolated made up about 20% of 'common air'.

The proximity of his house to a public brewery set the stage for many experiments on carbon dioxide, which he called 'fixed air'. These experiments led to an understanding of why water obtained from natural spas effervesced (fizzed). He found that the 'restorative sparkling beverages' that people drank at spas were simply water containing 'fixed air'. For this work he won the prestigious Copley medal from the Royal Society.

Priestley and scientists of his time did not have a periodic table as we have today. They also did not think about elements and compounds in the same way that we do. In Priestley's time the 'phlogiston theory' was the main theory that scientists used to explain their experimental findings. So when Priestley isolated oxygen and tested its properties, he called the gas 'dephlogisticated air'.

All the gases known by Priestley and his fellow scientists were thought to be different types of air, and the 'goodness' of air was measured depending on its 'respirability'. They carried out tests of 'goodness' by seeing if small animals such as mice could survive in a container of the gas.

| Gases in Priestley's time | Chemical formula |
|---|---|
| fixed air | $CO_2$ |
| reduced fixed air | $CO$ |
| nitrous air | $NO$ |
| phlogisticated air | $N_2O$ |
| acid air | $HCl$ |

In 1771, Priestley reported a new finding from his experiments. He had been experimenting on some 'injured air', which was air from which mice had already taken all the oxygen. Priestley found that if he put some green plants into a container of 'injured air' then the air's respirability returned. He tried this first with mint plants, then groundsel and then spinach. In all three experiments, he found that the plants changed the air.

He wrote:

'The injury which is continually done to the atmosphere by respiration of such a large number of animals … is, in part, regulated by vegetable creation.'

Priestley met with a fellow scientist, Lavoisier, who had been developing ideas on burning. Through their exchange of ideas, Priestley provided Lavoisier with a vital piece of evidence that enabled Lavoisier to overthrow the old phlogiston theory and revolutionise chemistry.

1 What was the phlogiston theory?
2 How did scientists in Priestley's time classify gases?
3 Why was living close to a brewery useful to Priestley's work, and what useful science did he discover from these experiments?
4 Explain how you might set up Priestley's famous experiment today to show the effect that plants have on 'injured air'.
5 Write out Priestley's quotes using modern language, and also explain the scientific reasoning in them.
6 What did Priestley's discussions with Lavoisier lead to?

## Rooted to the spot

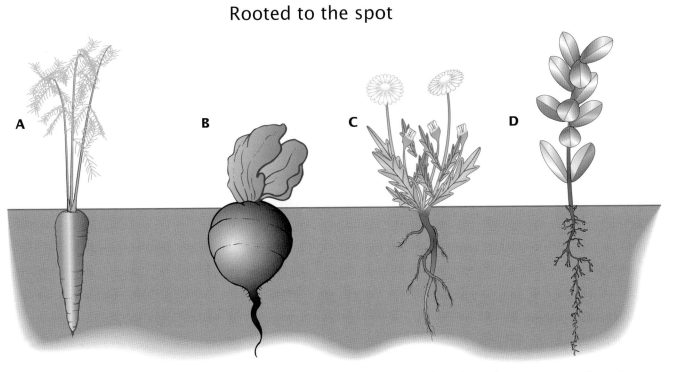

Roots are adapted for the jobs they do. Roots anchor the plant into the soil, which prevents the plant from being blown away, knocked over or pulled up easily. Plants also take in water and minerals through their roots. Some roots store starch from photosynthesis.

**42** Look at the roots pictured above. Decide which of them are:
  **a)** good anchors
  **b)** good for exchanging materials
  **c)** good for storage of starch.

Adaptation also takes place at the level of the cell. If you look closely at roots you can see that some of the root cells have tiny 'hairs' (They are clearly visible in this photograph). These are root hair cells, and they create a larger surface area for taking up water and minerals. While plants need moist soil, they do not work well in water-logged soil. This is because the root cells need oxygen for respiration. If all the gaps between the soil particles become full of water, the root hair cells die.

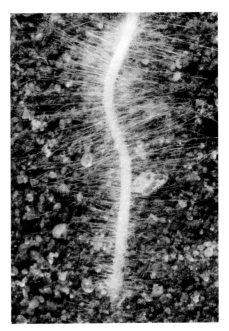

## *Reasoning* Mineral salts

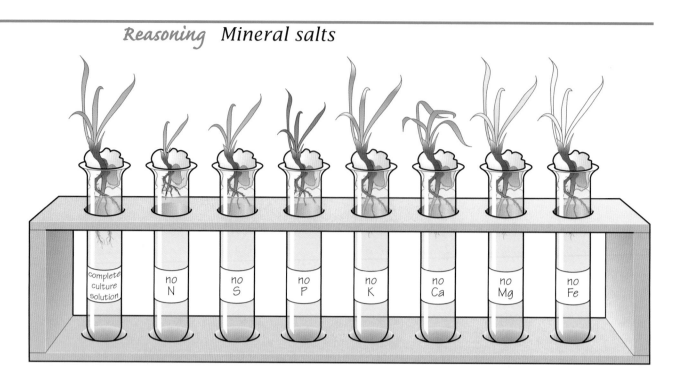

Look at this experiment which has been set up to find out which mineral salts plants need to grow healthily.

**1** Construct a table to record the results of this experiment.

**2** What has the scientist done to make this a fair test?

**3** What would be your conclusion to this experiment?

**4** How would you increase the reliability of this experiment?

## Why are green plants important to the environment?

**Key words**
∗ greenhouse effect
∗ global warming

Plants make food and materials for humans and other organisms. They also regulate the gases in our atmosphere. We get very worried today when people cut down forests. Sometimes it seems necessary to do so to make way for agriculture or roads. If the proportion of the world covered by plants decreases, then less carbon dioxide will be taken out of the air and less oxygen will be put back into it. In a similar way, if we continue to burn fossil fuels in factories and power stations we will be adding to the carbon dioxide and reducing the oxygen in the atmosphere. Increasing the carbon dioxide in the atmosphere can increase the **greenhouse effect**. This is one of the factors that may be causing climate change such as **global warming**.

*Reasoning*  ## Atmosphere model

The experimental set-up below models the role that plants play in maintaining the atmospheric gases.

sealed bell jar

1 Decide how effective this set-up is as a model, and explain your decision.

2 Invent some initiatives that would help people or countries to maintain the balance of gases in the atmosphere.

*Time to think*

- List the various topics covered in this chapter. Select two topics that you feel you need to do some more work on. Divide a page into four sections. In one section make notes on the main ideas of one of the topics you have selected. Repeat this for the second topic. In the remaining sections, write some questions that would test whether you now understand the two topics. Try these questions out on a small group of pupils. Discuss the answers they give and whether your questions were good questions. Now try to do the same with another pupil's chosen topics.

- Construct a concept map including the main ideas in this topic. Think how it links with other topics you have studied, and extend your concept map to include these. Compare your concept map with others in your group.

# 7 *Genes and inheritance*

**In this chapter you will learn:**

→ **that all living things contain genetic information**
→ **how offspring inherit characteristics from their parents**
→ **that genes are organised into chromosomes**
→ **that genes are made up of large molecules called DNA**
→ **how sex in humans is determined**
→ **the history of the development of genetics as a science**
→ **that variation is due to both inheritance and the environment**
→ **how knowledge of genetics is used in selective breeding and genetic engineering**

**You will also develop your skills in:**

→ **decision making – deciding what measurements to make in an investigation**
→ **sampling to get a 'picture' of a population's characteristics**
→ **collecting, organising and using large data sets**
→ **looking for patterns in data to determine what is due to probability and what is not**
→ **evaluating the strength of evidence**

---

## ➡ ➡ ➡ WHAT DO YOU KNOW?

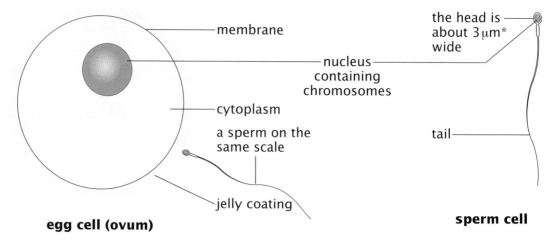

membrane

nucleus containing chromosomes

cytoplasm

a sperm on the same scale

jelly coating

**egg cell (ovum)**

the head is about 3 μm* wide

tail

**sperm cell**

*1 micrometre (μm) is one-thousandth of a millimetre (mm)

Here is a quick quiz to see what your group already knows about reproduction, inheritance and variation. Make one of your group the questioner and another the 'scribe' who will note down your group's answers. Your teacher will tell you how long you have to do the quiz. Groups can swap and mark each other's answers.

**1** What does 'inheritance' mean?

**2** How is a sperm cell adapted to its function? Where is it made?

**3** How is an egg cell adapted to its function? Where is it made?

**4** Why are brothers and sisters similar to each other and their parents in some ways?

**5** How are identical twins formed?

**6** What does 'unique' mean?

**7** A farmer harvested some wheat grain from a particular wheat plant and planted all the seeds in a plant pot. They germinated and he planted them out in a row in a field. When the plants grew to full size he noticed that they were all different heights. What factors might have caused this variation?

## Inheritance

**Key words**
* genetics
* inheritance
* offspring
* genes
* heredity
* traits
* characteristics
* generations

Read this paragraph to yourself and make some notes to help you remember the main points. For example, write down what you think are the meanings of each of the key words. Check that you know who Mendel was and why he is an important historical figure for biologists. Note down anything you do not understand. See if anyone else in your group can help you understand these topics. If not, make them into questions to ask your teacher.

**Genetics** is the scientific study of **inheritance**, or how plant and animal **offspring** obtain characteristics from their parents. Every organism on the planet has **genes**, even though scientists have only discovered them within the last 100 years.

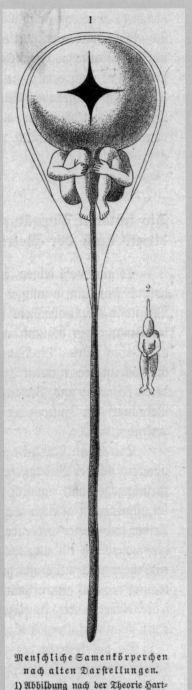

Menfchliche Samenförperchen
nach alten Darftellungen.

1) Abbildung nach der Theorie Hart=
foekers; 2) entpupptes Spermato=
zoon, welches Dalepabius (be la
Plantabe) in diefer Geftalt gefehen
haben wollte.

Nicolas Hartsoeker's drawings in 1694 of a human sperm cell containing a miniature adult called a homunculus.

Ancient Greeks had theories about **heredity** and why children resemble their parents. One of them, Hippocrates, recognised that the male contribution to a child's heredity is carried in the semen. He also thought that women had some similar fluid, and that the two fluids fought each other to produce **traits (characteristics)** to be shown by the offspring. For example, he thought that the eye colour part of the man's and woman's semen-like fluids fought each other and the stronger, winning fluid sent that parent's trait to be inherited by their offspring.

In the nineteenth century some scientists thought that the sperm cell contained a miniature model of an adult. This tiny thing was thought to grow inside the mother until it was born. The mother was not believed to contribute any characteristics to the baby.

Other scientists thought that the mother contained a seed that grew into the new child and that the father made no contribution to how that child looked. Of course we now know that both the sperm and the ova (egg cells) are important, each containing half a set of coded instructions that, when combined, form the embryo.

Gregor Mendel can be thought of as the person who started the new science of genetics in the 1860s. He was a peasant's son who became a monk and was eventually the abbot of a monastery at Brunn, in what we now call the Czech Republic. Like most scientific investigations, his investigation started with a question. The question was:

> How are the characteristics we inherit from our parents passed on to us, the offspring?

Mendel was not the first person to think about this question, but his curiosity and logical approach led him to develop systematic ways of testing out his ideas about inheritance. He was a keen gardener, as well as a mathematician. He had noticed how peas grown in the monastery's kitchen gardens showed variation. He had also noticed that he could predict some of the characteristics of adult plants grown from seeds where he had noted the parent's characteristics. He decided to record the characteristics for several **generations** of peas. He compared the numbers of different types of pea produced from the offspring of each generation, and looked for relationships between the parents and offspring over several generations.

Mendel published his work in 1866 but no one then really understood the importance of what he hypothesised. It was only in 1900, long after he had died, when the 'particles' that he identified were given the name 'genes' (from the Greek word 'genos' meaning descent), that his work received recognition.

# Chromosomes

**Key word**
* chromosomes

The invention of the microscope showed that organisms were made up of cells, but it was not until the end of the nineteenth century that strange thread-like strings were seen floating around inside the cells of worms that lived in horse intestines. When the cells divided (to reproduce) these threads seemed to go through a series of complicated movements, like a dance. They made copies of themselves so that each new cell had the same number of threads as the parent cell. This cycle was repeated over and over again. The dancing threads became known as **chromosomes**. The man who first described them was Thomas Hunt Morgan, a professor at Columbia University. The link had been made between cells dividing and how humans pass coded information from parent to child.

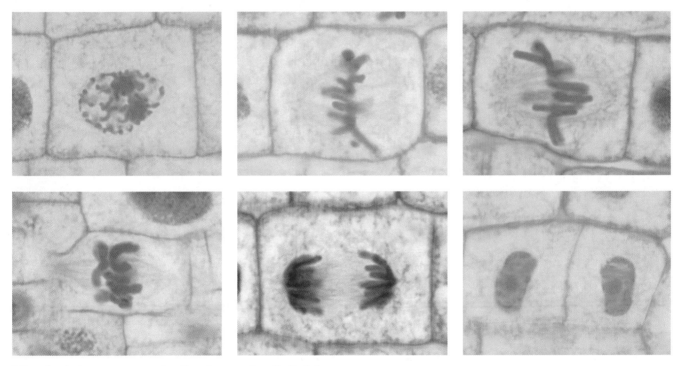

Mitosis – chromosome duplication and cell division.

1 Talk to a partner to help you 'think out loud' about Mendel's question: 'How are the characteristics we inherit from our parents passed on to us, the offspring?'. What answer would you give him?
2 Why do you think the name 'gene' was chosen for Mendel's 'particles'?
3 Could you think of a better name, one that more accurately describes the function of a gene?

# More about Mendel

Key words
* fertilised
* deduce
* self-pollinate
* self-fertilise
* cross-pollinating
* anthers
* stigma

To carry out his investigations Mendel had to know how plants are **fertilised**. He controlled the plants being fertilised so that he could breed together parent pea plants with different characteristics.

Mendel would not have been able to **deduce** as much as he did about inheritance if he had tried to study humans. The genetic make-up of humans is far more complex and the life cycle too long. He also could not have selected which parents could breed with each other! Peas were ideal organisms to investigate. Peas show easily observable, contrasting characteristics, for example, pea seeds are either round and smooth or wrinkled, and the height of the plants is either tall or dwarf. They can **self-pollinate**, so they **self-fertilise** even when the flower is unopened. When this happens, all the offspring contain all the genes of the parent. Mendel could interfere with this by **cross-pollinating** one plant with another. This is done by removing the **anthers** of one plant's flower before they can produce pollen to land on the nearby **stigma** of that same flower. He then dusted pollen from a flower on another plant onto the first flower's stigma.

**1** The immature stamens of a young flower are exposed

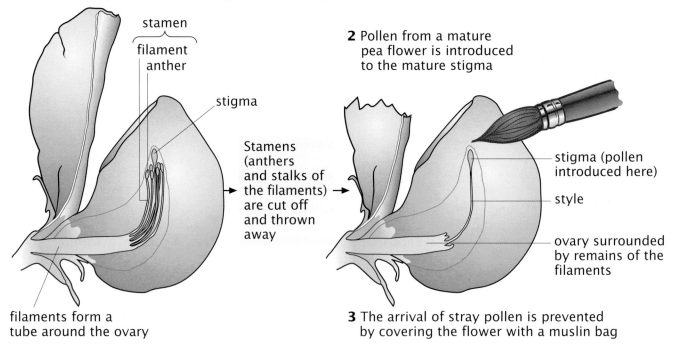

stamen
filament
anther

stigma

Stamens (anthers and stalks of the filaments) are cut off and thrown away

filaments form a tube around the ovary

**2** Pollen from a mature pea flower is introduced to the mature stigma

stigma (pollen introduced here)

style

ovary surrounded by remains of the filaments

**3** The arrival of stray pollen is prevented by covering the flower with a muslin bag

Cross-pollination of the pea plant.

Wind pollination.

Insect pollination.

4 Make sure you know the names of all the sexual parts of a flower.
5 Write a sentence that explains the difference between cross- and self-pollination.
6 How does cross-pollination happen naturally?
7 How do you artificially make sure a flower is cross-pollinated? Why would you want to do this?
8 Think of a way to test other people's knowledge about sexual reproduction in plants.

## *Reasoning* *Variation in populations*

Look at these drawings of a human population and a population of pea plants.

height

scale 1:40

height

scale 1:3

1 What do you notice about the heights in each of the populations? You may want to measure these pictures. They are drawn to scale.
   **a)** What is the range of heights in the human population?
   **b)** What is the range of heights in the pea plant population?

2 Why would it have been very difficult, if not impossible, for Mendel to have deduced his ideas about inheritance of characteristics from parents to offspring if he had looked at human populations instead of pea plants?

## Variables

In living things the **variation** of characteristics between individuals in a population can be described as **continuous** or **discontinuous**. Continuous variables are characteristics that have many different variations, each one only slightly different from the next one. For example, height is a continuous variable in humans. Discontinuous variables describe characteristics which are clearly one thing or the other, for example, male or female, able or unable to tongue-roll.

9 Which of these characteristics do you think might be continuous and which are discontinuous variables?

* length of a human hand
* width of a human hand
* number of people with blue eyes
* length of a worm
* number of peas in a pod
* length of pine cones
* number of people with grey eyes
* number of flowers on a bluebell stem
* number of petals in a daisy head

*Information processing* **Mendel's peas**

Here is an example of one of Mendel's pea-crossing investigations:

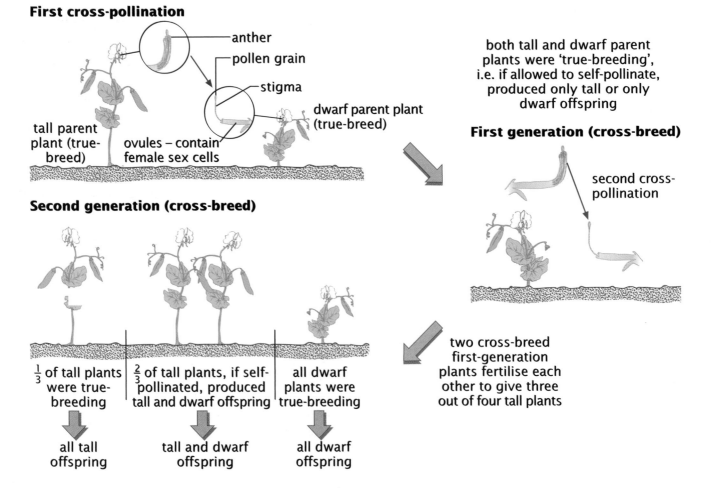

**First cross-pollination**

anther

pollen grain

stigma

dwarf parent plant (true-breed)

tall parent plant (true-breed)

ovules – contain female sex cells

both tall and dwarf parent plants were 'true-breeding', i.e. if allowed to self-pollinate, produced only tall or only dwarf offspring

**First generation (cross-breed)**

second cross-pollination

**Second generation (cross-breed)**

two cross-breed first-generation plants fertilise each other to give three out of four tall plants

$\frac{1}{3}$ of tall plants were true-breeding

$\frac{2}{3}$ of tall plants, if self-pollinated, produced tall and dwarf offspring

all dwarf plants were true-breeding

all tall offspring

tall and dwarf offspring

all dwarf offspring

**1** What do you notice about the ratio of tall to short plants in the offspring?

**2** Height in humans is a continuous variable; height in peas is a discontinuous variable.

  If you were plotting a graph to show the range of heights for a human population and for a pea population, which type of graph would you draw for each, and why?

## Collecting data

It is not always easy to tell if a characteristic is discontinuous or continuous. You would need to look at large numbers of individuals in a population to be sure. A frequency table is a good way to collect this kind of data; we call this a **data set**.

Here is a frequency table for the number of petals in a daisy head. Strictly speaking, a daisy head is not one flower but is made up of many little part-flowers. Each of these is called a 'ray floret'.

**Key words**
* data set
* sample

petals

a single
ray floret

A daisy head.

### Number of daisies with this number of florets

| Number of ray florets | Score (tallies) | Total |
| --- | --- | --- |
| 34 | 卌 II | 7 |
| 35 | 卌 II | 7 |
| 36 | 卌 卌 | 10 |
| 37 | 卌 卌 卌 IIII | 19 |
| 38 | 卌 卌 III | 13 |
| 39 | 卌 卌 I | 11 |
| 40 | 卌 III | 8 |
| 41 | 卌 II | 7 |
| 42 | 卌 II | 7 |
| 43 | IIII | 4 |
| 44 | IIII | 4 |
| 45 | III | 3 |
| Total in sample | | 100 |

**10** Plot a bar graph of these results.
**11** Why are you not asked to plot a line graph?
**12** What is the smallest number of ray florets?
**13** What is the largest number of ray florets?
**14** What is the range?
**15** What is the median?
**16** What is the average number of ray florets?
**17** How many individuals would you **sample** to find out about each of the characteristics for the organisms listed in Question 9? Why have you suggested that number?

*Enquiry* *Studying characteristics*

Think of a characteristic in an organism that you want to study and decide whether it is a continuous or discontinuous variable. You could select a characteristic from the list in Question 9 (page 194).

**1** What will you measure?

**2** How big will your sample need to be?

**3** How will you record your data?

Carry out your investigation of your chosen characteristic. Your work will be assessed on your ability to:

- decide what to measure and observe and how to do this in an efficient way, taking into account the time and resources you have available
- collect and record data appropriately
- identify and describe trends in your data
- evaluate the limitations of the evidence you have collected by thinking about your sample size and the possible effects of other factors
- use your scientific knowledge and understanding to interpret your data.

**Evaluation**

Looking back at your investigation, is there any way you could improve it if you were asked to do something like this again?

# → Sex cells

**Key words**
* cell division
* sperm
* ovum
* zygote
* embryo
* ova
* X chromosomes
* Y chromosome

Humans reproduce sexually and, unlike pea plants, never self-fertilise! Each of the nuclei in our normal cells contain 46 chromosomes. They pair up in 23 pairs during the process of **cell division**, when the genetic material duplicates itself so that each new cell will also have 46 chromosomes. To make a sex cell, a normal cell divides into two cells. Each new cell only has 23 chromosomes, half the number in the original parent cell. During fertilisation a **sperm** cell (with 23 chromosomes like the ones in the father's cells) fuses with an **ovum** (containing 23 chromosomes like the ones in the mother's cells). The new cell formed (a **zygote**) has 46 chromosomes so it can replicate and grow into an **embryo** with a full set of genetic instructions, half from the mother and half from the father. Each **ova** and each sperm cell contain a unique mixture of genes, so everyone is different.

One pair of chromosomes in each cell has the special function of deciding the sex of the embryo. They are called the sex chromosomes. Women's and girls' cells each contain two sex chromosomes of the same shape, called **X chromosomes**. Boys' and men's cells contain one sex chromosome like the female one, an X chromosome, and the other in the pair is different – it is a **Y chromosome**. Each fusion of a sperm and egg cell produces a genetically unique human, because it is not possible to predict which sperm cell will fertilise which egg cell.

*Reasoning*   *Same or different*

Copy and complete this table.

| Cells | Same or different genetic information? | Reasons |
|---|---|---|
| two cheek cells from the inside of Jane's cheek | cheek cells | |
| a cheek cell and a brain cell from Jane's body | brain cell<br><br>cheek cell | |
| a cheek cell and an egg cell from Jane's body | egg cell<br><br>cheek cell | |
| two egg cells from Jane's body | egg cells | |

## Determining the sex of a baby

We can use a simple table to help us show how sex cells determine if a baby is born male or female.

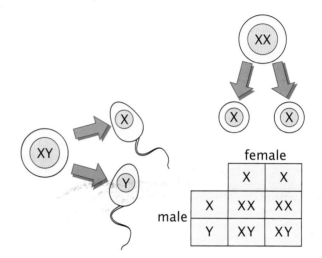

The table shows that 50% of the sperm cells contain an X chromosome and 50% contain a Y chromosome.

**18** What percentage of ova contain Y chromosomes and what percentage contain X chromosomes?

**19** Write down the **proportion** of babies that will be female and the proportion that will be male. The table gives you the answer.

## Probability

If you spin a coin, what are the chances (the **probability**) of its landing heads up? What are its chances of landing tails up?

**20** How would you prove this?

**21** Think of a way to use a coin to represent a genetic characteristic that is inherited. Write an activity using this model and give it to another group to try.

---

*Creative thinking* ## Boy or girl

There are lots of myths and superstitions (old wives' tales) about influencing the sex of a baby. Ask some older people in your community if they know any of these myths. They may also know some myths about how to tell the sex of a baby while it is still in the womb. You could also do some internet research. Write a story using one of these myths.

Now the sex of a baby can be **genetically engineered**. Make a mind map of what this term makes your group think of.

---

## Tests

A pregnant woman can have an amniocentesis test. This is recommended at about 16–18 weeks into pregnancy only if there is concern that the embryo may be carrying a genetic fault, for example, Down's syndrome or spina bifida. A long needle is pushed through the wall of the abdomen into the amniotic fluid surrounding the baby in the womb. Some fluid is drawn up into the syringe and then analysed to look at the chromosomes under a microscope. The baby's sex can also be identified.

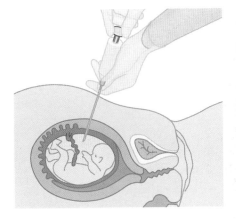

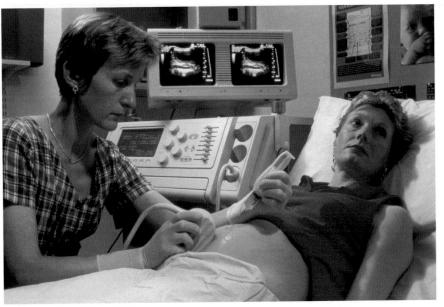

Amniocentesis.

# Some inherited diseases

## Cystic fibrosis

Symptoms: respiratory problems caused by overproduction of mucus which collects in the lungs. Poor digestion so nutrients are not absorbed from food.

Inheritance: from two genes, one from the mother and a similar gene from the father. Most common in people whose ancestors were from white northern European populations.

## Thalassaemia

Symptoms: red blood cells are destroyed too rapidly, before new ones are made in sufficient numbers to replace them.

Inheritance: from two genes, one from the mother and a similar gene from the father. More common in people whose ancestors were from Mediterranean and Indian populations.

## Sickle cell anaemia

Symptoms: red blood cells are not round but crescent-moon (sickle) shaped. This means that each blood cell can carry less oxygen.

Inheritance: inheriting two genes, one from the mother and one from the father, causes the serious form of the disease, but there are mild symptoms when only one disease gene is inherited and the other parent passes on a healthy gene. More common in people whose ancestors were from African and West Indian populations.

## Huntington's disease

Symptoms: slow degeneration of the nervous system. Symptoms appear in adults aged 30–40 years old.

Inheritance: only one disease gene is needed, from the mother or the father, to cause this disease in the offspring.

## Haemophilia

Symptoms: lack of a blood clotting factor so wounds do not stop bleeding.

Inheritance: the gene for this clotting factor is on the X chromosome. Males only have one X chromosome. If the clotting factor gene on the X chromosome inherited from the mother is defective, the male offspring will have haemophilia.

## Genetic carriers

People who carry a gene that causes an inherited disease but who do not suffer from the disease themselves are called **carriers**. Genes are instructions that control characteristics. **Genetic screening** and counselling is offered to people who have a family history of a particular disease and they may be advised on the chances of passing the disease gene on to any children they might have.

## Science and society

22 Think of one advantage and one disadvantage of allowing parents to choose the sex of their baby. Now ask other people in your group what they think. Are your views similar, identical or different?

23 Compile a whole class list of advantages and disadvantages and use this to ask everyone to vote 'YES' or 'NO' to giving parents the right to choose their baby's sex. How did the majority vote in your class?

24 Find out what the current law says about determining the sex of your baby by selecting embryos for implantation.

### Research

Select one of the diseases described here and research it so that you can make a leaflet suitable for a genetic counsellor to give to people planning to have a family but who have a family history of the disease.

**Key words**
* carriers
* genetic screening

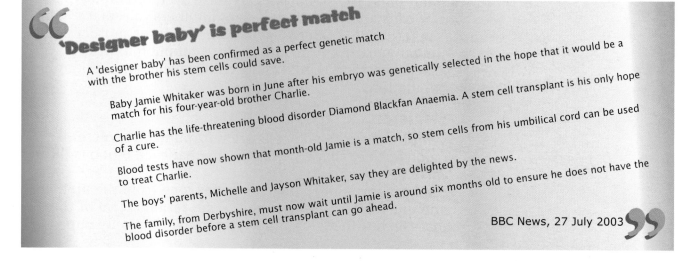

### 'Designer baby' is perfect match

A 'designer baby' has been confirmed as a perfect genetic match with the brother his stem cells could save.

Baby Jamie Whitaker was born in June after his embryo was genetically selected in the hope that it would be a match for his four-year-old brother Charlie.

Charlie has the life-threatening blood disorder Diamond Blackfan Anaemia. A stem cell transplant is his only hope of a cure.

Blood tests have now shown that month-old Jamie is a match, so stem cells from his umbilical cord can be used to treat Charlie.

The boys' parents, Michelle and Jayson Whitaker, say they are delighted by the news.

The family, from Derbyshire, must now wait until Jamie is around six months old to ensure he does not have the blood disorder before a stem cell transplant can go ahead.

BBC News, 27 July 2003

*Reasoning* *Twins and siblings*

**1** Why are identical twins more similar than brothers and sisters or non-identical twins?

**2** Can a boy and a girl born at the same time, to the same mother, be identical twins?

**3** Will multiple births from eggs fertilised outside the body *in vitro* then implanted produce identical or similar offspring?

*Word play*

Look at these pictures and decide which word goes with which pair: identical, similar or different.

In your group, write a paragraph containing all three words so that their meaning is clear.

*Creative thinking* *Male or Female*

Imagine your team have been asked to design and write an illustrated booklet for Year 6 pupils to explain inheritance and how we are born male or female. Write a draft manuscript and include the artwork for the booklet. The publishers have asked your team to think about using appealing colours and pictures, and making the reading level appropriate for this age range. You could make up the booklet using word processing techniques, graphic packages and image scanners. If you produce the booklet, see if your local primary school would like a copy for their library.

*Word play* List all the words, phrases or proverbs you can think of that refer to luck or chance. Here are some to start you off. Do you know these?

- Jammy
- Good luck!
- Break a leg!
- Luck of the devil
- Lucky in money, unlucky in love
- See a penny pick it up, all day long you'll have good luck

Proverbs are things people say that sum up a kind of truth. (Ask your English teacher what a proverb is if you are still unsure.)

*Reasoning* ## Exploring probability

1 Do you think of yourself as a lucky person?

2 What do other people in your group think?

3 What do you all mean by 'luck'?

4 Can you think of an investigation to find out if some people are luckier than others?

5 Using the idea of probability, explain why somebody is said to be lucky.

It is mostly a matter of chance whether a sperm containing an X chromosome or a Y chromosome fertilises the female sex cell.

25 Who do you think determines the sex of a baby, the mother or father?

## Environmental factors

Genes are not the only factor determining the way an organism looks and functions. Environmental factors can also play a role.

26 What conditions might affect the height of a plant other than its genetic make-up?

27 What environmental factors might inhibit normal physical and mental growth in a baby human?

Variations of characteristics in a population can be caused by the environment the organism lives in, by inheritance, or by a mixture of both.

28 Categorise each of these examples into groups according to the most likely cause of variation.

- Leaves of a beech tree growing in woodland are on average larger but thinner than leaves of the same species of tree growing in a garden with no shade.
- Seedlings of beans grown in a dark cupboard are white. Seedlings of beans grown on the windowsill are green.

- The banded snail shell has a range of different colours; they can be pink, yellow or brown, wherever the snails live.
- Supermarkets ask farmers to plant their dwarf carrot varieties very close together so that the carrots will be uniformly small and so that each row of carrots has a larger number of carrots than when spaced apart.
- Upland sheep have shorter legs than lowland sheep.
- At about 6 months old, breast-fed babies are larger on average than bottle-fed babies.
- People today are on average taller than their grandparents.

*Time to think*

Discuss in your group if you think environmental variation is due to chance or not. It all depends on what you think is the result of 'chance'. Think about how the environment might influence which male mated with which female organism. Think about the chances of a baby organism surviving to breeding age, and what helped that organism be successful in surviving.

**Key words**
* nucleus
* nucleic acids
* DNA
* double helix
* spiral

## DNA – life's spiral staircase

The first experiments on the nuclei of cells were carried out by the scientist Johann Friedrich Miescher in 1868. By analysing the pus cells from old surgical bandages, Miescher isolated the chemicals found in the cell **nucleus** and called these **nucleic acids**. In 1944 Oswald Theodore Avery, an American doctor, proved that genes were made up of nucleic acids.

In the late 1950s, James Watson, Francis Crick and Rosalind Franklin, British and American scientists, used X-rays to determine the chemical structure of one particular nucleic acid, deoxyribonucleic acid, **DNA** for short. Rosalind Franklin fired X-rays at crystals of DNA and took photographs showing the way the X-rays bounced off DNA molecules. From these photographs, Watson and Crick were able to build a model of DNA and worked out that to give the kind of pictures Franklin was recording, the molecule had to be a **double helix**. For this they received a Nobel Prize in 1962. Franklin had died at an early age in 1958, without being recognised for her work.

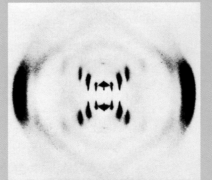

1 Some people call the DNA molecule 'life's **spiral** staircase'. Why?
2 Draw one spiral in your notebook. Now add a second spiral in another colour to make a double spiral or double helix, like the picture of DNA overleaf.

An X-ray photograph of DNA taken by Rosalind Franklin.

DNA is one of the largest known molecules. A DNA molecule weighs 100 000 times more than one sugar molecule.

**Key words**
* strands
* bases

DNA molecules are crammed tightly inside the cells that hold them because they are so long. If they were completely unwound they would be several thousand times the length of the cell. A DNA molecule consists of two long, thin **strands** that are wound around each other to form a double spiral or helix. The strands contain lots of chemical building blocks called **bases**.

Every strand of DNA contains about twelve billion individual bases. There are four different bases, A, G, C, and T, and they occur in various sequences of different arrangements of bases. The strands of a helix are held together by weak chemical bonds between paired bases. A G base will only pair up with a C base, and an A base will only pair up with a T base (for example, C can't pair with G).

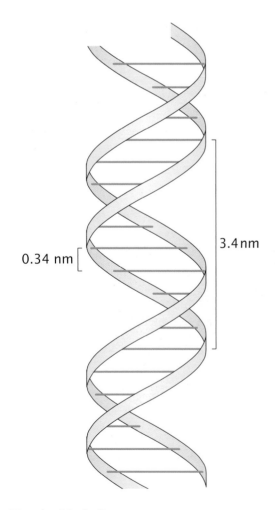

The double helix.

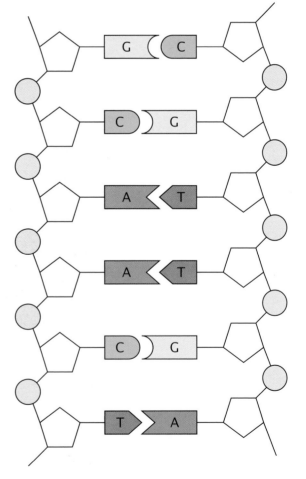

DNA base pairs on two strands of DNA.

## And now ... the Human Genome Project

Begun in 1990, the goals of the Human Genome Project are:

- to identify all the approximately 30 000 genes in human DNA ('the human genome')
- to determine the sequences of the 3 billion chemical base pairs that make up human DNA
- to store this information in databases
- to improve tools for data analysis
- to transfer related technologies to the private sector
- to address the ethical, legal and social issues (ELSI) that may arise from the project.

Source: *the Human Genome Project website*

The project was originally planned to last 15 years, but technological advances accelerated the process and the sequencing of the human genome was completed in 2003.

If you want to know more about this exciting project you can look it up on the Human Genome Project website – http://www.ornl.gov/hgmis/

## Cell division

When a cell starts to divide, the DNA inside the nucleus coils up very tightly into individual chromosomes which are visible under a microscope.

Every living organism has a certain number of chromosomes in each of its cells. A mosquito has six, and a cabbage has 18. Humans have 46.

Your father passed on the DNA that is contained in 23 of your chromosomes to you. The DNA contained in the other 23 chromosomes came from your mother.

*Research*

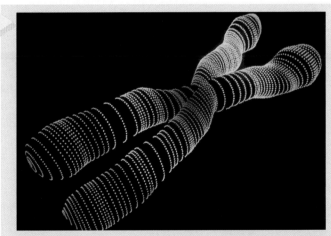

This close-up image of a chromosome looks a bit like a bar code on something you might buy. A bar code is a good analogy (model) for thinking about a chromosome. Find out what bar codes are for. In what ways is a bar code like a chromosome and how is it different?

# Gene mapping

It is possible that within the next ten years each person could have a personal 'map' of his or her **genome**. A genome is the whole set of genes contained in each of an organism's normal cells. It is probable that this will be an expensive process so is unlikely to be available for everyone. **Gene mapping** will be able to show people if they carried genes for a disease such as cystic fibrosis, Huntington's disease or an increased risk of breast cancer. However, depending on the disease, carrying the gene does not always mean a person will get the disease.

## *Creative thinking*   Gene map

1 Imagine you are making an application form for the health service to give to people who want to request a personal gene map. What questions would the form ask? Use ICT to design your form.

2 What do you think are the advantages and disadvantages of each person having the right to know what their genome is? Discuss this in your group.

    Write a letter summarising your class's views and send it to the Human Fertilisation and Embryology Authority (www.hfea.gov.uk/Home). This is the non-government body that licenses and monitors all human embryo research in the UK.

# Genetic engineering

Scientists have begun to change the genetic code by moving some genes within chromosomes. These genes are **transgenic** – they can be moved from one place to another and still function. In 1968 a Swiss scientist called Werner Arber discovered enzymes that could chop DNA into pieces which could be rejoined in different sequences. Once it was realised that **biotechnologists** could use this technique commercially, the **bioengineering** and genetic engineering industries were born.

Some bacteria have genes that cause them to produce a substance that kills insects. These bacterial genes can now be put into plant DNA so that if the insects eat the crop, they die. Human genes that control the immune response have been put into pigs. It is hoped that one day soon we will be able to transplant hearts and kidneys from such pigs into humans and the human body not reject the pig tissue as alien.

Barbara McClintock (1902–1992) was awarded a Nobel Prize in 1983 for her work with plants that showed how genes could be copied from chromosome to chromosome.

*Time to think*   Find the mind map your group produced earlier for the word 'genetic engineering'. Add your new knowledge to it.

    Use it to write a short article for the 'Science now' page of a popular teenage magazine.

## *Information processing* Gene model

Do you remember this gene model from Book 1? It gives an analogy for our current understanding of genetics.

**1** What labels should be used instead of the numbers?

**2** What is an analogy?

**3** Why are analogies helpful in understanding scientific theories and ideas?

① .................... are a bit like the letters of the ② ....................

| A<br>is for apple | B<br>is for book | C<br>is for cow | D<br>is for dog |

Letters make up words and sentences, as *genes* make up ③ ....................

'Once upon a time ...'

... and sentences make up stories just as chromosomes make up the story of the characteristics you will ④ .................... from your parents.

THIS IS YOUR LIFE
M.M. GENE & M. CHROMOSOME

An ⑤ .................... for genetic inheritance.

Genetic information (text) is organised into genes and stored in the DNA (a book). Each gene contains instructions (words) to make one product. The individual 'words' identify the materials to be used, and the word sequence details the order in which the materials are assembled. A very simple language (the genetic code) is used. This language has just

64 'words'. A huge number of different messages can be written with a 64-word vocabulary.

Every living thing uses the same language (genetic code) but different types of organisms use it to produce different sets of instructions, so there are many very different 'stories' written – a fish story, a tree story, a human story, etc. Because all living things use this same basic vocabulary, it is possible for different organisms to 'read' and understand genes for another organism. This is why genetic engineering is possible.

## Genetically modified crops

Known as GM crops, **genetically modified** crops are widely grown in some countries. The most common GM crops are modified to be herbicide tolerant or to produce their own insecticides. In Europe, GM crops still have to go through safety testing before they can be planted outside plant research institutions. Even then, small-scale field trials may have to be carried out before farmers can grow them.

The risks that concern scientists are:

- the GM crops' seeds may spread into the wild plant populations and become strong weeds, competing with the natural vegetation
- insects such as bees and butterflies may be affected in unpredictable ways because their food source has been changed
- the foods from GM crops may have long-term harmful effects on the health of humans or the domesticated animals that are fed on the crops
- GM plants might breed with wild plants and produce 'super weeds.'

The first two risks also apply to any new organisms that we might introduce into the environment. For example, rabbits were introduced to the UK by the Romans who bred them for food; some escaped and they are now widespread and very destructive.

Genes could spread via pollen from GM crops to wild plants and this might be undesirable, for example, if wild plants gained herbicide resistance from such cross-breeding. Making GM crops sterile through genetic engineering or harvesting them before flowering would reduce the risk of genes spreading from GM to wild crops. Most domestic crops are unable to breed with the wild forms and many cannot survive outside agricultural conditions.

It is very unlikely that eating GM food will transfer modified genes into our bodies. When we digest food the DNA it contains is broken down. We eat miles of DNA daily, and swallow whole genomes of many organisms such as oranges, apples and all the microbes we ingest. Our bodies would chemically treat (digest) modified DNA in the same way as it deals with DNA in other foods.

GM crops could be used to great advantage. For example, GM rice can produce a 35% bigger yield than existing rice varieties, which themselves have been selectively bred over many thousands of years from wild rice.

*Research* Collect information and opinion about GM crops from the news. Make a display to put up around the school so that other pupils and teachers can become more informed about the GM debate. Add three or four questions that people should think about to form their own opinions. In June 2003 the Government held a public debate about eating GM foods. Look at the website www.gmsciencedebate.org.uk to find out more about the GM debate.

*Creative thinking* *Company identity*

Imagine you have been asked to choose a name and design a logo for a new biotechnology company that specialises in genetic engineering. Use a computer graphics or design package to make a sample letterhead including the name and logo.

## Stevens and Wilson

Nettie Stevens (1861–1912) discovered that X and Y chromosomes determine gender. She was one of the first female scientists to become famous in her time. She was born in Cavendish, Vermont, USA. Her father was a carpenter and handyman. He was successful so could afford to send all his children to school. Nettie Stevens was a brilliant pupil, always coming top of the class. In 1896 Stevens went to California to university. Her study there involved lots of work with a microscope and precise, careful detailing of what she saw. This training in observation skills helped her in her later investigations of chromosome behaviour.

Edmund Beecher Wilson was born in 1856 in Geneva, Illinois, USA. He died in 1939. He was the son of a judge, but instead of the law, Wilson chose to study biology at Yale University. Wilson's training was in the field of embryology; genetics did not exist as a science at that time. Between 1885 and 1891 Wilson travelled to Europe to continue his investigations. Cytology, the study of cells, was becoming increasingly important, and Wilson soon became an expert in this new branch of science. He began investigating the role of heredity in cell development.

Wilson was asked to review Nettie Stevens' paper on the subject of sex cells. Wilson's own paper on the same subject was already about to be printed when he read Stevens' paper. Both Wilson and Stevens are credited with the theory of sex determination by chromosomes, which they arrived at independently.

This little piece of history shows that individual scientists can arrive at the same conclusions at about the same time.

1 Can you think of an example from your own experience when you discovered that your way of solving a problem or carrying out an investigation was similar to someone else's, even though you had not discussed it?

*Time to think*

**1** List these items in order of size, staring with the smallest: cell, chromosome, gene, DNA, nucleus, genome.

**2** Which of these statements are true and which are false?
- Genes are grouped together on chromosomes.
- Chromosomes are grouped together into genes.
- DNA is a larger molecule than sugar.
- A genome is a large gene.
- All living things contain genetic information.
- A double helix is shaped like a string of beads.
- DNA is found in the cytoplasm of a cell.
- A gene map would show what a genome contained.

---

**Key word**
* evolution

# Evolution

Geologists estimate that the world is 4500 million years old, and that life originated 3500 million years ago. Life on Earth changes constantly over time, and this change is referred to as **evolution**. Evolution is a process by which new types of organisms develop from existing organisms.

The naturalist Charles Darwin spent many years observing the great varieties of organisms. He realised that when organisms compete for food, any variation that enables an organism to survive will increase its chance of producing fertile offspring.

Darwin studied finches on the Galapagos Islands, and observed that from one island to another the birds were slightly different. He believed that they had developed from one kind that reached the islands from different lands a long time ago, and that they had evolved to feed on different foods.

In 1859 Darwin's work was published in *'On the origin of species by means of natural selection'*. This was met with some controversy, like Galileo's work was before him. Darwin's ideas did not agree with that of the Church, which followed the teachings of the Bible that the world and all the animals and plants in it had been created in seven days.

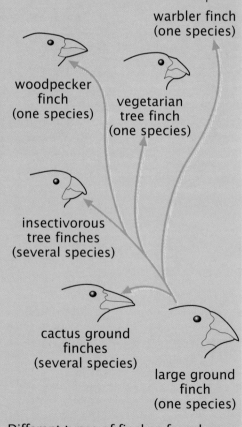

warbler finch
(one species)

woodpecker finch
(one species)

vegetarian tree finch
(one species)

insectivorous tree finches
(several species)

cactus ground finches
(several species)

large ground finch
(one species)

Different types of finches found on the Galapagos Islands, all originating from the large ground finch.

---

ON

# THE ORIGIN OF SPECIES

BY MEANS OF NATURAL SELECTION,

OR THE

PRESERVATION OF FAVOURED RACES IN THE STRUGGLE
FOR LIFE.

By CHARLES DARWIN, M.A.,

FELLOW OF THE ROYAL, GEOLOGICAL, LINNÆAN, ETC., SOCIETIES;
AUTHOR OF 'JOURNAL OF RESEARCHES DURING H. M. S. BEAGLE'S VOYAGE
ROUND THE WORLD.'

LONDON:
JOHN MURRAY, ALBEMARLE STREET.
1859.

*The right of Translation is reserved.*

*Information processing*

## What do you know?

In Years 7 and 8 you looked at the ways in which some plants and animals are adapted to suit their environments. In your group, list the adaptations you can remember for each of these:

- cactus
- fungus
- fox
- rabbit
- dandelion.

In Chapter 6 you read about the development of wheat (see pages 175–176). The first type of wheat plants grown were einkorn or emmer. How were these plants adapted by wheat-breeding programmes to produce better varieties for farmers to plant and grow?

Now assess your group's understanding of 'adaptation'. Which of these statements describe your group?

- We are very confident about the biological meaning of 'adaptation' and can give lots of different examples.
- We know what 'adaptation' means but we need to recall more examples.
- We are not sure we understand this – we need help!

*Word play*

Here are some sentences using forms of the word 'adaptation':

- The leaves of a cactus plant are adapted to reduce water loss in the desert.
- Shakespeare's plays have been adapted for television.
- People who climb mountains at high altitudes for several weeks adapt to the lower oxygen content in the air they breathe by producing more red blood corpuscles (cells).
- When you leave a dark room your eyes take a few seconds to adapt to bright sunshine.
- Fish are adapted to live in water.
- Old tractor tyres can be adapted to make containers to grow potatoes in.

These sentences use 'adaptation' in three different ways. In some of them 'adaptation' is used biologically to indicate a process of short-term change that is reversible. In others the use is still biological but the changes are long-term and not reversible – they indicate a process of natural selection. Some of the statements use adaptation in a non-scientific way.

Discuss the statements with a partner and decide which statements belong in each category.

# ➡ *Artificial selection*

**Key words**
* artificial selection
* cull
* selective breeding
* breeds
* species
* natural selection

Archaeologists have found dog remains from 10 000 BC in Israel and Iraq. There are now over 500 distinct **breeds** of dog.

**Artificial selection** refers to the process of deliberately modifying plants and animals so that they are more useful to humans than the wild form. It is a kind of speeded-up evolution. Over hundreds and perhaps thousands of years humans have controlled which wild plants and animals breed. We can mate the best males and females together, then look at the offspring and select the best characteristics for our purposes. We can '**cull**' (kill) offspring that are not suitable or are weak. If this is done repeatedly over many generations then there is deliberate genetic change in the population.

Darwin bred pigeons to show how **selective breeding** could lead to greater variety. All varieties of pigeons today come from the rock dove.

The dog was probably the first animal to be domesticated by humans. It was domesticated from the wolf about 13 000 years ago, by selective breeding.

*Research* Darwin argued that the great variety within domestic animal **species**, for example, pigeons and pigs, supported his theories about evolution. Do you think it does?

Find out more about **natural selection** and why modern understanding of genetics leads scientists to think Darwin's theories were largely useful and probably correct.

29 What features do all the dogs in the photographs and their wolf ancestor share?
30 Which features are unique to the collie (sheep dog), and which are unique to the greyhound?
31 Why do you think these features have been selectively bred into each of these dog varieties?
32 How do breeders make sure the right kind of puppies grow to adults and are used for reproduction?

## *Reasoning* *Better breeds*

Friesian cow.

Hereford bull.

A Friesian–Hereford cross.

**1** Look at the photographs and list the features that the offspring has inherited from the Hereford parent and the features it has inherited from the Friesian parent.

    Friesian cows are good milk producers, while Herefords are known for their beef. What do you think the cattle breeder is looking for in a good cross?

| | |
|---|---|
| **Organism** | |
| **Characteristic** | |
| **Why desirable/useful** | |

**2** In your group, imagine you are responsible for some plant- and animal-breeding programmes. Draw up a table like the one on the left.

For each of the following plants and animals, decide which characteristics you would try to develop by selectively breeding and why you think those characteristics might be desirable:

- pig
- sheep
- cow

- dog
- wheat
- tomato

- daffodil
- lettuce.

Some characteristics or variables can be observed easily, but others may be 'invisible', for example, resistance to mildew or cold, good flavour, faster or slower ripening time.

Different types of lettuce.

Different types of tomato.

*Enquiry* Peas

The photographs show a range of supermarket pea products. For each product specific characteristics have been bred into the peas.

Design an investigation to compare the characteristics of the different varieties, for example, taste, texture, size, tenderness, cooking time.

**1** Frame a question for your group to investigate.

**2** Will you look at all the pea products or just a few?

**3** How will you make sure the sampling method is representative?

**4** Decide on your method and apparatus.

**5** What do your data indicate? Evaluate your investigation process.

# Mutations

**Key words**
* mutate
* mutation
* mutant
* resistance
* gene pool
* hybrid
* gene therapy

Genes can **mutate**. A **mutation** is a spontaneous and sudden change in a gene which may produce a difference in the organism. Some mutations may be caused by environmental factors such as nuclear radiation; others seem to occur without any apparent external cause.

A **mutant** is an organism that carries a mutation. Most people think that a mutation is always a bad thing, but mutations may be bad or good for the organism or may make no difference. If a mutation gives an organism an advantage over the rest of the population then the mutation may be passed on to the offspring and, over time, may become a common characteristic. The development of **resistance** of some bacteria to antibiotics is an example of this.

The genomes of all the individuals in a population make up the **gene pool** for that population. Many mutations do not give advantages or disadvantages; they are simply variations of that characteristic in the population. If a mutation is a disadvantage for an organism then it is highly likely that the organism will die before reproducing, or be infertile, so that the mutation is likely to 'die out' of the population.

Find out about rare breed centres and national plant collections. Why do you think people put time, money and effort into creating them?

**TILGATE PARK**
**NATURE CENTRE**
*...a refuge for the rare*

Rare breed centre.

Forestry Commission

**BEDGEBURY**

The National Pinetum

and Forest Garden

A national plant collection.

**DID YOU KNOW?**

A 'gwan' is a rare animal with the body of a large black swan and the feet and honking noise of a goose. It is an infertile **hybrid** from goose and swan parents.

Many human diseases are caused by gene mutations. It may be possible to treat these by using human **gene therapy**. For example, if a protein is missing from the body because a gene is faulty, a good copy of the gene which makes that protein can be introduced into blood cells. The blood is then returned to the patient's body and the cells will multiply and make the required protein.

**DID YOU KNOW?**

In 1990 French Anderson and Michael Blaese treated 4-year-old Ashanti DiSilva using genetic engineering methods. She suffered from a genetic disease that kills T lymphocytes. This disease meant that even minor infections could be fatal for Ashanti. She had to live totally isolated from other people, in sterile conditions. After the genetic manipulation, Ashanti can now be hugged by her parents without any sterile barriers in the way, and goes to a normal school.

# *Cloning*

**Cloning** is reproduction which is **asexual** – it does not involve sex cells. Instead a cell divides so that each of the two 'daughter cells' still contains the identical number and type of chromosomes found in the original cell.

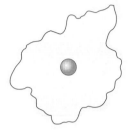 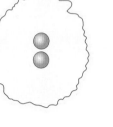 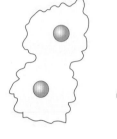 

parent *Amoeba*     nucleus divides     cytoplasm divides     daughter cells separate

Gardeners clone organisms regularly; they cut potato tubers in half to grow new potato plants that are identical in their genetic make-up to the original potato, and they take cuttings to propagate plants such as ivy and geraniums.

*Time to think*

This image shows the chromosomes from a human embryo. They have been arranged in pairs.

Look at the image of the human chromosomes.

1 What is special about the 23rd pair?
2 Is this embryo male or female? How do you know?
3 Can you tell which chromosome in each pair came from the sperm cell and which from the egg cell?

---

# STOP PRESS!

An American clinic is advertising a 'designer baby' service. For just $100 000 you can make sure your baby will look the way you want it to. All designer babies will be guaranteed free of inherited diseases.

---

4 Do you think this report is true?
5 If it is true, why do you think some people would want to close the clinic down? Do you think designer babies should be allowed?
6 If this article was about 'designer wheat' or 'designer rice', would you have a different opinion? Would people opposed to designer babies have a different opinion?
7 Make an animated PowerPoint presentation that your group could use to explain why Mendel's work with pea populations was so important for the understanding of the way inheritance works.
8 Evaluate each group's presentation using the 'traffic light' system:

Green dot = excellent use of animations to show how pea characteristics are inherited; clear explanations.
Amber dot = a good explanation but a bit boring.

Red dot = confusing and not very helpful for explaining Mendel's work.

# 8 Pressure and moments

**In this chapter you will learn:**

→ the key ideas about pressure
→ about the relationship between force, area and pressure between solids and within liquids and gases
→ about the action of levers, including examples in the human skeleton, in terms of the turning effect of a force
→ to use the principle of moments to explain balance and give examples of its application
→ the definition of pressure and how to use it in calculations to explain the operation of a range of devices
→ about the relationship of hydrostatic pressure and density in liquids and gases
→ to apply the principle of moments to explain a range of situations, including the action of levers

**You will also develop your skills in:**

→ planning investigations, making sufficient observations with precision, identifying patterns in results and using them to draw conclusions
→ accounting for anomalies in observations and evaluating your conclusions

---

## →→→ WHAT DO YOU KNOW?

**1** Construct a concept map to show your current understanding of forces. Think about different types of forces and how we deal with forces in our everyday lives.

**2** Some Year 6 children made the following statements:

'Weight is a type of mass.'
'Weight is a pull.'
'Weight is not affected by gravity.'
'An object has a mass whether or not there is gravity.'
'A falling mass has weight because of gravity.'
'Weight is a force.'
'An increase in gravity increases an object's mass and weight.'
'There is tremendous weight pushing down on the centre of the Earth because of so many people and things pressing down on it these days.'

Discuss in your group whether each of these statements is correct or not.

Examples of forces in action.

Forces and their effects is an important theme in science. In everyday language, we describe a force as a push or a pull. When forces act on something they can have different effects. For example, a force can change the direction of movement of an object.

**3** What other effects can a force have? For each effect, give an example to help explain it.

We can look at forces when objects are weighed in air and again in a liquid.

**4** How do the readings on a newton meter change when an object is weighed first in air and then in water?

**5** Suppose the object was weighed in a liquid less dense than water, such as methylated spirits. How would the new reading compare to the previous two readings?

**6** If you hold in your hand a ball that floats, and lower it into water, how do the forces acting on the ball change?

**7** When the ball is floating, what forces are acting on it?

**8** When you push the ball down to the bottom of the container, in which direction is the force acting? What is this force called?

# Floating and sinking

If you walk down the steps into a swimming pool you begin to float when nearly all your body is in the water. You feel lighter. This is because the water has **upthrust**.

*Reasoning*   *Floating in water*

Here is a sequence of drawings that shows the effect of upthrust on Peter as he walks into a pool full of water.

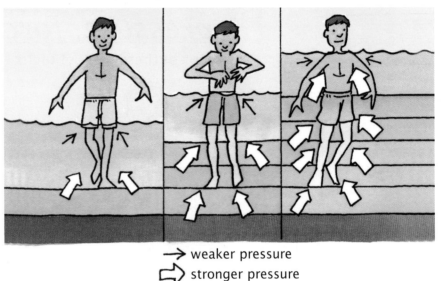

→ weaker pressure

⇨ stronger pressure

1 In pairs, discuss what is happening in each of the three drawings, and why Peter can float on his back.

2 If Peter weighs 500 N, what weight of water is **displaced** when he floats? Is it 50 kg, 50 N, 500 kg or 500 N?

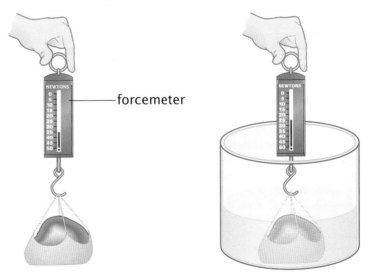

forcemeter

3 Why does the lump of rock have a different weight in the beaker of water?

4 Do objects float more easily in fresh water or salt water? Why?

*Word play*

As we have already seen, words can have a very precise meaning in science although they may be used in a more general way in everyday life. Force was one such word. Pressure is another.

Write down two sentences in which the word pressure is used scientifically, and another sentence in which it is used more generally. Compare your sentences with others in the group.

# ➡ The relationship between pressure, force and area

Look at these pairs of pictures.

**Key words**
* force
* area
* pressure
* pascals

plasticine

In each pair of pictures the effective **force** is the same. For example, in the first pair of pictures the force is the weight of the bag. However in the left hand picture the strap is cutting into the boy's shoulder and is therefore more uncomfortable than the strap in the right hand picture, which has a wide pad where it is in contact with the shoulder. In each pair of pictures, the **area** over which the force is acting differs. In the left hand pictures the area is smaller than in the right hand pictures. We say that the **pressure** is less in the right hand situations.

Pressure depends on two measurable variables – the area and the force applied to that area. Pressure is *force per area*, and is calculated as the ratio of force to area.

It can be written as a formula:

$$\text{pressure} = \frac{\text{force}}{\text{area}}$$

Pressure is measured in newtons per square metre ($N/m^2$), more usually called **pascals** (Pa). It is often more convenient to use a smaller unit, the newton per square cm ($N/cm^2$).

Pressure is a compound variable; it is made up from two other variables interacting together.

A neat trick is to show a ratio relationship using a triangle diagram. You have now got a kind of 'calculator'. The equation above is useful when tackling problems where you need to work out pressure and you know about the force being applied and the area it is being applied to. However, if you need to calculate force and you know the pressure and area, cover the letter F in the triangle and you will see that:

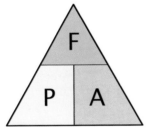

**F**orce = **P**ressure × **A**rea

1 Using the triangle, write a formula to find area.
2 Using the triangle, write a formula to find pressure.

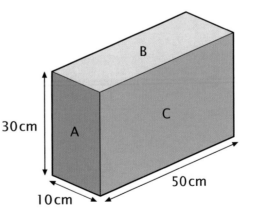

3 a) The diagram above shows a block. It weighs 25 kg (25 000 g). Calculate the area of each of the surfaces (A, B and C).

The block is placed on some sand.

b) Redraw the block to show which surface it should stand on to reduce how far it sinks into the sand.

c) Draw the block standing on the surface on which it would sink furthest into the sand.

d) On which surfaces would it exert the most pressure?

e) Calculate the greatest pressure and the least pressure.

_Research_ Why do you think the unit of pressure is called a pascal? How could you find out if you are right?

Blaise Pascal.
Born: 1623 in Clermont-Ferrand, Auvergne, France.
Died: 1662 in Paris, France.

Many other units for pressure are used in everyday life, and this makes the measurement of pressure quite complicated. For example, the pressure of a car tyre used to be measured in psi (pounds per square inch). In modern car handbooks the pressure may be quoted in 'bars'.

This table shows some of the units you may come across and their connection to the pascal.

| Name | Relation | Where it may be used |
|---|---|---|
| psi (pound per square inch) | 6895 Pa | car tyre pressure |
| atmosphere (atm) | 101 325 Pa | weather forecasting |
| bar (and millibar) | 100 000 Pa (exactly) | weather forecasting |
| mm of mercury (mm Hg) | 133.32 Pa | blood pressure older science books |
| inch of mercury | 3386.39 Pa | USA |
| torr (the same as 1 mm Hg) | 133.32 Pa | used in low-pressure engineering |

_Enquiry_  ## Planning an investigation

Look back at the bag and ski pictures on page 222. In your group, select one of these pictures to model in the classroom – you will not be getting the chance to go to the ski slopes to test out your ideas!

Plan an investigation to explore the effects of pressure. You will need to think about how to make simple models of bags or skis and snow shoes. Scale and proportion will be important. Remember to identify the dependent and independent variables, predict the outcome, and say how you will record your data.

# → Calculating pressure

In Book 1 we explained the difference between mass and weight. We also discuss it in this book in Chapter 4, Forces and space. Make sure that you are clear about the difference between mass and weight.

4 Write a sentence to explain the difference between mass and weight. Look at the explanation given by your neighbour and together produce a sentence to explain the difference.

The picture shows a shoe with a stiletto heel. The area of the heel is 1 cm². A girl who weighs 500 N wears the shoe.

To calculate the pressure she would exert let us say that she is standing with just her heels on the ground. They cover a total area of 2 cm². Pressure = force/area, so:

$$\text{pressure} = \frac{500}{2}$$

$$= 250 \, \text{N/cm}^2$$

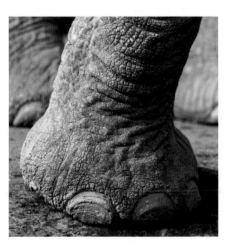

Now think of an elephant. The estimated size of this elephant's footprint is 400 cm². With all four feet on the ground the area in contact with the ground will be:

$$4 \times 400 = 1600 \, \text{cm}^2$$

An elephant will typically have a mass of 2 tonnes (2000 kg). It would exert a downward force on the ground of 20 000 N. So the pressure is given by:

$$\text{pressure} = \frac{20\,000}{1600}$$

$$= 12.5 \, \text{N/cm}^2$$

5 If you had laid a new wooden floor, who would cause most damage walking across it – the elephant or the girl wearing the stilettos? Why?

6 How could you model this to prove you are right?

A crazy thought – what pressure would the elephant exert if it could put on a pair of stiletto shoes? How did you work that out?

---

*Creative thinking*   ## Sinking competition

Hold a competition between the groups in your class to make a piece of plasticine sink as slowly as possible through a column of liquid. First make up a list of rules for the competition to make sure it is fair. After the competition, explain why some shapes were slow to sink while others were faster.

## *Enquiry* Force experiment

Look at the equipment shown in the diagram. It can be used to perform an experiment to look at the effects of force and surface area. As well as the newton balance, there are soft plasticine or modelling clay and a selection of dowel rods of different cross-sectional areas. Design an experiment to investigate the effect of (i) force, and (ii) area on the depth that the rods sink into the clay.

Here are some results obtained by a group doing an experiment using equipment similar to that described above. Each rod sank exactly the same depth into the clay.

| Cross-sectional area of rod (cm²) | Force (N) |
|---|---|
| 0.5 | 19 |
| 1 | 41.5 |
| 2 | 81 |
| 4 | 160.5 |

**1** What is the relationship between the variables?

**2** What type of graph would you use to show these results? Sketch the graph and label the axes remembering to include the units. Give your graph a title.

**3** If a rod with a cross-sectional area of 3 cm² was used, what force would need to be applied to produce the same indentation in the clay?

## *Creative thinking* Three-legged chair

Think about designing a three-legged chair. What would it look like? What are its advantages and disadvantages compared with a conventional four-legged chair?

# ➡ *Under pressure*

Look at these pairs of pictures.

7 For each pair decide which is the best option.

8 a) In your group, make a list of examples of situations where it is helpful to exert low pressure. Some examples have already been mentioned in this chapter.

b) Now make a list of examples that depend on applying high pressure.

c) Compare your group's lists with other groups', and make two large class posters of all the examples you have thought of.

*Creative thinking* ## Sports products

Read the article below from a financial newspaper and discuss the following questions with your partner:

1 What do you think about the company's new products? Would you invest your money in this company?

2 What properties would you want snow shoes to have, and why?

3 What properties would you want ice skates to have, and why?

4 Rewrite the article and rename the company so that their products stand a better chance of success.

---

## Expansion of sports manufacturer

**R**OLIF LOPA, the well known Italian sports manufacturer, has announced its expansion into the winter sports market with its new range announced today in Cortina. The initial range of products will include new cutting-edge technology snow shoes. These are constructed from high density copper and steel alloy with a smaller surface area than those produced by any other manufacturer. They guarantee faster sinking through snow and even mud and sand or your money back.

The company are also producing a range of ice skates with an innovative new base consisting of no less than three parallel blades per shoe, each constructed from flexible wide contact area plastic.

*Financial Review, 1ˢᵗ April 2003*

---

# ➡ Pressure of liquids

We know that the further a diver descends into the sea, the greater the pressure that he experiences. Pressure increases with depth. At 10 metres below the surface the pressure has increased to 2 atmospheres. Some watches are guaranteed to 5 atmospheres pressure. This means that they will work underwater at a depth where the pressure is five times greater than at the surface.

The picture shows a simple demonstration of this effect using a large plastic cola bottle with holes drilled in the side. In fact, the pressure depends not only on the depth, but also on the density of the liquid.

Another thing you should note is that the pressure of the water in the bottle is not only acting downwards, but on the sides as well. We can see this because the water is squirting out sideways from the holes.

A liquid under high pressure can dissolve more gas than a liquid at a lower pressure. When you open a bottle of lemonade, the pressure in the bottle is decreased. The liquid can no longer hold as much gas. The dissolved gas comes out of solution and rises to the surface of the liquid in bubbles.

*Reasoning*  Divers

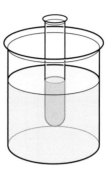

When the test tube is empty, it floats in the beaker, which contains 500 cm³ of water. When it is full of water it sinks.

David makes the test tube 'swim', neither floating nor sinking, so that it is in equilibrium. He does this by using a dropper to remove small amounts of water from the test tube until the tube just floats. You can see the air in the top of the test tube.

**1** Why do you think the test tube is swimming now?

David then adds one or two more drops of water to the tube so that it just begins to sink. Now it's a 'sinker'. He takes the tube out of the beaker and adds about four teaspoonfuls of salt to the water in the beaker. He stirs it until the salt dissolves.

**2** What do you think happens to his test tube when he puts it in the beaker now? Will it float or sink?

**3** Write down your group's prediction and explanation of why you think that.

**4** How could you test your prediction?

**5** You might need to know the volume of the test tube. How would you find this? Describe the method you would use. (HINT – Think of Archimedes.)

**6** What can you say about the density of the tube if it floats in water?

**7** What can you say about the density of the tube if it sinks in paraffin?

**8** Write a general rule that describes whether a solid object will float or sink in a liquid.

# ➡ *Liquid levels*

Read the following expression: 'A liquid always finds its own level.' From our knowledge of pressure, we can see why this must be so. In the diagram below the tap is initially closed. Water is then added into the left hand side. When the tap is opened, the water will flow into the right hand side as shown. The pressure depends on the height of the water. The pressure at X due to the column of water on the left will be the same as the pressure at Y due to the column of water on the right when the height of the water is the same on both sides.

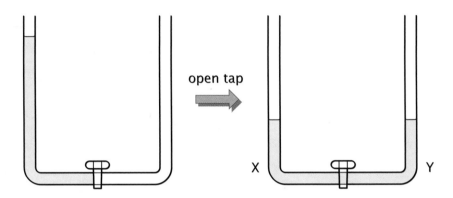

Look at the diagram below. If some water is poured into the right hand section of this strange container to the height shown, where will the water rise to in the other sections?

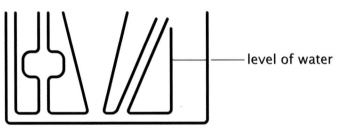

Builders often use the levelling effect of water during construction. A length of plastic tubing is filled with water and the two ends are placed apart at the two places where the heights need to be the same. The height of the water at the two ends is the same if the ground is level, so looking at the picture it follows that the ground here must be sloping.

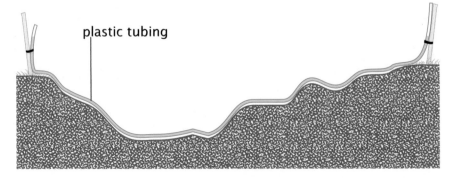

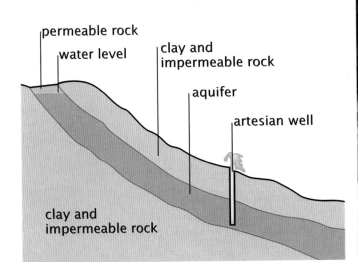

An artesian well.

Fountain at Witley Court.

Water for the fountain in the photograph above was pumped by a huge steam engine from the nearby Hundred Pool to a reservoir at New Wood, well above the height of the Court. This extra height was needed to maintain the pressure necessary to supply a fountain comprising 120 nozzles with a main jet capable of reaching over 100 feet (about 35 metres) into the air. The necessary pipe work was hidden away in tunnels so that the gentry could not see servants scurrying around to open the valves when the fountains played twice a week. Water from this fountain was 'recycled' to the smaller Flora or Triton Fountain on the east side.

9 Look at the pictures above and find out how each water feature depends on pressure for its operation. Write a paragraph that could accompany the pictures.

When reservoirs are constructed, the walls of the dam need to be very strong because of the large pressure exerted by water at the base. Reservoirs are a source of water for drinking and irrigation, and dams can be used to generate electricity.

Dam of the Clywedog reservoir, Wales.

wall of dam

Explain how our ideas of pressure can be used to explain the term 'upthrust'. Look back to the questions on page 220. If you answered these correctly you will know that the force acting upwards is upthrust. Use the drawing below to help you. Do the forces on the sides balance out? How about the forces on the top and bottom?

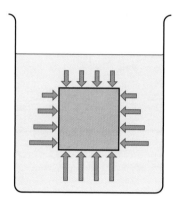

# → *Hydraulic systems*

**Key words**
* compress
* hydraulic press

You should already know that compared to gases, liquids are very difficult to **compress**. This is because the particles are much more tightly bound together in a liquid than in a gas. Liquids are more dense than gases. It is quite easy to put a cork into a bottle containing air, but if you try to push it into a bottle completely full of water it is impossible because you cannot compress the water.

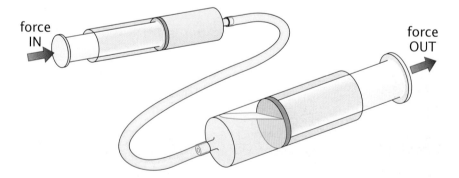

Look at the drawing above showing two syringes joined together. One syringe is large; the other is small. They are both filled with water. If you place your thumbs on the plunger of the syringes and press the plunger of the small syringe you can feel the forces. Water goes through the connecting tube into the large syringe. The pressure in the water is the same throughout, but the forces are different because of the different areas of cross-section of the syringes. This apparatus demonstrates the principle of the **hydraulic press**.

# Some applications of pressure

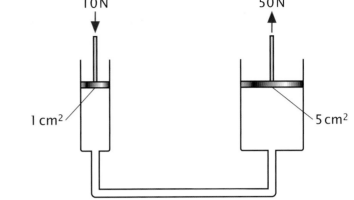

Joseph Bramah invented the hydraulic press around 1795. The principle is shown in the diagram above. If the force on the left hand side is 10 N, the pressure exerted on the water by the left hand **piston** can be calculated using the formula:

$$\text{pressure} = \frac{\text{force}}{\text{area}}$$

$$\text{pressure} = \frac{10}{1} = 10\,\text{N/cm}^2$$

As the pressure is the same throughout the liquid, the pressure exerted on the other piston is the same, i.e. 10 N/cm$^2$. Therefore, pressure out = 10 N/cm$^2$. As the pressure is constant, the greater the area of the piston, the greater is the size of the outward force.

As we saw on page 223, the pressure formula can be rearranged so we can use it to calculate the outward force:

force = pressure × area

force = 10 × 5 = 50 N

The hydraulic press is used extensively in industry. A similar device, the **hydraulic jack**, is used in garages. Here the force exerted is much less than the **load** (the car). Note, however, that the distance moved by the load is less than the distance the jack is moved by the person's force.

10 In the above example, the **effort** is 10 N and the load is 50 N. If the load moved up through 3 cm, how far would the effort have had to have moved?

In 1784 Joseph Bramah patented the Bramah safety lock. His lock was considered unpickable until it was finally picked in 1851. He also invented a beer pump, a quill sharpener and methods of paper-making, and improved fire engines and printing machines. In 1806 Bramah patented a machine for printing banknotes that was used by the Bank of England.

Joseph Bramah (1748–1814).

A car raised by an hydraulic jack.

The principle of hydraulics is also used in the brakes of a car:

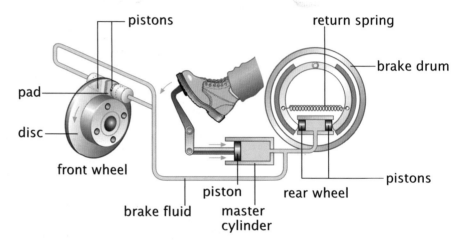

11 Explain the main idea behind hydraulic lifts and jacks.

# → *Pneumatic systems*

Differences in air pressure, just like differences in liquid pressure, can also be used to do work. Air-driven systems are **pneumatic**.

*Word play*

1 The French word *pneumatique* means relating to air or gas. In French, *pneu* is a tyre.
   The French word for a mattress is *matelas*. What do you think *matelas pneumatique* means?
2 In medicine, *pneumonia* refers to the air passages (lungs) being infected. What do you think *pneumothorax*, another medical term, means?

**Key words**
* vacuum
* atmospheric pressure

# Experiments on the atmosphere and atmospheric pressure

In the seventeenth century European scientists made many discoveries about air pressure. In France, work was done by Blaire Pascal. In Italy, Torricelli suggested ideas about a **vacuum**. In Germany, Otto von Guericke performed his now famous experiments with vacuums and, in England, Robert Boyle was working on gases.

1  The collapsing can experiment was described in Book 1. Explain what happened in this experiment? Why did it happen?

### Steam pressure

In 1712 Thomas Newcomen invented the first steam engine, which was used to pump water out of mines. The next major development came when James Watt invented a far more efficient steam engine with a separate condenser. He made big improvements to Newcomen's steam engine.

Many ideas led to the development of the steam engine: the concept of a vacuum and how to make one; an understanding of pressure; methods for generating steam; and the invention of the piston and cylinder.

The idea of using steam under pressure to do work had been around for some time before Newcomen began his investigations. One of the earliest records is of Hero of Alexandria in about 100 AD. In 1698 Thomas Savery, an English military engineer, had developed a steam-powered water pump.

In Newcomen's steam engine, steam passes from the boiler through a valve into the cylinder. This balances the **atmospheric pressure** on the upper side of the piston and allows the weight of the pump rod, connected to the piston rod by a beam balanced on a fulcrum, to raise the piston. This allows the valve between the boiler and the cylinder to close and a jet of water is sprayed into the cylinder. This produces a vacuum by condensing the steam, so the atmospheric pressure on the upper side of this piston forces it downward, lifting the pump rod by means of the beam. This whole cycle may be repeated.

### Vacuum pumps

You may have seen an experiment in which a balloon is inflated by removing the air from around it. A balloon is partially blown up (and tied off), then placed inside a bell jar. The air is then pumped out of the bell jar and the balloon inflates.

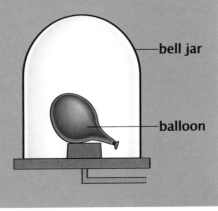
bell jar
balloon

2  Explain why the balloon inflates as the air is removed.

The German engineer and physicist Otto von Guericke (1602–1686) built the first vacuum pump and used it to create vacuums in various containers. Previously, it was thought that it was impossible for a vacuum to exist. In 1654, Guericke carried out his famous 'Magdeburg hemispheres' demonstration. This used two joined hemispheres from which the air had been removed. Two teams of eight horses could not pull them apart because the pressure of the Earth's atmosphere was acting on the outside of the spheres to hold them together.

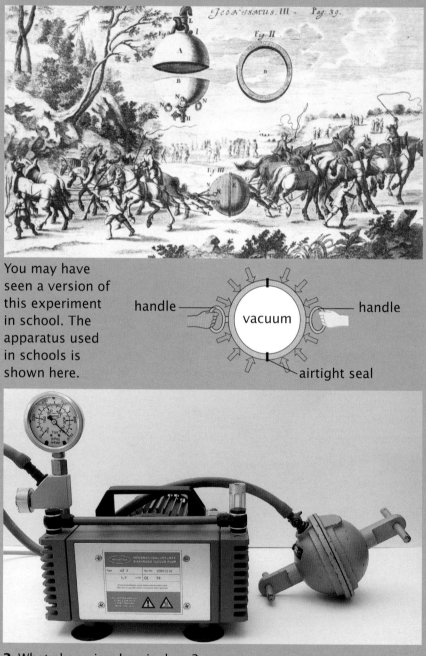

You may have seen a version of this experiment in school. The apparatus used in schools is shown here.

handle — vacuum — handle

airtight seal

3  What shape is a hemisphere?
4  Draw the school apparatus and add arrows to show where atmospheric pressure is acting.
5  What do you think is inside the hemispheres once the air has been removed?

*Enquiry* ## Rubber suckers

Design an experiment to investigate the action of rubber suckers. Think about a question you want to answer, for example:

- What would dislodge the rubber sucker?
- Do differently shaped suckers have different sticking properties, and if so, why?
- How do the different surfaces the sucker is attached to affect sticking time?

Write down full instructions for your experiment.

*Time to think*

The particle theory for pressure was first discussed in Book 1. We used the particle model to explain the different properties of solids, liquids and gases. Think back to your earlier work to explain the ideas of air pressure in terms of moving particles. Look at the sentences below and match each first half to its correct ending. Write the full sentences in your exercise book.

| | |
|---|---|
| Air consists of | with each other and everything around them. |
| The particles collide | different speeds. |
| Different particles move at | they bounce back with the same average kinetic energy. |
| When the particles hit the side of a container | a mixture of particles moving all the time. |

Now think about the particles of air contained in a tin can with a tightly fitting lid as it is being heated.

heat

| | |
|---|---|
| The air particles moving around inside the can will | they gain energy and move faster. |
| As the particles get hotter | the pressure inside the can increases. |
| They hit the sides of the container harder and | hit each other and the sides of the can. |

Now think about the collapsing can experiment again.

| | |
|---|---|
| In the collapsing can experiment, initially | there are no air particles hitting the inside of the can. |
| As the air is removed, | there is air inside the can exerting the same pressure as outside. |
| The pressure inside the can falls to zero because | there are fewer air particles hitting the outside of the can and the pressure inside the can decreases. |
| The pressure on the outside of the can | makes the can collapse. |

# The manometer

A U tube **manometer** is a useful device for measuring pressure differences. It may be used to measure gas pressures. It contains water which is forced to move when there is a pressure difference between the two ends of the tube. The difference between the two water levels is a measure of the gas pressure. A large version of this device can be used to measure your lung pressure.

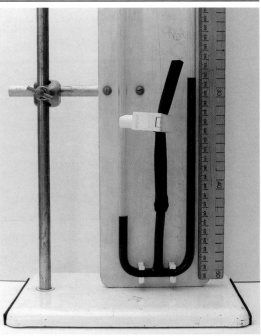

*Enquiry* Manometer

Devise an experiment to investigate whether there is any relationship between lung capacity and lung pressure.
Set up a spreadsheet exercise for this activity.

# The pressure exerted by the Earth's atmosphere

The Frenchman Blaise Pascal suggested that the air pressure decreases as we go higher. He and his father investigated this by measuring the pressure at the foot of the Puy-de-Dôme (a mountain in the Auvergne region of France) and the pressure at the summit. They found that the air pressure was less at the summit. If you have access to a digital pressure sensor, perhaps you could compare the pressure at the foot and at the top of a tall building.

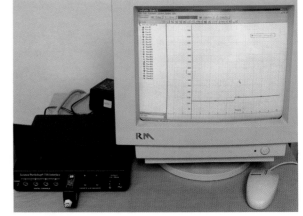

The pressure exerted by the Earth's **atmosphere** has been demonstrated by experiments such as the collapsing can. We effectively live at the bottom of an ocean of air. At sea-level, there is the maximum amount of air above us, so the air pressure is at its greatest. We now know that the pressure exerted by the air at sea-level is about 100 000 Pa. The pressure decreases as we go up – this is because the higher we go, the less tightly air particles are packed. In everyday language, we say that higher up the air is 'thinner'. Mountaineers carry oxygen supplies with them to help them to breathe at high **altitudes**. We know that our atmosphere extends to a height of several kilometres, and that air pressure falls as we go up. The atmosphere doesn't suddenly end, it just becomes less and less.

**DID YOU KNOW?**

New Zealander Sir Edmund Hillary and Nepalese Sherpa Tenzing Norgay scaled 8848 m high Mount Everest on 29th May, 1953. They are credited with being the first people to do so.

The photograph shows Sir Edmund Hillary wearing full climbing gear and carrying open circuit oxygen apparatus.

Peter Habeler, an Austrian, and Reinhold Messner, an Italian, were the first to reach the summit of Mount Everest without the aid of bottled oxygen, in 1978.

Sir Edmund Hillary, 1953.

*Information processing*    *Air pressure*

The data in this table show the variation of air pressure with height.

| Altitude (height above sea-level) (m) | Pressure (kPa) |
|---|---|
| 10 | 101 130 |
| 101 | 100 090 |
| 500 | 95 650 |
| 1005 | 90 290 |
| 2503 | 75 760 |
| 4002 | 63 240 |
| 5002 | 55 890 |
| 8001 | 37 890 |
| 10 003 | 28 730 |
| 12 502 | 19 800 |
| 15 967 | 11 100 |

1 Plot a graph of the data. You could use Excel or some other graphing package.

2 Use your graph to answer the following questions:
   a) Ben Nevis, the highest mountain in Scotland, is 1342 m high. Estimate the air pressure at the top of Ben Nevis.
   b) Mont Blanc on the French–Italian border is 4808 m high. Estimate the air pressure at the top of Mont Blanc.
   c) Everest is 8848 m high. Estimate the air pressure at the top of Everest.
   d) What do your answers to parts a–c suggest about some of the equipment needed by mountaineers?
   e) What is the air pressure at the top of the troposphere (16 000 m)?
   f) A Boeing 747 aircraft cruises at a height of 12 000 m. What is the air pressure at this height?

*Information processing*   *Altitude*

In an experiment to see how air pressure varies with altitude, a remote datalogger with a pressure sensor attached was taken on a flight in a hot air balloon. The data obtained are given in the table. Use them to plot a graph and answer the following questions.

| Altitude (m) | Pressure (kPa) |
|---|---|
| 149 | 99.6 |
| 500 | 95.7 |
| 800 | 92.4 |
| 1140 | 88.9 |
| 1300 | 87.2 |
| 1500 | 85.3 |

1 What would the air pressure have been at sea-level?

2 At what altitude would the air pressure have been 90 kPa?

3 Besides the pressure and altitude, what other measurements would have been of interest to a scientist?

4 Devise a scale that would allow you to extend the graph so that you could find the altitude at which the air pressure would be zero.

# → *The barometer*

**Key words**
* barometer
* mercury

A device that measures air pressure is called a **barometer**. Evangelista Torricelli (1608–1647) suggested the first **mercury** barometer. It consisted of a 1 m long glass tube sealed at one end. The tube was filled with mercury then turned upside down, with the open end dipping into a bowl of mercury. The mercury level in the tube fell a little but not all the way. It dropped until the height of the mercury column was about 76 cm. Air is pressing down on the surface of the mercury in the bowl. As no air was allowed into the tube, there is no air in the region labelled A in the diagram below. It is a vacuum.

The column of mercury is exerting a pressure at the bottom of the tube. This pressure must exactly balance the atmospheric pressure on the surface of the mercury.

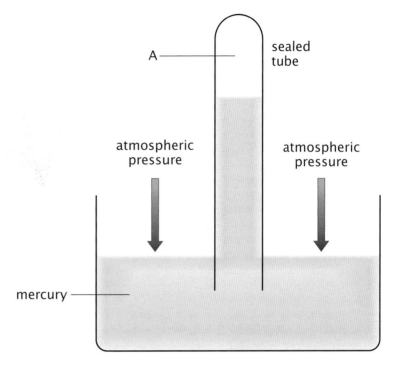

## The aneroid barometer

The aneroid barometer works on the same principle as the collapsing can. It consists of a metal box with strong sides and a spring lid, and it has had some air removed. A strong spring holds the lid to stop it being totally crushed. The middle of the lid is connected via levers to the pointer. As the air pressure alters, the lid flexes up and down. The levers magnify this movement and the pointer moves across the scale.

# Simple machines

We have seen that it is important to know the *direction* in which a force acts. We will now see that it is also important to know *where* forces act.

**Key words**
* lever
* pivot
* fulcrum

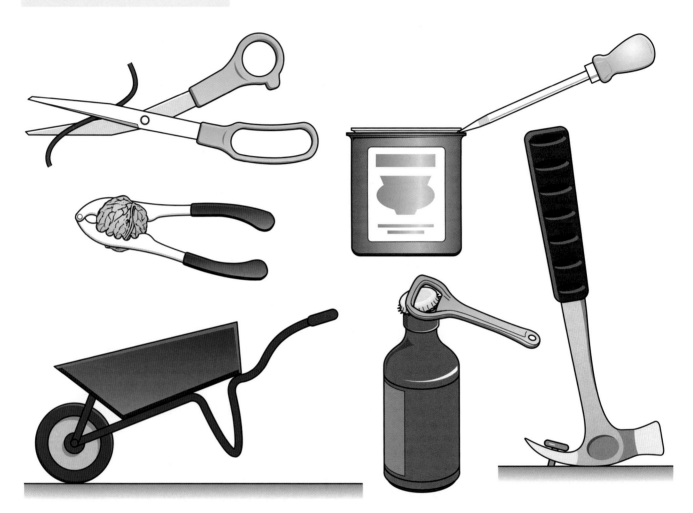

Look at the pictures of familiar objects. All these are examples of what we call a **lever**. A lever is a simple machine.

**12** A screwdriver is being used to open the lid of a tin of paint. If the tin were very tightly sealed, what sort of screwdriver would be better for levering the lid off?

**13** Where should our force be applied to lift this paving slab?

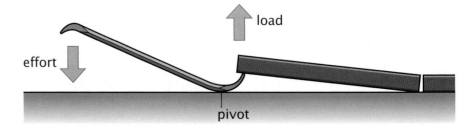

In the example in Question 13, the iron bar (crowbar) pivots around the point where it is in contact with the ground. (This **pivot** point is sometimes called the **fulcrum**.)

14 Look at the pictures opposite. In each case, identify where we should apply our force. (This force is called the effort). In each case, where is the pivot point and where is the load?

In the examples of the crowbar, the tin of paint, the claw hammer and the scissors, the effort is at one end, the load is at the other and the pivot is between the load and the effort (but closer to the load than the effort).

15 Look at the examples of the bottle opener, the wheelbarrow and the nutcrackers. Where are the load, effort and pivot in relation to each other in these cases?

There is a third group of examples, shown in the examples below. Here the effort is greater than the load. The pivot is at the opposite end to the load.

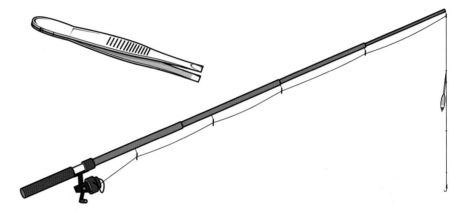

# Levers and joints

**Key words**
* contraction
* flexors
* extensors

Levers a little bit like the tweezers and fishing rod examples are found in the human body. One example is the biceps muscle in our forearm. Here, although the effort is more than the load, there is an advantage in the fact that a small **contraction** in the biceps moves the lower arm up through a large distance.

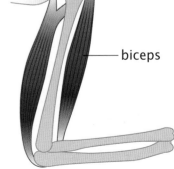

biceps

We can walk, run, lift objects, nod our heads and arm wrestle because we can move our bones against each other. Our bones and muscles make up a living system of levers. Muscles always work in pairs. **Flexors** bend limbs, and **extensors** straighten them.

The muscles in the thigh are the most powerful in the body.

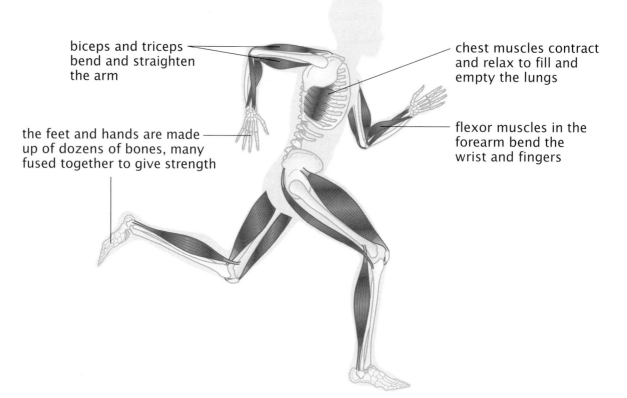

biceps and triceps
bend and straighten
the arm

chest muscles contract
and relax to fill and
empty the lungs

the feet and hands are made
up of dozens of bones, many
fused together to give strength

flexor muscles in the
forearm bend the
wrist and fingers

Some machines copy human systems. This mechanical
digger has pneumatic pistons and wires operating like
a hinge-jointed elbow and claws. Artificial limbs use the
same design.

**EXTENSION**

**Key words**
* anchorage
* antagonistic

## More details about the elbow joint and muscles

The movement of the arm about the elbow joint is brought
about by the contraction of several muscles that are
attached to the bones. The muscles are attached to the
bones by tendons. The main muscles are the biceps, the
triceps and the brachialis. The points of **anchorage** are on
the scapula (shoulder blade), the humerus and the radius
and ulna. The humerus is the bone connecting the scapula

to the elbow joint. The radius is the larger of the two bones in the forearm. As the muscles can only exert a force through contraction, there are two opposing muscles connected across the joint. One pulls in one direction and the other in the opposite direction. Muscles that are arranged in a pair like this to have opposite effects are called **antagonistic** muscles. The biceps cause the arm to be raised when the muscle contracts. It is the flexor muscle. (In fact, the biceps is not the only muscle that helps to bend the elbow. There is another muscle, called the brachialis, which is attached to the humerus and the ulna). When the triceps muscle contracts it causes the arm to straighten. The triceps is the extensor muscle. There are several such pairs of muscles in the human body.

The bones, muscles and elbow joint act like a lever in which the pivot is the elbow joint, the weight in the hand is the load and the effort is applied through the biceps to lift the arm. The muscles receive their instructions through impulses along the motor nerves.

*Information processing*

## How the arm moves

Copy the diagram below. Re-read the passage above and use the information to label the diagram. Now annotate the diagram to show which muscle raises the lower arm and which muscle lowers the arm. Also mark in where the load is acting. Show the distance of the load from the pivot. Draw and label an arrow to show the direction in which the arm moves when the triceps muscle contracts.

Write a sentence to explain what antagonistic pairs of muscles are.

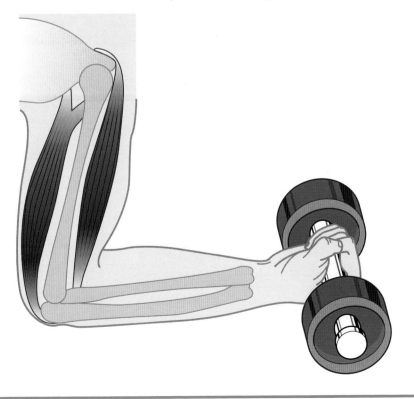

# Turning moments

When you exert a force on one end of a bar, it produces a **turning effect**. Think about pushing open a heavy door. To open the door you would push as far away from the hinge as possible. You could of course push in the middle of the door but it would be much harder.

The turning effect of a force depends not only on the size of the force, but also how far away the force is acting from the pivot point. We call this turning effect the **moment** of a force. The turning effect or moment of a force is calculated by multiplying the size of the force by the distance between the force and the pivot. (The angle at which the force acts is also important. The distance we measure is that drawn at right angles between the force and the pivot.)

*Time to think*

A moment is a compound variable. It is made up of two simple variables multiplied together. What other compound variables can you name?

# Balance

The turning effect that tends to pull down one side of the bar of the see-saw is called the moment on that side of the bar. When a system is in **balance** we call this being in **equilibrium**.

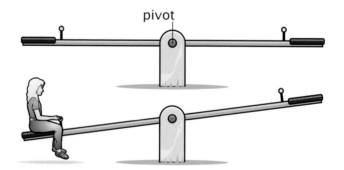

pivot

Look at the picture of the see-saw. In the second diagram a girl is sitting on the left hand side. It goes down, turning around the pivot. To return the see-saw to balance, someone would have to sit on the right hand side. This person would also produce a turning effect or moment.

16 When the see-saw is in equilibrium, what do you notice about the moment on the left hand side and the moment on the right hand side?

17 Make up a general rule to say what you need to do to keep a system in equilibrium if you change any of the variables.

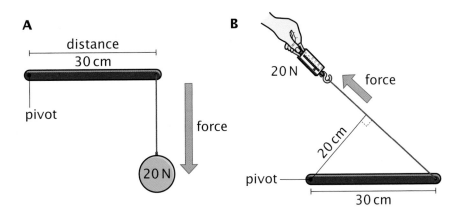

In diagram A above, the moment is given by:

moment = force × distance
moment = 20 N × 30 cm
   = 6 Nm

In diagram B, the force is provided by someone pulling on the thread with a force of 20 N again. The thread is attached at a distance of 30 cm from the pivot, but the distance from the direction of the force at right angles is 20 cm. So in this case, the moment of the force is:

moment = force × distance
moment = 20 N × 20 cm
   = 4 Nm

---

*Information processing*   ## Wire cutters

The diagram shows a pair of wire cutters being used to cut a piece of wire.

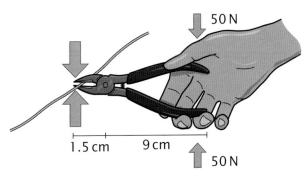

Davinda is pushing the handles of the wire cutters together with a force of 50 N on each handle.

**1** What is the turning moment of each handle about the pivot? Don't forget to include the correct units.

**2** What is the force applied to the wire by each blade?

Lewis used the same pair of wire cutters. He is putting a force of 200 N on each blade, and the area of contact between each blade and the wire is 0.0005 cm².

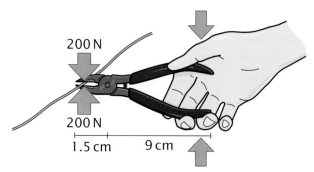

**3** What is the pressure of each blade on the wire? Give the unit.

**4** As the blades sink deeper into the wire, their pressure will decrease. Explain why this happens.

**5** Make up a new problem like the one above, this time using nail clippers rather than wire cutters. Here is a scale drawing to help you. Get another group to solve your problem.

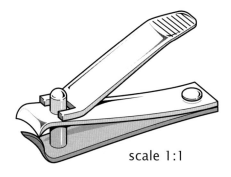

scale 1:1

---

*Enquiry*   *Data analysis*

Look at the apparatus shown below. You may have used similar equipment. It can be used to investigate the rules of balancing about a pivot.

A load is placed on the left hand side, and a different load is placed on the right hand side at a different distance from the pivot so that the beam balances.

You can make this apparatus balance in four different ways, starting from this arrangement. (Keep the 200 g weight on the left hand side and the 100 g weight on the right.)

**1** What are the four ways?

**2** What are the four variables you can alter to make the beam balance?

Groups of pupils used this equipment using different loads and distances. Baljit used a load of 3 N and placed it 40 cm from the pivot on the left hand side. She found it was balanced when she placed the 4 N as shown.

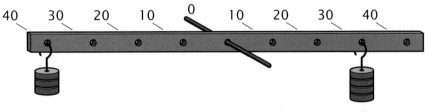

Look at the drawings of the results obtained by other pupils.

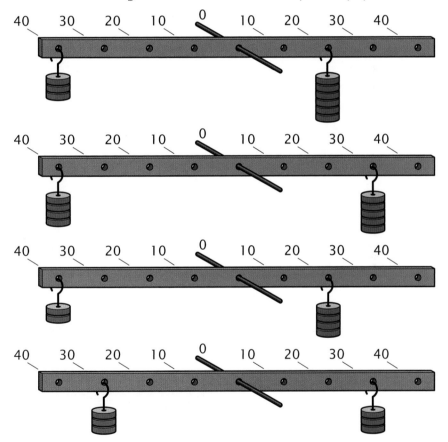

**3** From the diagrams, produce a table of the pupils' results.

**4** What do you notice about the product of mass × distance?

**5** One of the pupils did not get their beam to balance. Which one did not balance? What would you do to make it balance?

**6** What is the relationship between masses and distances in the table?

If you have a smaller mass, you can compensate for it by hanging it further from the pivot.
    If you can only hang the mass a short distance from the centre, you can compensate for this by using a heavy mass.

*Reasoning* *Find the mystery data*

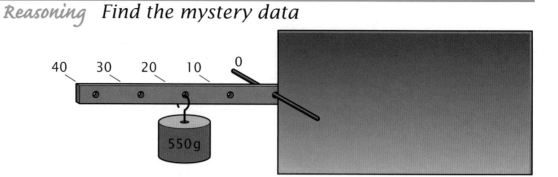

**1** The beam is balanced by a mystery mass at an unknown distance behind the screen. Copy and complete the table.

| Mass (grams) | Distance (hole) | Mass × distance |
|---|---|---|
| 550 | 20 | ? |
| ? | 50 | ? |

**2** What masses at what distances could be hidden behind the screen?

**3** How did you work this out?

*Time to think*    Michael has made a toy butterfly on a spring to give to his mother as a present.

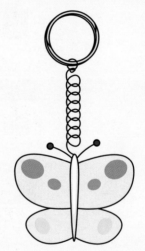

**1** Copy the diagram into your book and draw in an arrow to show the force of gravity.
**2** His mother hangs the toy up and pulls the butterfly down. Add a sketch of her hand to your drawing and show with an arrow the direction of the force of her pull.
**3** Use a different coloured pencil to show how the butterfly begins to move when she lets it go. What makes the butterfly move in this direction?

**4** The butterfly bounces up and down for about 20 seconds, then stops. Why does it stop moving? Discuss each of these possible answers in your group, then vote on the most likely answer:

- Air resistance slows it down.
- It gets heavier.
- It gets lighter.
- Gravity decreases.
- The spring stretches.
- The spring tightens.

This photograph shows a balanced crane. The crane is lifting a load, which is counterbalanced by a counterweight that the crane driver can move along the short arm.

**5** Where is the pivot?

**6** Why is the counterweight on the short arm and not the long arm?

**7** If the crane driver starts to move the load out towards the end of the arm, what must he or she do to the counterweight to stop the crane tipping over?

**8** Imagine the load is 6000 N and it is moved 8 metres out from the pivot. The counterweight is 11 000 N. What is the turning moment of the load?

**9** How far from the pivot must the counterweight be to keep the crane balanced?

**10** If the counterweight was placed at 3 metres from the pivot what would happen?

**11** Look at the pictures below. Make sketches with force arrows and notes on them to explain how each object remains balanced.

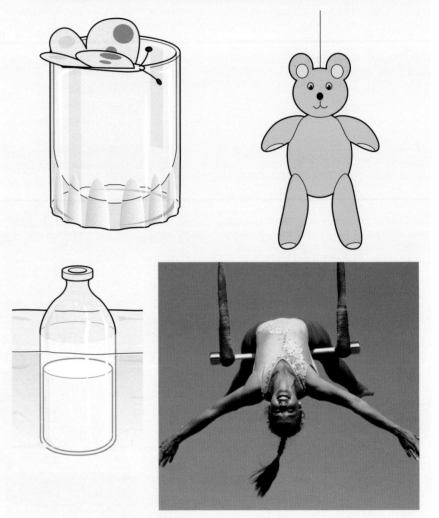

**12** Professor Swot is in the process of making a helpful dictionary for physics students on her course. She keeps the key words and their definitions on separate cards. Unfortunately she dropped all the cards, and the key words and their definitions are now muddled up. Here is a list of all her information. Put the key words into alphabetical order, then match each with its correct definition. You might want to divide up the key words between the members of your group and put the list back together when you have all finished your set of words.

**Key words**

**a)** mass
**b)** barometer
**c)** lever
**d)** manometer
**e)** inertia
**f)** momentum
**g)** pivot

**h)** newton
**i)** pressure
**j)** density
**k)** floating
**l)** balance
**m)** force

**n)** air resistance
**o)** free fall
**p)** upthrust
**q)** weight
**r)** hydraulics
**s)** pneumatics

**Definitions**

1 The SI unit used to measure force.
2 The science of gases doing work by using pressure changes.
3 A simple machine that helps us do work with less force because the force is applied around a pivot.
4 A property of an object that relates to its mass.
5 This is an indication of how much force is need to stop a moving object. It is related to the object's mass and how fast it is moving.
6 The downward force on an object caused by gravity.
7 The science of water doing work under pressure.
8 The compound variable describing a force and the area it is being applied to. It may be measured in psi.
9 This happens when the upthrust of the liquid equals the downthrust of the object in the liquid so the forces are balanced.
10 The friction force on bodies moving through the air. It is a compound variable relating to both the speed and the shape of the object and its speed.
11 The ratio of mass to volume.
12 This acts to change the shape or movement of an object. For each one of these there is another that is equal and opposite.
13 Objects are doing this when they fall towards Earth under the effects of gravity.
14 An instrument that measures air pressure.
15 This is sometimes called the fulcrum.
16 Another word for this is equilibrium.
17 The force of a fluid pushing up against an object due to its density.
18 The amount of 'stuff' in an object.
19 A useful device for measuring pressure differences.

# 9 Using chemistry

**In this chapter you will learn:**

→ about the chemical reaction which takes place when a fuel burns
→ how chemical reactions are used as energy resources
→ how new materials are made through chemical reactions
→ what happens to atoms and molecules when new materials are made
→ to represent chemical reactions by word and symbol equations
→ how accurate measurements have played a key role in scientific research
→ how mass is conserved during chemical reactions
→ the different stages of development of a new product

**You will also develop your skills in:**

→ making measurements of temperature, voltage and mass with sufficient accuracy
→ identifying questions that are suitable for a scientific enquiry
→ recognising the scientific method
→ using models to explain key ideas in chemistry
→ investigating how you can compare new materials with existing ones

→ → → WHAT DO YOU KNOW?

**1** This information was collected by a group of pupils investigating fuels.

| Fuel burnt | Limewater test | Cobalt chloride paper test | Observations |
|---|---|---|---|
| wood spill | ✓ | ✓ | yellow flame, some soot |
| methylated spirit | ✓ | ✓ | blue flame, no soot |
| hydrogen | ✗ | ✓ | blue/clear flame, some condensation |
| firelighter | ✓ | ✓ | yellow flame, soot |
| candle wax | ✓ | ✓ | yellow flame, lots of soot |
| powdered charcoal | ✓ | ✗ | slow burning, glows red, yellow flame |

**a)** Which gas does limewater test for?

**b)** What would you see happening to the limewater if the gas was present?

**c)** Which liquid/vapour does cobalt chloride paper detect?

**d)** What would you see happening to the test paper if that liquid/vapour was present?

**e)** What are the two main products when a fuel burns?

**f)** Which of the fuels above are the odd ones out?

**2** Look carefully at the apparatus used by the class.

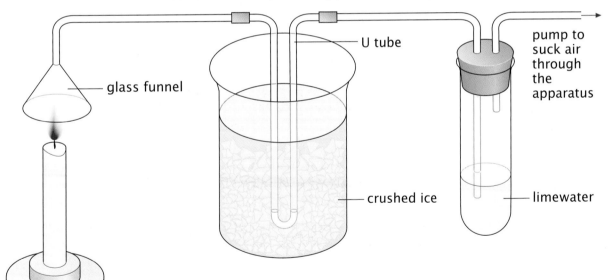

**a)** What might the liquid in the bottom of the U tube be?

**b)** Why is the U tube in a beaker of ice?

**c)** Why is the U tube placed before the tube containing limewater?

**d)** Why does the position of the funnel explain some of the observations made by the class?

**e)** Suggest why the class needed to use powdered coal for this experiment.

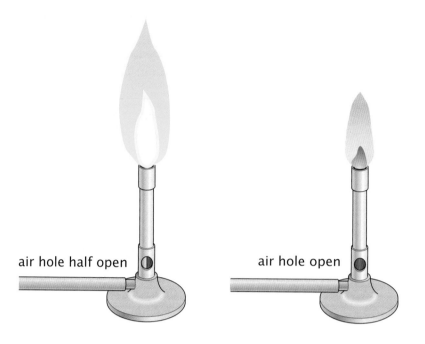

**3 a)** What energy transfer takes place when natural gas burns in a Bunsen burner?

**b)** Copy and complete this Sankey diagram to show the energy transfers taking place to produce a blue flame.

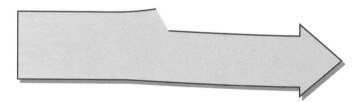

**c)** What would the Sankey diagram look like for a yellow flame?

**d)** Look back to the examples in the photographs on page 254 and state what energy transfers are taking place.

**4** What are the main differences between physical and chemical changes?

**5** Match up the key words in the table with the most helpful definitions.

| Key word | Definition |
|----------|------------|
| **1** Atom | **A** At least two different types of atoms bonded together |
| **2** Molecule | **B** Two or more substances together, not chemically combined |
| **3** Compound | **C** The smallest part of an element which can exist |
| **4** Element | **D** This is formed when atoms are joined by a bond |
| **5** Mixture | **E** Pure substance made of one type of atom |

**6** In the following table the answers are provided but not the questions!

| The answer is... | What was the question? |
|---|---|
| atoms | |
| easily separated | |
| the particles are moving more quickly | |
| the burning candle is extinguished | |
| a mixture | |

In pairs, write out a suitable question to fit each answer. In your group, decide on the best questions and add three extra questions. Give another group your questions to answer for homework.

**7** Divide a page into four sections and write one of the following headings in each section: atom, element, compound, molecule. Write down three things you know about each under the headings. Where would you put the term mixture?

# What happens when we burn a fuel?

A **fuel** is a substance which burns to release energy.

**Key words**
* fuel
* hydrocarbons
* oxidation
* complete combustion
* incomplete combustion

**1** List the fuels that:
• heat your home
• get you to school
• help you exercise.

Here is the first verse of the well-known Christmas carol, 'Good King Wenceslas'.

*Good King Wenceslas looked out on the Feast of Stephen*
*When the snow lay round about, deep and crisp and even.*
*Brightly shone the moon that night, though the frost was cruel,*
*When a poor man came in sight, gathering winter fuel.*

**2** What sort of fuel was being gathered? What other sorts of fuels could they have used?
**3** Which fuels do we use today?
**4** Compare your list with other groups. How can we classify fuels? Decide on different ways of classifying fuels. Which method is the most useful?

The fuels we burn today contain compounds consisting mainly of hydrogen and carbon – these fuels are called **hydrocarbons**. The main products of burning (combustion) are water and carbon dioxide. Other unwanted substances are also produced.

Remember: when elements burn in air or oxygen, oxides are produced. The reaction of substances with oxygen is called **oxidation**.

Good King Wenceslas (c.907–929).

The word equation describing the **complete combustion** of a hydrocarbon fuel is:

hydrocarbon fuel + oxygen → carbon dioxide + water

The simplest hydrocarbon molecule is methane (natural gas). This is the gas used in domestic cookers and also in Bunsen burners.

The balanced symbol equation for the combustion of methane is:

$$CH_4 + 2O_2 \rightarrow CO_2 + 2H_2O$$

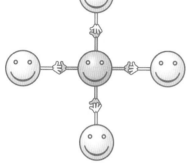

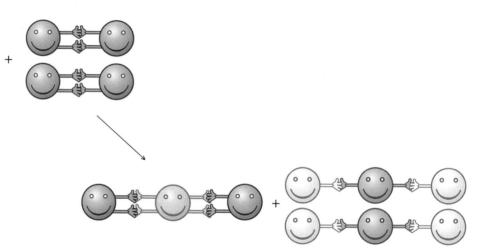

5 Write a key to show which colour has been used for each element in the diagram above.

6 Propane ($C_3H_8$) is a useful fuel and is used for camping cookers. Copy, complete and balance the word and symbol equations for the complete combustion of propane in air:

propane + oxygen →

$$C_3H_8 + ?O_2 \rightarrow ?H_2O + ?CO_2$$

## Incomplete combustion

Soot is produced if a hydrocarbon is not completely oxidised during burning – it is the product of **incomplete combustion**. For example, if a yellow Bunsen burner flame is used for heating, a layer of soot forms on the glassware. This is unburnt carbon which has collected on the glass surface. The reaction also produces water vapour.

7 Write the word equation for this reaction.

Petrol does not burn completely in a car engine. It produces carbon monoxide instead of carbon dioxide. Again, water vapour is produced.

8 Write the word equation for this example of incomplete combustion. Add the correct state symbols (s, l, g).

# Hydrogen as a fuel

Hydrogen is used in fuel cells. Fuel cells use the energy from fuels to provide electrical energy. A fuel cell provides a continuous source of electrical energy, as long as the fuel and oxygen are constantly supplied. Fuel cells were an important feature of the Apollo space programme which landed people on the Moon.

Hydrogen has the following properties:

- colourless
- odourless
- very low density
- highly explosive when mixed with air.

9 This is the symbol equation for the combustion of hydrogen. Try to balance it.

$$?H_2 + O_2 \rightarrow ?H_2O$$

Some fuel cells use methane as the fuel instead of hydrogen.

Methane has the following properties:

- colourless
- odourless
- low density
- moderately explosive when mixed with air.

**EXTENSION**   10 Make a list of the products of the combustion of methane. Include products of both incomplete and complete combustion. What effect might these products have on:
   **a)** our respiratory system
   **b)** our circulatory system
   **c)** our climate?
   **d)** Why do many conservationists recommend the use of hydrogen rather than methane?

*Research*   Find out how we get the hydrogen that is used in fuel cells. Where do we get methane from?

11 Why might plants growing near a smoky factory find it harder to carry out photosynthesis than plants growing in the countryside?
12 Evaluate the evidence for hydrogen being the cleaner choice for fuel cells.

These diagrams compare the energy transfers that take place in a fuel cell compared to those in a power station.

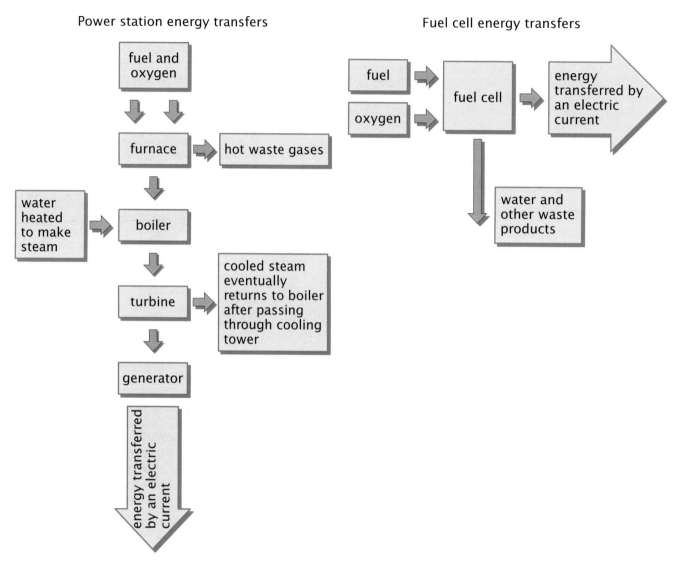

Power station energy transfers

Fuel cell energy transfers

**13** Study these two diagrams. Which of these systems is likely to be the more efficient? Give as many reasons as you can.

**Key words**
* friction
* safety matches
* flammable
* ignites

## How do matches work?

These days you can buy two different types of match. Before the development of matches, making fire was both difficult and unreliable. **Friction** matches can be struck on anything to light them. They were invented by the British chemist John Walker in 1827. **Safety matches** were invented in 1855 by a Swede called Johan Lundstrom. They can only be struck on a special surface on the side of the box.

### How do safety matches work?

Lundstrom's matches are safe because the **flammable** chemicals are separated. One is found on the match head and the other is on the special striking surface on the side of the matchbox. The match head contains potassium chlorate, sulphur and some red colouring. The gritty material on the side of a matchbox is coated with red phosphorus.

When the match head rubs against the box, friction **ignites** the mixture of phosphorus and potassium chlorate. The potassium chlorate contains lots of oxygen which supports the combustion, allowing it to burn long enough to set fire to the wooden matchstick. Also present on the match head is sulphur, which reacts with the oxygen provided to produce enough energy for the wooden match to light up. And there you go – instant fire!

The friction matches that you can light on any rough surface work on the same principle. The red phosphorus on the striking surface is replaced by phosphorus sulphide (in one form or another) in the match head. This decomposes and burns at a relatively low temperature and sets fire to the rest of the match.

1 List all the chemicals named in the passage and classify them as elements or compounds.
2 For any compound you identified, name the elements it contains.
3 Name the likely products of the combustion of phosphorus sulphide. Write a word equation for this reaction.
4 Fumes from burning matches are acidic. Suggest which of the products of combustion would be acidic.
5 How did Lundstrom adapt the original match to make it safer? Explain why his changes produced a safer match.

**Key word**
✳ decomposes

*Word play*

The phosphorus sulphide **decomposes** during the lighting process. Can you think of other words or phrases that could be used in this context? How else is the word decompose used in science? Would these words be suitable in this circumstance?

**DID YOU KNOW?**

During 1888, workers at the match makers Bryant and May went on strike for better pay and conditions. The women were working 14 hours a day for a wage of less than 5 shillings per week. It was also discovered that the health of the women had been severely affected by the phosphorus that they used to make the matches. It caused yellowing of the skin, hair loss and phossy jaw, a form of bone cancer. The whole side of the face turned green and then black, discharging a foul-smelling pus before the affected woman finally died. Campaigns continued against the use of yellow phosphorus.

In 1891 the Salvation Army opened its own match factory in Old Ford, East London. Using only harmless red phosphorus, the workers were soon producing six million boxes of matches a year.

*Time to think*

The combustion of a typical hydrocarbon, methane, depends on the amount of oxygen available. A group of pupils looked at the different products produced when the amount of oxygen varied. This table shows the results of their research.

| Conditions | Reaction products with formulae |
|---|---|
| little air | soot (C), water vapour ($H_2O$) |
| more air | carbon monoxide (CO), water vapour ($H_2O$) |
| plenty of air | carbon dioxide ($CO_2$), water vapour ($H_2O$) |

1 How would the pupils test for water vapour? What result would you expect?
2 What reagent would they use to test for carbon dioxide? What result would you expect?
3 What evidence is there to suggest that methane is a hydrocarbon? (HINT – Look at the reaction products.)
4 Explain the differences between the reaction products and the conditions for burning.
5 a) Match up each of the symbol equations below with the correct conditions in the table.
  b) Decide which equation is not correctly balanced and try to balance the reactants and products. Add state symbols for both reactants and products:
  (s) = solid, (l) = liquid, (g) = gas.

$$CH_4 + 2O_2 \rightarrow CO_2 + 2H_2O$$
$$2CH_4 + 3O_2 \rightarrow 2CO + 4H_2O$$
$$CH_4 + O_2 \rightarrow C + H_2O$$

# → *How else are chemical reactions used to supply energy?*

## Fireworks

Some fireworks contain fine powders of metals, such as magnesium metal. Magnesium is an element that reacts rapidly with oxygen, especially when the powder is suddenly exposed to oxygen – the oxygen causes it to burn.

Magnesium is the element that gives off the bright white lights in fireworks. Different colours can be created depending on what combinations of other metals are used. Creating firework colours is complicated, requiring considerable skill. Fireworks generally require an oxygen-producer, fuel, a colour producer and a binder (to keep everything where it needs to be).

## *Reasoning* *Fireworks*

This table shows some of the chemicals used to produce the different colours displayed in fireworks.

| Colour | Compound |
|--------|----------|
| red | strontium or lithium salts:<br>lithium carbonate, $Li_2CO_3$ = red<br>strontium carbonate, $SrCO_3$ = bright red |
| orange | calcium salts:<br>calcium chloride, $CaCl_2$<br>calcium sulphate, $CaSO_4$ |
| yellow | sodium compounds, for example, sodium nitrate, $NaNO_3$ |
| 'electric white' | white-hot metal, such as magnesium or aluminium<br>barium oxide, BaO |
| green | barium compounds:<br>barium chloride, $BaCl_2$ = bright green |
| blue | copper compounds:<br>copper(I) chloride, CuCl = turquoise blue |

1 Which compounds might each of these fireworks contain?

2 Write the word equation for the burning of magnesium.

3 Which combination of metal compounds would you use to produce purple?

4 Look at the periodic table (page 13) and place the metals from the table above, and their compounds, into groups. Is there a pattern? Where in the periodic table are most of the metals located? Find out the names of these groups of metals.

5 Suggest three other salts that might be used instead of lithium carbonate.

6 Copy and complete this table. The first row has been done for you.

| Compound | Formula | Number of elements | Number of atoms |
|----------|---------|--------------------|-----------------|
| lithium carbonate | $Li_2CO_3$ | 3 | 6 |
| strontium carbonate | | | |
| sodium nitrate | | | |
| copper chloride | | | |

**Key words**
* combustible
* rate

The process that causes any type of firework to go off is a chemical change that can happen very rapidly.

A sparkler consists of several components:

- an oxidiser
- a fuel
- metal such as iron, steel and aluminium
- a **combustible** binder.

A typical sparkler therefore contains the following ingredients: charcoal, sulphur, starch, potassium nitrate and any one of a number of metals to produce the sparks.

The reason why a rocket-type firework takes off with such force is because the chemical reaction produces hot gases, which push the rocket upwards.

Bangers are fireworks that explode noisily. The chemical reaction takes place very quickly, with the rapid release of hot gases in a very short period of time.

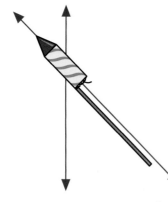

**14 a)** Explain, using the diagram opposite, how the rapid release of gases results in the rocket taking off with great force.

**b)** What effect will the release of gases have on the mass of the rocket?

**15** Match up each of the sparkler components with an ingredient from the text. Set out your answer as a table:

| Component | Ingredient |
|-----------|------------|
|           |            |

**16** Fireworks rely on chemical reactions taking place at the right speed (**rate**) in order for the fireworks to work properly. Place the three fireworks described in the text above in order of rate of chemical change, with the most rapid reaction first. Justify your order, including the relevant information given in the text.

**Key words**
* phlogiston
* caloric
* accurate
* oxygen theory

## Burning ideas

Burning has been important to people ever since early humans learnt how to control fire. But HOW do things burn? This was a question that took hundreds of years to answer. By the seventeenth century, scientists were beginning to realise that the burning of fuels, the reactions of metals in air and the breathing of animals all had something in common – they were all faster or slower versions of the same type of reaction.

Scientists observed that wood turns to ashes when it is burnt, and some metals become powders when they are heated. Some of the metal powders can be converted back into the metal by heating the powder with charcoal, but ashes cannot be converted back into wood.

An explanation was provided by Georg Stahl (1660–1734) and Johann Becher (1635–1682). They thought that burning could be explained by the removal of a substance, and they called that substance **phlogiston**. Stahl developed this idea, which became known as the 'phlogiston theory', and it became the scientific explanation for burning for around 100 years.

According to the phlogiston theory:

- metals and all other combustible substances contain a substance known as phlogiston, which is released into the air on burning, along with **caloric** (heat)
- substances lose mass burning because they lose phlogiston.

There were lots of problems with the theory, but it was better than no theory at all! A theory helps scientists to explain observations, and it allows them to make predictions.

### Enter Antoine Lavoisier

Antoine Lavoisier (1743–1794) was a French chemist. Like many other scientists of his day, Lavoisier was investigating burning. However, unlike them, he insisted on carrying out experiments involving **accurate** measurements. To help him, Lavoisier developed a balance that could weigh to 0.0005 g, so that he could accurately measure the changes in mass during his experiments.

Using his highly sensitive scales he showed that when he heated mercury oxide there was a loss in mass as the oxide released its oxygen. He also showed that when metals were heated in air the increase in mass was equal to the mass of oxygen taken from the air.

In another experiment, he heated charcoal with a number of metal oxides in closed containers, and found that with each oxide the total mass of the container was the same before and after heating.

1 Explain why having a very accurate set of scales was so important for his investigations to succeed.
2 Why was accurate mass measurement particularly important when reactions with gases were involved?

Lavoisier also investigated the combustion of phosphorus and sulphur, and discovered that after burning the mass of the material was greater than it had been at the start.

3 According to the phlogiston theory what should have happened?

### With a little help from his friends

After a meeting with Joseph Priestley, Lavoisier went on to show that air was a mixture. He did this with a series of careful experiments which showed that air was made up of several *different* components. From air he isolated the gases we now call oxygen, nitrogen and carbon dioxide, and showed that carbon dioxide could be produced by burning charcoal in air. He determined the proportion of oxygen in the air, and showed that oxygen was removed from the air during the process of burning.

4 What is the proportion of oxygen in air?

As a result of his work, Lavoisier developed the '**oxygen theory**': that when substances burn in air they combine with oxygen from the air and form an oxide (a compound containing oxygen).

Antoine Lavoisier.

*Evaluation* ## Does the phlogiston theory or the oxygen theory best explain how things burn?

Think about what takes place when a piece of magnesium ribbon burns in air.

**1** Make a list of everything you might expect to see.

Method 1.

Method 2.

The teacher provided the class with two different balances. She suggested that the groups heating the magnesium in the tongs would need the more accurate instrument.

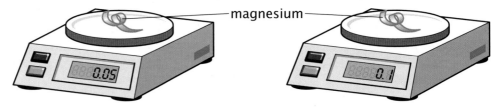

magnesium

Here are the results of their experiments:

| Method 1 | Set 1 | Set 2 | Set 3 | Set 4 |
|---|---|---|---|---|
| **Mass of magnesium ribbon before burning (g)** | 0.05 | 1.0 | 0.04 | 0.03 |
| **Mass of ash after burning (g)** | 0.03 | 0.0 | 0.01 | 0.01 |

**2** Look at the results for Method 1. What seems to happen to the mass of the magnesium after burning?

**3** Which theory do these results appear to support?

**4** Can you explain what has happened to data set 2?

**5** Which set of results is anomalous? Suggest a reason for this result.

| Method 2 | Set 5 | Set 6 | Set 7 | Set 8 |
|---|---|---|---|---|
| **Mass of test tube, mineral wool and magnesium ribbon before burning (g)** | 15.50 | 16.60 | 15.92 | 14.30 |
| **Mass of test tube, mineral wool and contents after burning (g)** | 15.60 | 16.80 | 15.92 | 14.41 |

**6** Look at the results for Method 2. What happens to the mass after burning?

**7** Suggest what might have happened to the group that collected data set 7.

**8** Which theory do these results appear to support?

**9** Nita says that Method 2 is an improvement on Method 1 and provides more useful data. What do you think she means? Compare the methods carefully and make a list of advantages of Method 2.

**10** Lavoisier insisted on making accurate measurements. How did this disprove the phlogiston theory?

*Reasoning*  ## Oxygen theory

In its day the phlogiston theory was used to explain many observations about combustion. These explanations may sound improbable to us now. Here are four explanations of well-known scientific observations using the phlogiston theory. Rewrite them using our current understanding of the oxygen theory.

**1** Substances lose mass on burning because they lose phlogiston.

**2** A candle flame goes out (is extinguished) in a gas jar because the air becomes saturated with phlogiston.

**3** Charcoal leaves hardly any ash when it burns because it is almost all pure phlogiston.

**4** A mouse would die in an airtight container because the air is saturated with phlogiston.

*Enquiry*  ## Making measurements

Nita suggested that if the mass of the reactants and products were measured carefully then the results would be more reliable. She suggested using this apparatus:

crucible          tongs          scales
(ceramic container)

**1** What piece of apparatus is missing? Write it down, then:

- think up a plan using this apparatus
- include all the measurements that you would make
- make a prediction about what will happen using your method
- explain how your results would help support the oxygen theory
- get your plan checked before proceeding.

*Creative thinking* **Letter to Georg Stahl**

Imagine that you are a scientist working in the eighteenth century. Write a letter to Georg Stahl to persuade him that Lavoisier's results are not good news for supporters of the phlogiston theory.

DID YOU KNOW?

On 8th May 1794, Lavoisier was executed by guillotine. He pleaded for more time to finish a vital scientific experiment, but the judge replied, 'The Republic has no need for scientists'. As one of Lavoisier's friends said, 'It took only an instant to cut off that head, and another hundred years may not produce another like it.'

# → Theory of conservation of mass

**Key words**
* reactants
* products
* particles
* conserved

Lavoisier suggested that the mass of the **reactants** is the same as the mass of the **products** after a chemical change. This is the 'theory of conservation of mass' which states that:

- Mass is neither created nor destroyed in a chemical change.
- When a reaction happens, the bonds holding the atoms together in the reactants break and the atoms are rearranged into products by making new bonds.

The theory of conservation of mass also applies to physical changes such as melting, dissolving and evaporation.

**17** Write a word and symbol equation for this reaction.

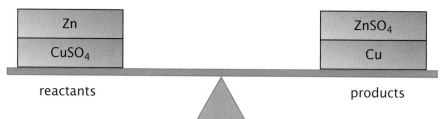

reactants                                          products

**18** Using the key idea of **particles**, explain why the mass inside Lavoisier's containers is **conserved** (remains the same).

**19** When acids react with metals or metal carbonates there appears to be a decrease in mass. Here are two examples:

zinc + sulphuric acid → zinc sulphate + hydrogen

copper carbonate + hydrochloric acid → copper carbonate + water + carbon dioxide

Can you explain this apparent loss of mass?

**20** Look back at page 265. What measurements would Lavoisier have made in his famous experiment that helped him to formulate this idea of conservation of mass? Write word and symbol equations for the two chemical changes taking place in Lavoisier's experiments.

## Even geniuses make mistakes!

Lavoisier burned lots of substances in oxygen to provide evidence for his oxygen theory of burning. He found that the oxides of some elements were acidic. From this he suggested that all acids must contain oxygen. Many years later the English chemist Humphry Davy (1806–1885) showed that hydrochloric acid did *not* contain oxygen.

21 Which elements does hydrochloric acid contain?
22 Which group of elements burn to produce acidic oxides?
23 Which other acidic compounds do not contain oxygen?

➡ # How else are chemical reactions used as energy resources?

**Key words**
* exothermic
* molten
* redox
* reduction
* reduced
* oxidised

Chemical reactions other than combustion can be used to supply energy. In Chapter 5 you studied displacement reactions. Many of these produce a rise in temperature. Reactions which produce a rise in temperature are known as **exothermic** reactions. An example of an exothermic reaction is the Thermit reaction. It produces a supply of **molten** iron which can be used to repair cracked railway lines (see page 147).

The word equation for the Thermit reaction is:

aluminium + iron oxide → aluminium oxide + iron

24 Which element are the two metals in this reaction competing for?

Displacement reactions take place because of the relative positions of the metals involved in the reactivity series. Metals high on the activity series displace less reactive metals. This is a kind of competition.

25 In the Thermit reaction, which metal is higher up the reactivity series? How do you know?
26 Where else in science have you learnt about competition?
27 Here is a pupil's attempt to balance the symbol equation for this reaction.

$$Al + Fe_2O_3 \rightarrow Al_2O_3 + Fe$$

Use the chemical equation balance from Chapter 1 to check whether or not there are equal numbers of each atom on each side of the arrow. Decide whether the equation is balanced, and make any necessary changes to ensure that it is.

The Thermit reaction is also classified as a **redox** reaction because it involves the transfer of oxygen.

**Reduction** is a process which results in the *loss* of oxygen. Chemicals are **reduced** by losing oxygen.
Oxidation is a process which results in the *gain* of oxygen. Chemicals are **oxidised** by gaining oxygen.

28 Look carefully at the Thermit reaction. Where is each of these processes taking place? Identify which reactant is oxidised and which reactant is reduced.

---

*Reasoning* ## Redox

Three metals, W, X and Y, form oxides WO, XO and YO.
Hot, finely powdered W will displace the metal from YO but not from XO.
Starting with the most reactive, what is their order of reactivity? Use the order to predict the result of reacting:

- powdered Y with XO
- powdered Y with WO.

---

*Information processing* ## Interpreting data: Patterns in displacement reactions

This table shows the results of mixing metals and salt solutions. The maximum temperature change for each mixture was recorded.

| Metal \ Salt solution | silver nitrate | zinc nitrate | copper nitrate |
|---|---|---|---|
| magnesium | 4 °C | 1 °C | 3 °C |
| iron | 3 °C | | 2 °C |

1 What else would pupils see during the displacement reactions?

2 Suggest the order of reactivity based on these results.

3 One of the metals did not react every time. Which one? How do you know?

4 Write word equations for the reactions recorded in the table.

5 You are asked to include aluminium and tin as well as magnesium and iron in your investigation. You are provided with suitable salt solutions – iron nitrate, tin nitrate and aluminium nitrate. How many possible combinations could you investigate?

6 What temperature changes would you expect with the new combinations?

7 Copy and balance these displacement reactions. Include state symbols. (Use 'aq' for an aqueous solution.)

$$Zn + AgNO_3 \rightarrow Zn(NO_3)_2 + Ag$$
$$Al + Cu(NO_3)_2 \rightarrow Al(NO_3)_3 + Cu$$

# → *Comparing handwarmers*

**Key words**
* supersaturated
* quicklime
* slaked lime

You may have come across small packages in camping shops which help to warm your hands in winter. You may also have used a pack to heat up canned food. These bags rely on chemicals mixing and heating the surroundings in the process. These are exothermic processes.

There are three different combinations which are used:

* the crystallisation of **supersaturated** sodium acetate solution
* dissolving calcium chloride in water
* the combination of calcium oxide in water (also called lime slaking – used for producing hot coffee in a can).

**29** Classify these combinations as either physical or chemical changes. Give as many reasons as you can.

**30** What do you think is meant by the term 'supersaturated'?

*DID YOU KNOW?*

An early chemist called Joseph Black, working at the same time as Lavoisier, thought that while calcium oxide was absorbing water, swelling and giving out heat it appeared to be alive. They called calcium *oxide* **quicklime**. Calcium *hydroxide* was called **slaked lime** because calcium oxide reacts vigorously with water to form it. Quicklime seems to be thirsty for water. In 1787, Lavoisier suggested that scientists agree names for chemicals because of this habit that scientists had of making up such unusual names.

*Word play*

The old-fashioned meaning of quick is alive. Slaked is an old-fashioned word for absorbing water. Can you suggest why calcium hydroxide was called slaked lime and calcium oxide was called quicklime?

# → *Generating electricity using metals*

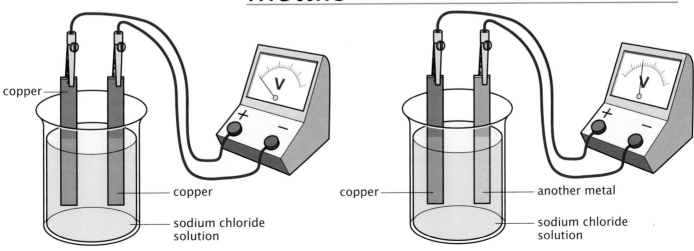

copper

copper

sodium chloride solution

copper

another metal

sodium chloride solution

In the electrolysis experiment (pictured on the previous page), the salt solution is called the **electrolyte** – any salt solution will work. The solvent in these salt solutions is water, so these are called **aqueous solutions**. An electrolyte is a chemical compound which conducts electricity and is split up by it. Strong acids and alkalis are also good electrolytes. When two strips of the same metal (in this example, copper) are placed in a salt solution the voltmeter does not register any **voltage**, but if one of the strips of copper is replaced with a different metal a reading registers on the voltmeter. The metal strips are the **electrodes**, which carry the electricity in and out of the electrolyte.

*Reasoning* *Electrolysis*

The experiment just described was repeated with a number of different pairs of metals, using sodium chloride solution as the electrolyte. The table shows the voltage recorded with each pair:

| Electrode 1 | Electrode 2 | Voltage (V) |
|---|---|---|
| zinc | copper | 1.1 |
| iron | copper | 0.78 |
| lead | copper | 0.47 |
| magnesium | copper | 2.71 |
| magnesium | zinc | 1.61 |
| zinc | iron | 0.32 |

**1** What is the input (independent) variable?

**2** What is the outcome (dependent) variable?

**3** Which variable(s) would you need to keep fixed?

**4** Put the metals used in descending order of reactivity.

**5** What pattern do you notice in the voltage readings? Compare your answer with others in your group. Do you agree? Select the best answer from your group and share this with the whole class.

**6** What voltage value would you predict if the experiment was repeated with:
**a)** iron and lead
**b)** magnesium and iron?

**7** What voltage would you predict with aluminium and copper? Explain how you decided on this value. How did the position of aluminium in the activity series influence your thinking?

**Key words**
* battery
* electrolysis

## New electricity

Around 1791, Luigi Galvani (1737–1798), an Italian anatomist from Bologna, reported on a series of experiments he had been conducting since 1780 when an assistant accidentally observed that a frog's legs contracted violently if a metal scalpel were touched to a certain leg nerve during dissection. In other experiments he showed that contractions were produced if the frogs were placed on an iron plate and if a brass hook, making contact with a nerve, were simultaneously pressed against the iron. He observed that the effects were most pronounced if two different metals were used. With non-conductors, the effects did not occur. He concluded that it was the muscles in the frog that contained the electricity.

On 20th March 1800, in a famous letter from Alessandro Volta to the Royal Society, came one of the greatest breakthroughs in the electricity experiments. A professional disagreement between Galvani and Volta over the results of an experiment led Volta to prove that when certain metals and chemicals come into contact with each other they will produce an electric current. He had already developed very sensitive instruments for detecting electric charge (electrometers), but did not detect any electric charge stored in animal tissue. He came to the conclusion that the contractions noticed by Galvani depended on the presence of the direct contact between two different metals.

He placed together several pairs of silver and zinc discs separated by paper soaked in salt water, and an electric current was produced. Volta had produced the first **battery**. The 'voltaic pile', which we now recognise under the name of 'electrical battery,' was produced, and within a short time scientific apparatus makers were offering 'Volta's piles' as regular items of equipment for research and demonstrations.

Very shortly after receipt of Volta's letter in London, William Nicholson and Anthony Carlisle constructed a Volta's pile. They connected conductors from the ends of the pile into a container of water, acidified to make it a better conductor, and detected hydrogen being produced at one conductor and oxygen at the other. Nicholson and Carlisle had carried out the **electrolysis** of water into its component gases.

**1** Write the word and symbol equations for the electrolysis of water.

Let's remind ourselves of how scientists go about their work.

1 Make observations or measurements.
2 Invent a tentative explanation (hypothesis), that is consistent with what has been observed thus far.
3 Use the hypothesis to make predictions.
4 Test those predictions by experiments or further observations, and modify the hypothesis in light of the results obtained.
5 Modify or revise the hypothesis and try predicting again.

**2** What observations did Galvani make?
**3** What was his hypothesis? What other conclusion could Galvani have reached about his work?
**4** Imagine you are Galvani. What would you predict would happen if different muscle tissues were used?
**5** What further experiments did he perform? Suggest extra work that Galvani might have carried out to support his idea that the electricity was contained in the muscle tissue.
**6** Volta repeated Galvani's experiments but with important improvements. What did Volta measure and how did this affect his conclusions? How did Volta use his electrometer?
**7** Galvani noticed that non-metals did not produce the muscle twitching. Name some non-metals that he could have used. (HINT – This was 1791.)
**8** Why do you think that Nicholson and Carlisle added acid to the water?

Humphrey Davy.

*Word play* Electro*lysis* is the breaking down of compounds, either molten or dissolved in water (aqueous), by passing an electric current through them. 'Lysis' means to break down. Look up the meaning of:

- plasmolysis
- haemolysis.

## Humphry Davy

Humphry Davy (1778–1829), in his chemical researches at the Royal Institution, seized upon the discovery of electrolysis for decomposing other materials, and used electrolysis to discover the metals sodium and potassium. He eventually achieved these great discoveries by using molten salts instead of aqueous solutions.

These are Davy's own notes on the experiment which resulted in the discovery of the group 1 metal potassium:

*As soon as the current was turned on the solid melted both at the top where there was a conducting wire and at the bottom that rested on a disc of platinum connected to the negative side of the battery. Around the wire at the top there was a vigorous bubbling with gas being given off. At the lower surface no gas formed, but small globules, having a high metallic lustre and looking much like mercury, appeared. Some of the globules burned with an explosion and bright flame as soon as they formed. Others remained and were merely tarnished and finally covered by a white film which formed on their surfaces.*

*At ordinary temperatures, if kept away from the air, the metal product is a soft and malleable solid, which has the lustre of polished silver. In contact with a few drops of water it decomposes the water with great violence. An instantaneous explosion is produced and a brilliant flame; a solution of pure potash lye is formed.*

Michael Faraday (1791–1867) was an apprentice of Davy at the Royal Society and went on to make many discoveries of his own. It was Faraday who gave the name 'electrolysis' to the process of splitting compounds with electricity.

31 Read Davy's notes again. Construct a table showing which properties of potassium you consider to be typical of a metal and those properties which are 'unusual' for most metals. Davy described the metal product as having *lustre* and being *malleable*. Which modern words could you use instead?

32 What evidence from the text suggests that potassium is a reactive metal?

33 What is the modern name for the chemical potash lye?

34 Why was it important to carry out the electrolysis on molten salts rather than solutions?

*Research* What other pairs of metals could Davy have used? Which metals did he discover using this new technique of electrolysis?

Where in the activity series are these metals to be found? Can you suggest a reason why these metals are difficult to extract?

## Using chemistry to make useful products

### Polymers

We do not know the exact number of chemicals people have produced as the number is increasing year by year, but there have been half a million new chemicals developed since 1965 alone. Many of these have been different types of **plastics**. Plastics play a big part in our lives because they have special properties. Our whole world seems to be wrapped in plastic. Almost every product we buy, most of the food we eat, and many of the liquids we drink come to us encased in plastic.

Plastics are all man-made (**synthetic**) materials called **polymers**. There are some very important polymers which occur naturally in living organisms, for example, proteins, DNA, starch and cellulose.

**35** What are the functions of each of these important natural polymers?

*Word play*

'Poly' means many. A *poly*mer is made from lots of smaller molecules bonded together.

Make a list of words beginning with the prefix 'poly'. Write down their meanings.

'Mono' means one. The small molecules which join together to produce polymers are called **mono*mers***.

Make a list of words beginning with the prefix 'mono'. Write down their meanings.

**36** Look carefully at the information on polymers above. Using the information, draw a table with these headings:

| Natural polymers | Synthetic polymers |
|---|---|
|  |  |

Add to each column using examples from the text and add as many others of your own as you can. Compare your table with other pupils'. Share ideas and add them to your table.

All polymers are synthesised (made) by the joining together of thousands of small molecules called monomers. Each polymer is made from a different monomer.

| Monomer molecules | Polymer |
|---|---|
| nucleic acids | DNA |
| ethene ($C_2H_4$) | polyethene |
| propene ($C_3H_6$) | polypropene |
| glucose | starch |
| vinyl acetate | PVA |

**37** Copy and complete this table using the information in the previous table:

|  | Ethene | Propene |
|---|---|---|
| formula |  |  |
| total number of atoms in formula |  |  |
| total number of elements in formula |  |  |
| element/compound |  |  |
| atom/molecule |  |  |

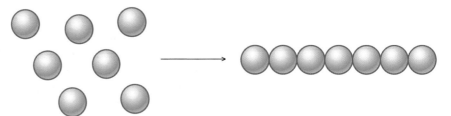

Monomers joining together to form a polymer.

**38** Danny said that making a polymer is a bit like threading beads to make a necklace.

Is this a useful model? Are there any other models that you could use to explain how polymers are made?

**39** What sort of molecules are ethene and propene?

**40** Predict the products of the complete combustion of polyethene and polypropene.

**41** Write balanced symbol equations for the complete combustion of each of these monomers. Write word equations for the complete combustion of each polymer.

The first man-made plastic was made by Leo Hendrik Baekeland in 1907. He called it Bakelite.

Radio with a Bakelite case.

Plastic packaging provides excellent protection for products: it is cheap to manufacture and seems to last forever. Lasting forever, however, is proving to be a major environmental problem. Packaging is the largest market for plastics, accounting for over a third of the consumption of raw plastic materials.

Disposable nappies contain synthetic polymers. A baby will use 7000 nappies which will take 500 years to decompose. This is because synthetic polymers are chemically unreactive.

## Biodegradable plastics

Another problem is that traditional plastics are manufactured from **non-renewable** resources – oil, coal and natural gas. Unfortunately, each year each person in the UK will use the energy equivalent of 3.5 tonnes of oil. In an attempt to solve this environmental problem, scientists have been developing **biodegradable** plastics that are made from **renewable** resources, such as plants. The term biodegradable means that a substance is able to be broken down into simpler substances by the activities of living organisms, and therefore is unlikely to remain in the environment for a long period of time.

One type of biodegradable plastic has small amounts of starch added to the plastic. Bacteria in the soil feed on the starch, breaking down the plastic.

The reason traditional plastics are not biodegradable is that their long polymer molecules are too large and too tightly bonded together to be decomposed. However, plastics based on natural plant polymers derived from wheat or corn starch have molecules that are readily attacked and broken down by microbes.

A biological reactor that converts a slurry of food waste into a biodegradable plastic has been developed by scientists in Hawaii, providing a use for the large amounts of food that more economically developed countries throw away every year. This polymer could be used to make greener packaging, disposable products such as bottles, or even pills that dissolve slowly to release drugs in the body.

There are many different standards used to measure biodegradability, with each country using its own. The requirements range from 90% to 60% **decomposition** of the product within 60–180 days of being placed in a standard composting environment.

42 What does 'biodegradable' mean?
43 A lot of plastic packaging is often unnecessary. Imagine that you are in charge of a newspaper campaign to persuade your local readers not to waste plastic. Prepare a leaflet and a full page advert to get your point across.
44 How do you think scientists compare how biodegradable different plastics are?
45 Explain why microbes are unsuccessful in breaking down synthetic polymers.

**Types of biodegradable plastic**

*Type 1*

In type 1 biodegradable plastics, starch is only used as a filling material – its polymeric properties are not used. Examples include 'biodegradable' plastic bags. These bags are not fully biodegradable, however, since they consist of mainly non-biodegradable synthetic polymers such as polyethene or polypropene, and only 5–20% starch. Under special conditions, the starch degrades and the plastic falls apart into small particles. The small plastic particles will last for many years although they will not be visible.

*Type 2*
In these plastics the starch is used for its polymeric properties. It is blended with synthetic polymers and contributes to the strength of the material. These plastics can be 50–80% starch, but still a large part is not biodegradable.

*Type 3*
This plastic is completely biodegradable – it is made from pure starch.

46 It has been suggested that biodegradable plastics are not as strong as non-biodegradable plastics. Design an investigation to test this.
47 Make a list of the properties of a plastic that would be suitable for producing
   a) carrier bags
   b) picnic plates.

# Medicines

**Key words**
* clinical trials
* placebo

Medicines from natural materials have been used for thousands of years. Many of them have been extracted from plants. The table shows some plants and their medicinal uses.

| Plant extract | Use |
|---|---|
| feverfew | migraine treatment |
| ginger | seasickness prevention |
| garlic | to lower blood pressure |
| Saint John's wort | antidepressant |
| ginseng | exercise performance enhancer |
| echinacea | immune system stimulant (upper respiratory infections) |

With the onset of new and deadly diseases and the increase in the world's population, scientists are having to invent new drugs all the time. However, a drug has to be thoroughly tested before it can be used, at a cost of millions of pounds, years of research and **clinical trials**.

## What is a clinical trial?
Scientists have made great progress in discovering ways to prevent, screen for and treat cancer. The key feature of these discoveries is the clinical trial – a carefully designed study that evaluates such things as promising new screening tests or medications, surgical procedures, and even lifestyle changes.

Let's look at the trials for a new cancer treatment. No new cancer treatment can be made available unless it has undergone careful testing through clinical trials to ensure that it is both safe and effective.

## How a clinical trial works

Each trial is designed to test a particular treatment on a specific type of cancer, often at a particular stage of the cancer's development. The trial might be designed to test whether the new treatment makes people feel better. Each clinical trial can take many years to organise and carry out. It involves several steps known as 'phases':

**Phase 1**

This first study evaluates a drug's safety and determines how best to provide it, such as how much to give, how often, and by what means (i.e. injection, orally).

**Phase 2**

This next step continues to test the drug's safety and begins to evaluate how well patients respond to it.

**Phase 3**

This stage of study expands the testing to include a larger number of patients and to compare the new drug with treatments already available to see if it produces better results. Cancer trials are different to other clinical trials in that cancer patients are never given a **placebo** if a standard treatment is available. A placebo looks, feels and smells like the drug under review, but it is a dummy, it has no real effect.

**Phase 4**

This final stage takes place after the drug has received government approval outside the experimental setting. The purpose of this study is to monitor the drug for long-term effectiveness and side effects.

48 What is a placebo?
49 Why do you think that placebos are not used during cancer trials?
50 Construct a table to summarise the main activities during each phase (stage) of a clinical trial for cancer.
51 During phase 2 of a clinical trial for a treatment for eczema, the doctors noticed significant improvements in those patients receiving the trial cream. One consultant suggests that *all* the patients be given the new cream. You have to make the final decision. Discuss this dilemma in your group. What do you decide?

*Time to think*

1 Make up a useful revision question for each of the key words listed below. Test a partner to see if they know the answers. Agree on the best question for each key word and make a loop game for the words.

- displacement
- oxidation
- exothermic
- synthesis
- reactants
- products
- molecules
- element
- compound

2 Look back through this chapter and write out the word equations for all the key chemical changes that have been discussed. Annotate each word equation with the key words from the list in Question 1. Produce a poster to help with your revision.

3 Scientists are always looking to use chemical reactions in new and useful ways. Explain how scientists have used chemical reactions in the following examples:

- fuel cells
- batteries
- plastics.

4 Joseph Priestley always remained convinced that the phlogiston theory was true.

Imagine you are Lavoisier. Write a letter to Priestley trying to convince him of the new oxygen theory of combustion. Include as much evidence as you can to support the theory.

# Index